The Impact of Religiosity on the Marketing
of Religious Iconography

By

Peter P. Madrid Jr.

Royal Premier Publishing
Grandville, MI

Published by Royal Premier Publishing
Madrid,Jr, Peter P.
The impact of religiosity on the marketing of religious iconography Peter P. Madrid Jr.
 Library of Congress Control Number: 2012906689
Includes Bibliographical references and index.
 ISBN 978-0-9854247-0-1

10 9 8 7 6 5 4 3 2 1

ABSTRACT

THE IMPACT OF RELIGIOSITY ON THE MARKETING

OF RELIGIOUS ICONOGRAPHY

By

Peter P. Madrid Jr.

May 2011

This study attempts to establish, identify, and classify target markets for the purchase of religious iconography based on past purchasing behavior and other consumer social behaviors perceived as religious vices. This study also distinguishes the likelihood of future purchases of religious iconography for the study, "demographics." The CAGS sample consisted of students from California State University, Long Beach ($n = 494$), and University of Arkansas, Fayetteville ($n = 216$).

The student respondents completed a self-administered questionnaire during the period of September 2004 through June 2006. The study methodology introduces a multidimensional religiosity index as an improvement over past studies, which employed unidimensional religiosity measures. The study reports that the consumer marketing behaviors perceived as religious vices can be used to determine the likelihood of purchases of religious iconography. The implications of this study are that business enterprises can better identify target markets for religious iconography products using the multidimensional religiosity index. This study also allows marketing plans for religious iconography products to leverage the religiosity index data to produce new quantified cross-advertising fields. Additionally, new potential marketing fields can also be developed by church groups, charities, and other non-profit organizations by using this scale in the advertising of religious iconography products and recruitment purposes.

The items included in the survey upon which this study is based have been divided into two categories: traditional and non-traditional, and this study makes a distinction between "Traditional Christian Iconography" and "Non-traditional Christian Iconography."

Keywords: religiosity, multidimensional religiosity index, religious iconography, consumer marketing, church recruitment, charity fundraising, target marketing

THE IMPACT OF RELIGIOSITY ON THE MARKETING

OF RELIGIOUS ICONOGRAPHY

A THESIS

Presented to the Department of Religious Studies

California State University, Long Beach

In Partial Fulfillment

of the Requirements for the Degree

Master of Arts in Religious Studies

Committee Members:

Peter Lowentrout, Ph.D. (Chair)
Edward Hughes, Ph.D.
Alan E. Ellstrand, Ph.D.

College Designee

Mark Wiley, Ph.D.

By Peter P. Madrid Jr.

M.A., 2004, California State University, Long Beach

ACKNOWLEDGEMENTS

Peter Phillip Madrid, Jr., College of Liberal Arts, Department of Religious Study and the College of Business Administration, at the California State University, Long Beach, Sam M. Walton College of Business, University of Arkansas.

I wish to thank all those who helped me, mostly importantly Darshan Sachdeva, Ph.D., California State University, Long Beach, College of Business Administration, for his survey coordination and guidance. Additionally, and round of thanks for the statistical verification and critiquing of the manuscript by Stafford G. Cox, Ph.D., California State University, Long Beach. Thanks also go to retired English Professor Mrs. Phillip K. (Tessa) Dick, Chapman University, and retired *Press-Telegram* Composing Room Proofreader John L. Roberts for grammar, punctuation, spelling, and formatting. A thoughtful thanks to Douglas C. Wallace for the currier and transportation service he provided. In particular, I wish to acknowledge the encouragement and inspiration to complete my graduate college education by my mother, Helen R. Madrid.

This manuscript utilizes a survey referred to as the California Arkansas Graduate Survey of Religion and Marketing (CAGS) by Peter P. Madrid, Jr., M.A., and Michael S. Rahlwes, M.A., California State University, Long Beach, and supplemented at University of Arkansas, which has been used by Peter P. Madrid, Jr., and Michael S. Rahlwes for their graduate theses. This is stated as a disclaimer as required by the American Psychological Association.

TABLE OF CONTENTS

APPENDICES

PREFACE

The following research study The Impact of Religiosity on the Marketing of Religious Iconography, also referred to as Marketing of Religious Iconography is a second edition. It remains the same as the first in subject content of a Master's Thesis study by the same name. The only change that is unique to the second edition that were done was for cosmetic and commercial value. The cosmetic changes included the formatting of tables and asked from formal academic requirements to a more aesthetic format unique to popular literature. To enhance the commercial value of this study, this edition includes an author's note, and promotional information and listing of other publications written by the author.

In short, this research study provides and encompasses a concise comparison and contrast between unidimensional and multidimensional religiosity indexes and their accuracy using Cronbach Alpha levels, as a standard (as shown in the Cronbach alpha level tables). The use of multidimensional religiosity indexes are original and proven valid through Cronbach alpha calculations and the statistical analysis of the survey data. Little research has been published concerning the use of multidimensional religiosity indexing and their potential use in other disciplines such as business marketing.

A major focus of the thesis focuses in two areas a person's religiosity level and their possession or purchasing habits of religious iconography. An affinity analysis establishes a link to a person's religiosity index level and comparable advertising forums for potential use outside of the religious studies discipline.

A establishment of an 11 variable religiosity index related to religion and spirituality supported by quantitative research studies and national polls to constitute a more accurate multidimensional religiosity index than those available at the time of this research (as seen in the religiosity index tables and methodology sections).

To quantify the strength of the relationship between an individual's religiosity and the possession of religious iconography both in traditional and nontraditional states, 13 items that are universally focused on religion and spirituality were correlated to an individual's religiosity index level and their purchasing history of religious iconography (as shown in the correlation tables of the religiosity index levels and congruent possession or purchasing of religious iconography).

While not a major focus of this research study, an analysis of a person's religiosity index level and vices and virtues showed a unlikely links that in many cases the higher a person's religiosity index the more likely the person's participation in vices dominate (as shown in the regression tables).

The frequency tables in total allow the reader a snapshot view and comparison / contrast of multi variant variables between the eclectic California State University Long Beach and the more homogeneous University of Arkansas.

While this study does not address the findings as shown in the comparison / contrast of the frequency table of both universities reflected in the study, it is addressed in a separate publication entitled "Today's Youth, God and the War on Religion" by Peter Madrid. This separate information utilizes the comparison contrast tables to address their present day impact. The publication "Today's youth, God and the War on Religion" is written for commercial purposes and does not reflect the idiomatic terminology used in scientific academic writing.

The second major focus of the thesis provides ground breaking quantitative findings that validate predictor variables in various advertising forums and their target market groups. This affinity analysis establishes a link to a person's religiosity index level and comparable advertising forums for nonreligious items establishing product relations with the 13 religious iconography items used in this study, thereby opening of a more novel and widespread advertising base for the marketing of religious iconography.

CHAPTER 1
INTRODUCTION
The Impact of Religiosity
on the Marketing of Religious Iconography

Mass secularization of Christianity has given rise to mass marketing of religious iconography, including but not limited to images, films, print media, music, and jewelry. By definition, iconography consists of those images or symbols associated with religious or legendary subjects. Marketers face the problem of defining the target population for religious iconography in its many forms and manifestations. Factors affecting the marketing mix include religiosity, defined as the level or intensity of an individual's religious beliefs, as well as preferences for specific items of religious iconography, current ownership of such items, and willingness to purchase. In order to formulate a viable business plan to market religious iconography, private enterprises need to identify, define, and focus on their target market. This study contends that religiosity and the social behaviors that some churches consider more vice than virtue constitute major factors affecting the response of consumers to marketing efforts.

The discipline of Business Marketing seldom acknowledges the significance of the religious aspects affecting marketing plans; this study combines the disciplines of Business Marketing and Religious Study to establish the validity of religiosity as a major factor in the target marketing aspect of the promotion and selling of religious iconography products. This study provides a systematic study of problems associated with the lack of combined research studies of both the discipline of Business Marketing and the discipline of Religious Study. More importantly, this research study introduces a unique and reliable scale of the depth of a person's religiosity as it relates to those Consumer Marketing Behaviors that some churches consider more vice than virtue. While measurement of the depth of a person's religiosity is as difficult to quantify as any other behavior, for example, "Although political behavior in organizations is ubiquitous, measuring it is often difficult," as Kacmar and Ferris (1991), demonstrated in their study. This study, however, has developed a quantifiable measure to gauge an individual's level of religiosity.

The items included in the survey upon which this study is based have been divided into two categories: traditional and non-traditional.

1

In order to arrive at these conclusions, the study utilizes a survey referred to as the California Arkansas Graduate Survey of Religion and Marketing (CAGS) by Peter P. Madrid, Jr., and Michael S. Rahlwes, using students from California State University, Long Beach ($n = 494$) and University of Arkansas, Fayetteville ($n = 216$). The respondents included both graduate students and undergraduates ranging in age from 18 to 60. The sample included males and females, as well as all ethnicities (17). Long Beach, California, is a major suburb of Los Angeles, and the University of Arkansas is in the city of Fayetteville, the third most populous city in Arkansas.

Affinity analysis is also employed in this study to correlate purchases of religious iconography to 16 (perceived vices) and 4 (perceived virtues). As consumer social behaviors, which are perceived as vices or virtues by most denominations, these behaviors provide a measure of religious tenet adherence or lack thereof. By definition, affinity analysis is:

> Understanding the relations between one's products, as determined by customer buying patterns, can yield potentially useful insights into customer behavior and need. Such information can be useful and for discovering cross-selling opportunities and for determining how to more effectively promote one's products. In a B2B context, where a significant part of a sales organization's activities may be oriented to providing customers with detailed product information and application support, being able to introduce a customer to appropriate new products both creates new sales opportunities and can increase the effectiveness of the sales organization." (Ramsden, 2009).

Previous religiosity studies have used a unidimensional scale, employing church attendance as the sole measure of religiosity. This research study is unique in that it presents evidence that attests to a more precise, multidimensional method for establishing the level of consumer religiosity and a historically exact purchasing pattern of the acquisition of religious iconography as reliability statistics are defined in Table 1 in this study. Secondly, the study correlates the survey respondents' consumer social behaviors (survey vices and virtues—survey questionnaire items 71 through 90) to the consumer multidimensional religiosity index in an affinity analysis to provide combined target market group fields. Both of the above-stated elements provide new and original marketing research using the CAGS survey, which was specifically designed for this research. As of August 2010, "The role of religiousness as a variable in models of consumer behavior is not well-established. Research findings in this area tend to be sparse and conflicting, and measurement issues have yet to be addressed." (Wilkes, Burnett & Howell, 1986)

TABLE 1. Reliability Statistics

Cronbach's Alpha	N of Items
.797	11

The survey questionnaire consisted of 51 questions with a possible 111 responses related to consumer social behaviors (Appendix K). Questions concerning consumer purchasing of religious iconography are asked, as well as questions concerning Consumer Social Behaviors.

Religious iconography covered in this study includes 13 products: Religious DVD or VHS; Religious Music CD; Religious Painting or Print; Religious Statuette; Religious Pendant or Medal; Religious Jewelry; Other; Religious Holy Book; Religious Book; Other; Religious Bumper Sticker; Cross; Crucifix; Rosary; and Other Religious Iconography.

The consumer social behaviors (survey questionnaire items 71 through 90, 16 vices, 4 virtues) include the following behaviors:

1. I enjoy cigarettes/cigars
2. I enjoy dancing
3. I enjoy beer, wine, etc.
4. I enjoy concerts
5. I enjoy night clubbing
6. I enjoy video games
7. I enjoy TV shopping
8. I enjoy the computer/Internet
9. I enjoy self-improvement
10. I enjoy cultural events
11. I enjoy casino gambling
12. I enjoy lottery/sweepstakes
13. I enjoy astrology/horoscope

3

14. I enjoy tarot cards
15. I enjoy psychic readings
16. I enjoy worship/Bible
17. I enjoy politics
18. I enjoy donating to charity
19. I enjoy hunting/shooting
20. I enjoy watching/playing sports

Since the CAGS was conducted, a recent study employing a multidimensional religiosity index appeared in *Journal for the Scientific Study of Religion,* (Collett & Lizardo, June 2009). However, the variables employed in that religiosity index produce a moderate Cronbach's Alpha (rating of .64, compared to this study's multidimensional religiosity index rating of .797, (Table 1). Additionally, Collett and Lizardo (2009) employed different variables in their religiosity index, compared to this study. In alignment with their focus on gender with regard to power and control, Collett and Lizardo's study used three variables in their religiosity index: (1) Church attendance, (2) Frequency of prayer, and (3) Strength of affiliation.

In contrast, this thesis (CAGS) study used eleven variables:

1. Clergy Influence, item 16a
2. Influence of church education, item 20a
3. Influence of religious printed media, item 23a
4. Spiritual value, item 29a
5. Purchased item for worship purposes, item 46a
6. Purchased item for special enlightenment purposes, item 47a
7. Respondent classified themselves as seriously religious, item 51a
8. Respondent classified themselves as very religious, item 51b
9. Respondent enjoys worship/Bible, item 86a
10. Respondent believes in life after death, item 129a
11. I attend church services weekly, item 103a

"A unidimensional religiosity index using only church attendance is clearly insufficient ... Many surveys and polls have shown a distinct noncorrelation to individual spirituality, i.e., and strength of church affiliation." ("Divided: Survey finds split commitments," 1995).

> Large majorities of Americans say they're religious and think
> spirituality is important, but that doesn't translate into commitment
> to a single religion or house of worship, a MacArthur Foundation

survey has found. More than seven out of 10 Americans surveyed said they are religious and consider spirituality to be an important part of their lives. But about half attend religious services less than once a month or . . . (Journal Gazette—April 23, 1995).

A unidimensional religiosity index using only church attendance is clearly insufficient. Many surveys and polls have shown a distinct noncorrelation to individual spirituality and strength of church affiliation. The following survey shows split commitments:

Large majorities of Americans say they're religious and think spirituality is important, but that doesn't translate into commitment to a single religion or house of worship, a MacArthur Foundation survey has found. More than seven out of 10 Americans surveyed said they are religious and consider spirituality to be an important part of their lives. But about half attend religious services less than once a month or . . . ("Divided: Survey finds split commitments," 1995).

Polls in the late 1990s shows a trend that extends from the West Coast to the Bible Belt, as supported by the *Birmingham News* (AL):

Church attendance has suffered a five-year decline and sunk to its lowest level in two decades, according to research by the Barna Research Group of Glendale, California.

It's a trend that has been noticed even in the buckle of the Bible Belt, as Alabama churches feel the pressure to come up with innovative ways of keeping people coming to church. From the early '80s to the early '90s, there has been a definite change . . . Many more polls and surveys support the fact that church attendance is not a good indicator of religiosity. (Barna Research Group of Glendale, California, 1996).

5

CHAPTER 2

LITERATURE REVIEW

The student survey data collection method was carefully evaluated, since it represents a pivotal point in the research process. Both the modified personal interview and the Web-based survey methods were evaluated for use in the student assessment survey. Those areas affecting the evaluation process concerning the choice of collection methods are concisely discussed here. Areas or factors which tend to make one collection method preferable over another vary greatly. It is common knowledge within the discipline that no one data collection technique or system is consistently superior over the other. Rather, it is the demographics within the target group sought that dictates the most beneficial method. It is a generally accepted practice to adapt a particular method to one or more circumstances that are unique to the target group. Moreover, according to authors Kumar, Aaker, and Day (2002), in the book *Essentials of Marketing Research*:

> . . . the telephone and the mail survey methods are the dominant methods for conducting surveys. In the 1990 Walker Industry Image Study, it was found that 69 percent of the respondents had participated in mail surveys, 68 percent had participated in telephone surveys, 32 percent in mall-intercept surveys, and 15 percent in door-to-door interviews. However, both in academic and business environment and fax services . . . are being used increasingly.

The modified interview method employed here is similar to the executive interviewing method:

> Executive Interviewing—The term executive interviewing is used by marketing researchers to refer to the industrial equivalent of door-to-door interviewing. This type of survey involves interviewing business people at their offices concerning industrial products or services and virtues. (Kumar et al., 2002).

This modified interview method did provide help with questions; however, the CAGS study participants had few questions, since there are no open-ended

6

questions requiring clarification. In addition, the fact that there were no open-ended questions reduced the possibility of interviewer bias.

CHAPTER 3

SURVEY

The participants for this study were drawn from the California State University, Long Beach (CSULB), and from the University of Arkansas (U of A) Sam M. Walton College of Business. All were students of their respective universities. There were a total of 710 participants completing the survey from CSULB ($n = 494$) and the U of A ($n = 216$). All participants were selected as convenience samples. When professors were amenable, students were invited during classroom time to complete the survey questionnaire.

Survey Questionnaire

The study developed and administered the California Arkansas Graduate Survey CAGS Religion and Marketing survey at CSULB and the U of A between September 2004 and June 2006. There were a total of 51 questions with several having multiple response categories.

The first question asks, "Do you own, or will buy, or don't own/won't buy any of the following items." These items represent the consumer purchasing behavior of religious iconography:

Religious DVD or VCR movie

1. Religious Music CD
2. Religious painting or print
3. Religious statuette
4. Religious pendant or medal
5. Any other religious jewelry
6. Holy book
7. Religious book
8. Religious bumper sticker
9. Cross
10. Crucifix
11. Rosary
12. Other religious iconography

For those who own religious iconography, the tables in Appendix B compare CSULB with the U of A by the number of participants. Subsequent questions were related to purchasing preferences displayed in distribution percentage tables in Appendix B.

The question related to the Consumer Social Behaviors viewed as vices by some religious groups consisted of a multiple response whereby the participant could answer "yes" to all or none of the choices.

The survey questionnaire statement was worded, "I enjoy" with the following choices (Appendix K, questions 71 through 90):

1. Cigarette/Cigar
2. Dancing
3. Beer, Wine, etc.
4. Concerts
5. Night clubbing
6. Video Games
7. TV Shopping
8. Computer/Internet
9. Self-improvement
10. Cultural Events
11. Casino Gambling
12. Lottery/Sweepstakes
13. Astrology/Horoscope
14. Tarot cards
15. Psychic Readings
16. Worship/Bible
17. Politics
18. Donating to Charity
19. Hunting/Shooting
20. Watch/Play sports

Correlation tables 7–13 and 15–33 compare this list of consumer social behaviors for CSULB and U of A by cases.

CHAPTER 4

PRIMARY AND SECONDARY HYPOTHESES

The primary hypothesis of this study is that religiosity correlates with the purchasing behavior with regard to religious iconography. The secondary hypothesis includes the assertion that consumer social behaviors labeled by certain churches as "vices and virtues" also correlate to purchasing behavior of religious iconography. Likewise, both hypotheses, as they relate to purchasing behavior, are affected by current ownership status and level of religiosity, holding true across demographic factors, such as age and gender. Further, this study looks at both traditional and non-traditional forms of iconography.

This suggests that religiosity has a direct impact on consumer spending, or in the case of this study, purchase of religious iconography.

Objective Links to Theory

This study provides numerous primary research data unique to the customer or consumer profile. "The results suggest that religiosity is a viable consumer behavior construct in that it (1) did correlate with the lifestyle variables selected; (2) contributed directly to the model along with sex, age, and income; and (3) was successfully operationalized through multiple measures." (Wilkes et al., 1986). This suggests that religiosity has a direct impact on consumer spending, or in the case of this study, purchase of religious iconography.

In this research study, Affinity Analysis, or more simply put, is a form of analysis that:

> . . . provides insights into consumer co-purchasing behavior and market basket affinities. This analysis helps consumer products manufacturers determine which items to promote or to create pull-through. Affinity Analysis helps consumer products manufacturers answer key questions that can help them optimize their sales and marketing strategies." (DemandTec Inc., 2009).

With regard to the survey activities (consumer social behavior questions 71 through 90), the affinity analysis will help not only religious iconography product manufacturers but also advertising marketing strategies by establishing.

10

"Which set of products makes up common consumer solution sets? Which item of the solution set is the 'anchor' that drives sales of other items?" (DemandTec Inc., 2009).

A typical example that illustrates DemandTec Analytical Services' statements above is more simply stated by:

> Dr. Larose who [sic] received his Ph.D. in Statistics from the University of Connecticut in Storrs in 1996. He designed, developed, and directs the data mining programs at CCSU, including the world's first online Master of Science program in data mining. He is a consultant in data mining and statistical analysis . . . (Larose, 2006).

In Professor Daniel T. Larose's book, Discovering Knowledge in Data, An Introduction to Data Mining, the example is about how:

> . . . a particular supermarket may find that of the 1000 customers shopping on a Thursday night, 200 bought diapers, and of the 200 who bought diapers, 50 bought beer. Thus, the association rule would be: If buy diapers, then buy beer, with a support of $50/1000 = 5$ percent and a confidence of $50/200 = 25$ percent. Examples of association tasks in business and research include . . . Finding out which items in a supermarket are purchased together, and which items are never purchased together" (Larose, 2005).

CHAPTER 5
STUDY HYPOTHESES

The general null hypothesis for this study states that there are no significant relationships between the religiosity index and the individual Consumer Social Behaviors and religious iconographic ownership variables. This study utilized Statistical Package for the Social Sciences (SPSS) software to conduct the statistical analysis.

Subsequent to establishing the religiosity index, the survey population was classified in regard to their levels of religiosity. Affinity analysis was then applied, drawing bivariate correlations among religiosity index, Consumer Social Behaviors, and religious iconographic ownership variables. This process ascertains the existence of correlated relationships observed between religiosity and these variables.

A correlation is also frequently called the Pearson product-moment correlation or the Pearson r. Although the Pearson r is predicated on the assumption that the two variables involved are approximately normally distributed, the formula often performs well even when assumptions of normality are violated or when one of the variables is discrete. (SPSS for Windows Step by Step, Fifth Edition Darren George, and Paul Mallery, Boston, Pearson 2005).

So, while the religiosity index is a continuous variable, the individual Consumer Social Behaviors and religious iconographic ownership variables are dichotomous.

Study Analysis

The research design was formulated to provide a "market basket analysis" that will permit an analytic market examination of effective correlated "consumer marketing behavior" variables. These variables are product-specific to religious iconography products that will promote bivariate correlated "cross-advertising fields"[1] "affinity analysis."[2] These cross-advertising fields are examined by

---

[1]Cross-Advertising Fields — For the purposes of this study, cross-advertising fields refer to target market groups that share two or more Activities, Interests, and Opinions (AIOs).

[2]Affinity Analysis is a "Causal relationship or connexion (as flowing the one from the other, or having a common source), or such agreement or similarity of nature or character as might result from such relationship if it existed; family likeness." (Affinity, (2011).

analyzing the relationship between consumers' acquisitions (religious iconographic variables) and the religiosity index.

Moreover, in the correlational analysis between the religiosity index and the participants' consumer marketing behaviors, which are perceived as vices by the majority of religious groups, the affinity analysis of this study provides an integral micro-level of granularity for cross-advertising marketing plans that can provide new marketing strategies. The study analyzes participant/consumer historical purchasing patterns against their levels of religiosity. Moreover, this process depicts what religious iconography products, such as "Holy Books," which are historically purchased by those who buy, will correlate, for example, to the purchase of "Video Games." In addition, this study provides analysis enabling the determination of Item Affinity; in short, the probability of two or more products being purchased at the same or a later historical time may be determined using this research design.

An Affinity Analysis helps to provide the analytical approach to access relevant marketing data that identifies cross-item purchases, aka market basket analysis.

A market or shopping basket typically arises as the result of a consumer's multicategory decision on the choice or non-choice of items among retail assortments during a shopping-trip. We demonstrate the adoption of selected data mining techniques for analyzing such market baskets using real-world supermarket transaction data. The employed methods are comprised of onventional affinity analysis. (University of Wollongong [UOW], n.d.).

Covariates and Measures

For every cross-selling transaction in the user's shopping history, the item Affinity Engine derives its calculations from the correlated number of times respondents select a product and activities in the affinity analysis group (survey consumer marketing behavior vices and virtues questions 71 through 90) as defined in this research study. Item affinity is calculated from the correlational analysis comparing relationships among the religious iconographic variables and the Consumer Social Behaviors. In addition, the historical variables provide multivariate predictions for the purchase of religious iconography products as defined in this research study, based on the respondent's level of religiosity.

Employing the probability of two or more products being purchased at the same or at a later historical time is a unique method similar to "The use of eminent people for the promotion of a brand, which is . . . the use of celebrities because many consumers identify with the celebrities, and it is a general psychology to emulate the person one identifies with. Celebrities are widely admired and hence prove highly effective in advertising, e.g., a religious consumer who smokes and would buy a cigarette lighter with an engraved cross on it. (Buzzle.com, 2010).

In addition, the affinity analysis allows the cross-advertising fields to identify shared target market groups that will allow advertising campaigns that target two or more unrelated items that share the same target groups or AIOs.[3]

The study variables were inter-correlated and included the religiosity index, the iconography purchase variables, and the consumer social behavior variables. Viewing these correlations as advertising variables, the correlations (the 11 variables comprising the religiously scale) of respondents who have been analyzed with the religiosity index. The thesis study (CAGS) used 11 variables.

The utilized variables are (1) Clergy Influence, 16a; (2) Influence of church education, 20a; (3) Influence of religious printed media, 23a; (4) Spiritual value, 29a; (5) Purchased item for worship purposes, 46a; (6) Purchased item for special enlightenment purposes, 47a; (7) Respondent classified themselves as seriously religious, 51a; (8) Respondent classified themselves as very religious, 51b; (9) Respondent enjoys worship/Bible, 86a; (10) Respondent believes in life after death.

The 13 religious iconography items are as follows:

Any other religious jewelry, 6a; (7) Holy Book, 7a; (8) Religious book, 8a; (9) Religious bumper sticker, 9a; (10) Cross, 10a; (11) Crucifix, 11a; (12) Rosary, 12a; (13)

The 20 consumer social behaviors include:

Cigarette / Cigar, 71a; Dancing, 72a; Beer, Wine, etc., 73a; Concerts, 74a; Night clubbing, 75a; Video Games, 76a; TV Shopping, 77a; Computer / Internet, 78a; Self-improvement, 79a; Cultural Events, 80a; Casino Gambling, 81a; Lottery / Sweepstakes, 82a; Astrology / Horoscope, 83a; Tarot cards, 84a; Psychic Readings, 85a; Worship / Bible, 86a; Politics, 87a; Donating to Charity, 88a; Hunting / Shooting, 89a; and Watch / Play sports, 90a.

Marketers can use affinity analysis to set an advertising strategy that will define a common interest in a religious iconography product with one or more of the consumer marketing behaviors. This would allow a dual advertising marketing plan that may, with high probability, interact with the greatest majority of viable consumers. It will raise and answer the question whether high levels of consumer social behaviors, which are perceived as human vices / virtues, will be statistically significantly related to historical purchasing patterns for religious iconography. From this analysis, the study proposes to extrapolate viable target marketing groups and project probable sales.

---

[3]AIO "Activities, Interests, and Opinions . . . shows a number of variables for each of the AIO dimensions—along with some demographics used to add detail to the lifestyle profile of a target market" Perreault & McCarthy, 2006, exhibits 5-6 on pp. 116–117).

[4](1) Religious DVD or VCR movie, 1a; (2) Religious Music CD, 2a; (3) Religious painting or print, 3a; (4) Religious statuette, 4a; (5) Religious pendant or medal, 5a; (6) Other religious iconography, 13a.

CHAPTER 6
METHODOLOGY
Survey Sample

The Methodology Survey Sample was selected from students at California State University, Long Beach, and students at University of Arkansas. The purpose of this sample was to draw upon the cultural diversity of the two distinctive regions of the country. CSULB is an urban university with a large commuter student population, whereas the U of A is a rural school with a more traditional student population. Data collection consisted of 3 phases, starting with a self-administered questionnaire and modified personal interview.

First, a protocol was developed using a combination of the personal interview with a semi- self-administered questionnaire (Phase 1). Since the participants would be surveyed in the classroom setting, administering the questionnaire would be efficient. The coordination of the classes at CSULB was accomplished with the assistance of Dr. Darshan Sachdeva for the College of Business Administration and Dr. Carlos Piar at the College of Liberal Arts in the Religious Studies department. In the case of University of Arkansas, Dr. Alan Ellstrand coordinated the data collection.

At both universities, the greatest number of responses was gathered at the Colleges of Business Administration. In all classes, the interviewer provided the participants with an opportunity to ask questions and helped to pass out and collect the completed survey questionnaires. Since the students were a captive audience, there were no long delays and no cancellations.

The participants were provided verbal instructions and answers to their questions concerning the questionnaire and purpose of the study. They completed the survey in about one hour, using Scantron answer sheets to score their responses.

Phase 2 consisted of reading the answer sheets using Scantron's Parscore software and a Scanmark 2260 scanner. Phase 3 was when the data cleaning and scale and variable construction occurred using Microsoft Excel and SPSS (Statistical Package for the Social Sciences). In total there were 710 student surveyed, 494 from CSULB and 216 from the U of A. (See the protocol statement in Appendix J that was read to each group/class.)

Study Construct

The multi-dimensional measurement of religiosity was developed using 11 questionnaire items. These items were related to the following categories, resulting in a religiosity index ranging from 0 to 12 points.

Categories:

A. Who or what influenced your decision to purchase iconographic items.

B. Reasons for having purchased iconographic items.

C. Perceived Level of Religiousness

D. Self-Reported Religious Behaviors

Within category A, 4 questions were asked:

1. "Which if any of the following persons' recommendations influenced your decision to purchase the items from the product list?" If the subject marked "clergy," the item was scored "1."

2. "Did your Sunday School / Church Education influence your decision to purchase?" If the subject marked "yes," the item was scored "1."

3. "Which of the following forms of printed media influenced your decision to purchase?" If the subject marked "church newsletters," the item was scored "1."

4. "Which of the following influenced your decision to purchase items from the product list?" If the subject marked "spiritual value," the item was scored "1."

Within category B, 2 questions were asked:

5. The question read, "Select all the purposes for which you purchased the items listed in the product list." If the subject marked "worship," the item was scored "1."

6. The question read, "Select all the purposes for which you purchased the items listed in the product list." If the subject marked "special enlightenment," the item was scored "1."

The focus of Category C was on the "Perceived Level of Religiousness." Two questions were asked:

7. "I classify myself as (a) seriously religious, (b) very religious, (c) somewhat religious, (d) not religious, (e) unsure." If this item was marked "seriously religious," the item was scored (3), seriously religious, (2) very religious, (1) somewhat religious, (0) not religious, (0) unsure.

8. "Do you believe in life after death?" (a) yes, (b) no, (c) unsure, (d) N/A. This item was scored (3) yes, (2) unsure, (1) no, and (0) N/A.

Category D covers the area of self-reported religious behaviors. Three questions are included.

9. If the participant attends church services and answered the question, "I attend church services (a) more than weekly; (b) weekly; (c) 1 or 2 times a year; (d) less than weekly but more than twice a year; (e) N/A." Then the item was scored (4) more than weekly; (3) weekly; (2) less than weekly but more than twice a year; (1) 1 or 2 times a year; (0) N/A. "more than weekly," the item was scored.

10. If the respondents answered the question, "I enjoy workshop / Bible," then the item was scored "1."

11. If the participant attends religious services and answered the question, "How often do you attend religious services?" (a) Less than once a month, (b) Occasionally attend, (c) Nearly every week or more often, and (d) N/A. Then the item was scored (1) Less than once a month, (2) Occasionally attend, and (3) Nearly every week or more often, and (0) N/A.

CHAPTER 7
RELIGIOSITY INDEX

The religiosity index is comprised of the following indicators, based upon the CAGS survey questions, possible responses, definition of germane and non-germane variables (survey responses), interpreted relevance as an indicator and supporting polls and/or surveys. The weight given to each indicator is reviewed and supported, with regard to past polls and published studies.

---

1)   16a   *Clergy Influence*

Which if any of the following persons' recommendations influenced your

decision to purchase the items from the product list?

(Select ALL that apply.)

14a   Religious leader, non-clergy

15a   Friend/acquaintance

16a   Clergy

17a   Family

18a   N/A

FIGURE 1. Clergy Influence

Response 16a Clergy is a germane variable used in the linguistic context of "recommendations that influenced a decision to purchase religious iconography" and how this sphere of influence extends beyond influencing religious purchases, as substantiated by a poll, survey, or study which serves as its authoritative construct. In the case of "clergy influence," the *San Jose Mercury News,* a renowned California newspaper, reported that "Americans are far more likely to consider religion central to their lives and to support giving clergy a say in public policy than people in nine countries that are close allies, according to an AP-Ipsos poll." ("Americans more likely, " 2005).

The probability that Americans can be swayed to accept politics in religion would show a vast influence in all areas, including purchases of religious iconography. To this day, long-deceased clergy are still influencing Americans, as stated in an article by *Watertown Daily Times*:

> The 76th anniversary of the Rev. Martin Luther King Jr.'s birth, local clergy reflected on the civil rights leader's enduring influence. Clergy said they often quoted and sought to emulate the Rev. Mr. King, who had a gift for making biblical messages of hope and inclusiveness relevant to modern audiences. One pastor said the Rev. Dr. King inspired him to consider preaching on overcoming the social divisions parishioners encounter in everyday life. These are only two of many observations accepted as authoritative citation. (This is from the San Jose Mercury article, as provided in the Watertown Daily News Times, Watertown, NY).

Relative to Clergy Influence variables, 14a religious leader, non-clergy, 15a Friend/acquaintance, 17a Family, and 18a N/A are not germane in the linguistic context of "recommendations that influenced a decision to purchase religious iconography." The germane variables are mutually exclusive; the respondent is influenced by clergy or is not. The weighting of the variable is displayed in Table 2 in relation to all other Religiosity Index Elements such as variables 20a, Influence of religious printed media; 23a, Spiritual value; 29a, Purchased item for worship purposes, 46a 6). Purchased item for special enlightenment purposes; 47a, Respondent classified themselves as seriously religious; 51b, Respondent enjoys worship/Bible; 86a, Respondent believes in life after death, 129a.

2)   20a   *Influence of church education*

Did your Sunday School / Church Education influence your decision to purchase?
(Select only ONE.)

20a   Yes

20b   No

20c   Never attended Sunday School / Church Education

FIGURE 2. Influence of church education

This is a germane variable used in the linguistic context of "recommendations that influenced a decision to purchase religious iconography" as substantiated by a poll / survey / study, which serves as its authoritative construct.

3)   23a   *Influence of religious printed media*

Which of the following forms of printed media influenced your decision to purchase? (Select ALL that apply.)

21a   Books

22a   Magazines

23a   Church newsletters

24a   Other printed media

25a   N/A

FIGURE 3. Influence of religious printed media

Relative to the influence of church education, variable 20c, Never attended Sunday School/Church Education, is not germane in the linguistic context of "recommendations that influenced a decision to purchase religious iconography." The germane variable is mutually exclusive; the respondent is influenced by Sunday School/Church Education or is not. The weighting of the variable is displayed in Table 2 in relation to all other Religiosity Index Elements such as variables (23a, Spiritual value; 29a, Purchased item for worship purposes; 46a 6). Purchased item for special enlightenment purposes; 47a, Respondent classified themselves as seriously religious; 86a, Respondent believes in life after death, 129a.

This is a germane variable used in the linguistic context of "recommendations that influenced a decision to purchase religious iconography," as substantiated by a poll/survey/study which serves as its authoritative construct.

Relative to the influence of religious printed media, variables 21a Books, 22a Magazines, 24a Other printed media, and 25a N/A, are not germane in the specific linguistic context of "recommendations that influenced a decision to purchase religious iconography." Germane variables are mutually exclusive; the respondent is influenced by Church Newsletters or is not. The weighting of the variable can be found on Table 2 of the religiosity index, since the response choices were "Yes or No," such as variables 20a, Influence of church education; 29a, Spiritual value; 46a, Purchased item for worship purposes; 47a, Purchased item for special enlightenment purposes; 51b, Respondent classified themselves as seriously religious; 86a, Respondent enjoys worship/Bible; and 129a, Respondent believes in life after death.

4)　　$\boxed{29a}$　*Spiritual value*

Which of the following influenced your decision to purchase items from the product list?
(Select ALL that apply.)

$\boxed{29a}$　Spiritual value

$\boxed{30a}$　Tradition

$\boxed{31a}$　Guilt

$\boxed{32a}$　N/A

FIGURE 4.　Spiritual Value

This is a germane variable used in the linguistic context of "recommendations that influenced a decision to purchase religious iconography," as substantiated by a poll/survey/study which serves as its authoritative construct.

Relative to Spiritual value (please note that question answers 5 and 6 were taken from the question, "Select all the purposes for which you purchased the items listed in the product list. [Select all that apply]) variables, 30a Tradition, 31a Guilt, and 32a N/A are not germane in the linguistic context of recommendations that influenced a decision to purchase religious iconography. The germane variables are mutually exclusive; the respondent is influenced by Spiritual value or is not. The weighting of the variable is displayed in Table 2 in relation to all other Religiosity Index Elements such as variables (20a, Influence of religious printed media; 23a, Spiritual value. 29a; Purchased item for worship purposes; 46a 6). Purchased item for special enlightenment purposes; 47a, Respondent classified themselves as seriously religious; 86a, Respondent believes in life after death; 129a.

5)　　[45]　*Purchased item for worship purposes and special enlightenment purposes*

(Select all the purposes for which you purchased the items listed in the product list. (Select ALL that apply.)

[45a] Display only

[46a] Worship

[47a] Special Enlightenment

[48a] Wear/jewelry

[49a] N/A

FIGURE 5. Purchased item for worship purposes and special enlightenment purposes

Questions 46 Worship and 47 Special enlightenment are both germane variables, and for the purposes of this study, they were weighted equally, even though they were presented to the survey respondent as two parts of one question. Relative to worship purposes and Special enlightenment variables, (see above: 45 Display only, 48

Wear/Jewelry, and 49 N/A), these items are not germane in the linguistic context of "recommendations that influenced a decision to purchase religious iconography." Whether the germane variables are mutually exclusive, the respondent is influenced by clergy or is not. The weighting of the variable is displayed in Table 2 in relation to all other Religiosity Index Elements.

6) | 51 | *Respondents classified themselves as seriously religious*

I classify myself as:

| 51a | Seriously religious

| 51b | Very religious

| 51c | Somewhat religious

| 51d | Not religious

| 51e | Unsure

FIGURE 6. Respondents classified themselves as seriously religious

This survey question allows the respondents to rate themselves on a mutually exclusive scale ranging from seriously religious, very religious, somewhat religious, not religious, and unsure. For the purposes of this study, this variable was scored "3," "2," "1," "0," (51a, Seriously religious; and 51b, Very religious; 51c, somewhat religious; 51d, not religious; and 51e, unsure) with those marking "not religious" or "unsure" assigned "0."

The weighting of the variable is displayed in Table 2 in relation to all other Religiosity Index Elements such as variables 20a, Influence of church education; 29a, Spiritual value; 46a, Purchased item for worship purposes; 47a, Purchased item for special enlightenment purposes; 51b, Respondent classified themselves as seriously religious; 86a, Respondent enjoys worship/Bible; and 129a, Respondent believes in life after death.

This survey question allows the respondents to rate themselves on a mutually exclusive scale ranging from seriously religious, very religious, somewhat religious, not religious, and unsure. For the purposes of this study, this variable was scored "3," "2," "1," "0" (51a Seriously religious, and 51b Very religious, 51c somewhat religious, 51d not religious, and 51e unsure with those marking "not religious" or "unsure" assigned "0."

25

7)　　　$\boxed{129}$　*Respondent believes in life after death*

I classify myself as:

$\boxed{51a}$　Seriously religious

$\boxed{51b}$　Very religious

$\boxed{51c}$　Somewhat religious

$\boxed{51d}$　Not religious

$\boxed{51e}$　Unsure

FIGURE 7. Respondent believes in life after death

Relative to the respondents' belief in life after death variables 129a, Yes; 129b, No; 129c, Unsure; 129d, N/A are germane in the specific linguistic context of the religious belief in life after death and its relation to religiosity.

The germane variables are mutually exclusive; the respondent believes in life after death or does not. The weighting of the variable is displayed in Table 2 in relation to all other Religiosity Index Elements.

8)   103   *Respondents attend church services*

I classify myself as:

103a More than weekly

103b Weekly

103c 1 or 2 times a year

103d Less than weekly but more than twice a year

103e N/A

FIGURE 8. Respondents attend church services

This survey question allows the respondents to rate themselves on a mutually exclusive scale ranging from more than weekly, weekly, 1 or 2 times a year, less than weekly but more than twice a year, or N/A. For the purposes of this study, this variable was scored more than weekly (4), weekly (3), 1 or 2 times a year (1), less than weekly but more than twice a year (2), or N/A (0).

10).   86a   Respondent enjoys worship/Bible.

Relative to the enjoyment of religion, all variables 71a and 90a, except for 86a (Worship/Bible), are not germane in the specific linguistic context of the enjoyment of religion and its relation to religiosity. The germane variables are mutually exclusive; the respondent enjoys religious worship and/or Bible or is not. The weighting of the variable is displayed in Table 2 in relation to all other Religiosity Index Elements such as variables 16a, 20a, 23a, 29a, 46a, 47a, and 129a.

9) |127| *Respondents attend religious services*

I classify myself as:

|103a| Less than once or twice a year

|103b| Occasionally attend

|103c| Nearly every week or more often

|103d| N/A

FIGURE 9. Respondents attend religious services

This survey question allows the respondents to rate themselves on a mutually exclusive scale. For the purposes of this study, this variable was scored less than once a month (1), Occasionally attend (1), Nearly every week or more often (3), and N/A (0). The weighting of the variable is displayed in Table 2.

TABLE 2. Religiosity Index

	Range	Point Value
Clergy influence purchase	0–1	1
Religious education influence purchase	0–1	1
Church newsletters influence purchase	0–1	1
Spiritual value influence purchase	0–1	1
Purchased for worship	0–1	1
Purchased for special enlightenment	0–1	1
Level of religiousness	0–3	3
Enjoy worship/Bible	0–1	1
Attend church services	0–4	4
Attend religious services	0–3	3
Belief in life after death	0–3	3

NOTE: The religiosity index can range from 0 to 20.

Highest religiosity levels

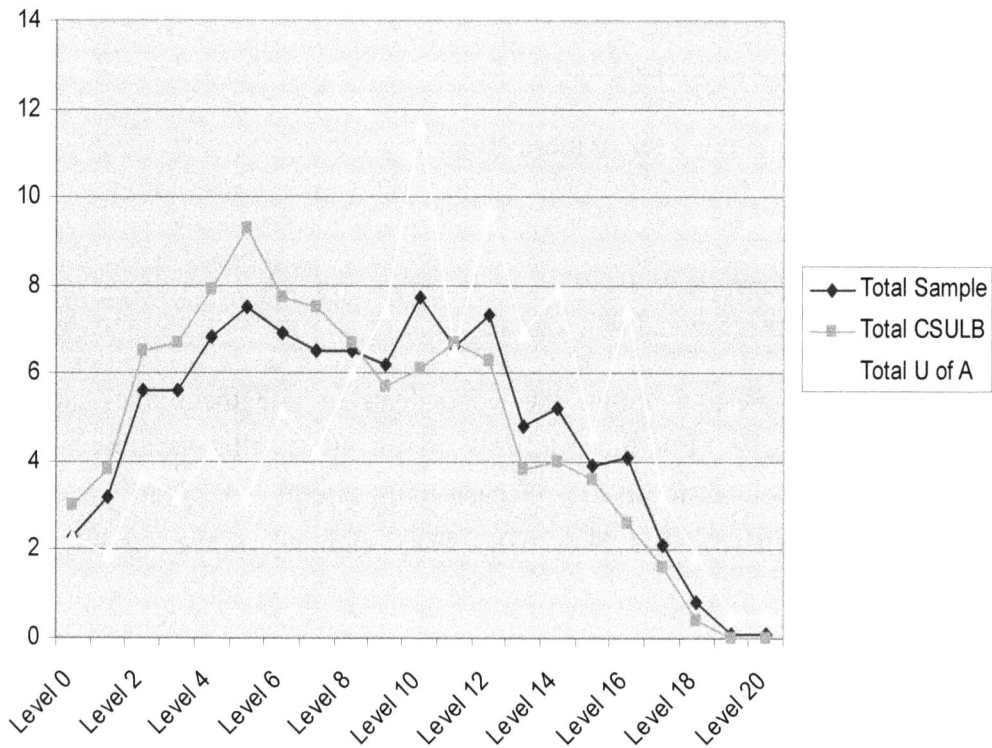

FIGURE 10. Highest religiosity levels

Levels 10 through 17 are the highest religiosity levels found for total sample population,
U of A. Levels 5 through 8 are the highest religiosity levels found for total sample population, CSULB.

CHAPTER 8

TRADITIONAL AND
NON-TRADITIONAL ICONOGRAPHY

For the purposes of this paper, religious iconography refers to religious social stratification, which is equivalent to social status within the religious community. Defining these subgroups allows a market segmentation strategy that would separate the homogeneous subgroups into segment markets used to promote iconography.

Also, for the purposes of this study, religious iconography must be defined beyond its normal parameters. For many individuals, religious iconography can mean many things, with both a religious and secular meaning or perceived purpose. To clarify the meaning used in this study, we must first eliminate those uses or definitions that do not apply. Some have perceived iconography as pictures or images more than other types of representation as sacred or religious. More complex meanings include icon representation as a point of view for yet another purpose or objective, by virtue of a similarity, tradition, or analogy to another more important event or use. This type of use or meaning usually implies a psychological representation, thought, or conception that is unique to a discipline or field within the religious community.

This study reinforces that in its "commercial product form," religious iconography such as the cross, provides a value to the consumer beyond the cost of the materials used in its manufacture, as described by distinguished scholar William C. Spohn not only in spiritual meaning, but also in motivation both inside and outside the Christian community since motivation:

> . . . cannot be so readily separated from moral content, since why we do something often inners into the very meaning of what we are doing. Often, different motivation changes the meaning of the action. Nonviolence understood as participating in the cross of the Christ as a meaning different from Gandhian nonviolence. They are not the same moral practice, outfitted in disposable rhetorical garments" (Spohn 2007).

It is apparent that this study must first identify the distinction between religious iconography in the broader sense of the word and in its meaning within the confines of this study. This section defines Christian iconography within the parameters of the CAGS survey used in this study. Once this section has defined the parameters of Christian iconography, insofar as the definitions relate from the broader sense to the confines of this study, it then defines the forms of symbolism and how they relate to the sacred within the confines of the study of religious iconography. The items included in the survey upon which this study is based have been divided into two categories: traditional and non-traditional.

While religious iconography in the broader sense can include a wide variety of objects, actions, and experience, this study is limited to 13 items that have some commercial value as consumer goods, e.g., items of mass production and marketing. Religious iconography can take many forms, and each individual form can change in meaning over time," since their relationship to what is symbolized is conventional or intentional rather than necessary, and shifts in usage are commonplace. For example, during the Vietnam War, the forming of the fingers in a V-shape was employed in the peace movement to symbolize peace; the same gesture during World War II represented victory." (Schmidt, 1988). Nevertheless, the individual items included in the survey retain their character as either traditional or non-traditional iconography.

Religious Statuettes: Just as doctrinal symbolism can take a visual form that is portrayed in paintings or prints, so can it manifest itself in religious statuettes (e.g., Sacred Heart), such as was an item included in the survey used in this study. Beyond statuettes, the survey also dealt with religious pendants or medals (e.g., St. Christopher, Virgin Mary, others), as well as other forms of iconography which have contributed to the mass production stage that religious iconography has reached, as referenced within this study.

We have clearly defined the respondent's choices of religious iconography as presented in this study, based primarily upon the survey of 494 students of California State University, Long Beach (CSULB), and 216 students of the University of Arkansas, both combined in the CAGS survey, in predominantly general education courses. By restricting the survey to those students enrolled in predominantly general education courses, this study was broad based and representative of the University demographic populations.

The 710 students that responded to the survey were more than sufficient to represent in varying demographics the general populations of both universities. The surveys administered at the University of Arkansas were focused on the College of Business, and, therefore, contained special characteristics of business major students that may not be representative of all students at the university. However, for the purposes of this research, the specific characteristics of business major students shall not be addressed.

The administration of the survey at the University of Arkansas was delegated to resident graduate students who were supervised and coordinated by the MBA director, Dr. Alan Ellstrand, and coordinated within the parameters of this study, as prescribed by CSULB graduate student Pete Madrid. The smaller number of respondents at the University of Arkansas do not impair or reduce the number required to achieve a plus or minus 3 percent representation of the student body of the University of Arkansas, since the University of Arkansas population is substantially smaller then the California State University.

This section further addresses each of the 13 choices or forms of Christian iconography that were studied within the confines of the survey as presented to the respondents. Among the 13 items, both traditional and non-traditional Christian iconography were represented. This section identifies which of those 13 items are traditional forms of iconography and which are forms of non-traditional iconography. It further defines each item's broader definition and specified definition in the context of the survey for the purposes of this study. Moreover, the individual items as discussed in this section are expounded upon to the same extent that the interviewer verbally expounded upon each of the examples and what it entails. For example, item 10 "a cross," was explained as a form that could represent any one of several representational crosses, such as the Latin cross, or St. Anthony's cross, Cross of Calvary, cross Lorraine, Patriarchal cross, Greek cross, St. Andrew's cross, cross potent, papal cross, Maltese cross or Celtic cross. Just as crosses were discussed in their broader meaning and their specified meaning in the context of the survey, so were all individual items in the survey. This chapter deals with each of the 13 items in detail.

Iconography can be defined as representational symbols; that is, "symbols that function religiously point to the holy . . . intended to draw humans from their rootedness in the ordinary to the transcendent or enable them to experience transcendence within the ordinary. They must point beyond themselves to a mysterious reality that lies beyond the limits of language. Anything can serve as a symbol of the sacred because as a great many traditions teach, holiness is present or can be manifested in everything. The test of all religious symbols and lying leads is their power to illumine the sacred. Symbols are like Windows; they not only connect experience to the meaning of the experience but also provide a fields of vision through which humans can explore different worlds of meaning, including religious ones." (Schmidt, 1988).

Representational and Presentational Iconography:

Symbols of the holy that depend on the likeness between symbol and symbolized all are indispensable to religious expression. The likeness can be an iconic or pictorial resemblance — for example, paintings or sculptures that depict some event in Jesus in his life — or metaphorical, for example, symbolizing the divine energy through an analogy to sexual energy. Iconic likenesses are evident in anthropomorphic images of divinities as well as in images of such historical master figures as Buddha and Christ. Anthropomorphic images of the holy suggests that human beings resemble the holy, a conviction evident in the Christian doctrines suggests that humans beings are created in God's image and that the divine become flesh in Jesus of Nazareth. (Schmidt, 1988).

Depending on the context, iconic likenesses may be representations of a sacred subject or a focused presence of the holy. Although there are traditions of true images of sacred figures ... such as images of Christ on the Shroud of Turin and Veronica's Veil, most depictions are not portraits but expressions of how such figures are known in the life of the spirit. (Schmidt, 1988).

Distinctions Between Traditional and Non-Traditional Iconography

For the purposes of this study, it is paramount that a decisive distinction is made from "Traditional Christian Iconography" and "Non-Traditional Christian Iconography." Through the ages, an evolution of iconography has coalesced into what we define today as traditional iconography. This traditional iconography is in use in the predominant, mainstream denominations of Christianity. This research study focuses on a total of 13 religious forms of iconography, seven of which are defined as traditional forms of religious iconography, and six as non-traditional. In its utmost use, all forms of religious iconography have been utilized as representational, Doctrinal, or Conceptual forms of Christian.

33

Religious Iconography

The description of "traditional iconography," as presented in the survey

A religious painting or print (e.g., Last Supper, angels)

A religious statuette (e.g., Sacred Heart)

A religious pendant or medal (e.g., St. Christopher, Virgin Mary, others)

A holy book (e.g., Bible, Book of Mormon, New Testament, other Holy
Books)

A cross

A crucifix

A rosary

Traditional iconography as defined in this study includes both presentational and representational symbols.

Representational religious symbols are words, gestures, or things that by custom or stipulation stand for or represent something sacred. Depending on the context, the same symbol may function either representationally only or presentationally. (Schmidt, 1988).

For example, while a cross or rosary would be representational, a holy book such as the Bible is defined as presentational.

The description of "non-traditional iconography," as presented in the survey:

1. A religious DVD or VCR movie (e.g., Passion of Christ, Ten Commandments)
2. Any religious music CD
3. Any other religious jewelry
4. Any other religious iconography
5. A religious book (e.g., Billy Graham, Chuck Missler, Hal Lindsey)
6. A religious bumper sticker (e.g., fish)

Non-traditional iconography as defined in this study includes both representational and presentational symbols. For example, while other religious iconography and other religious jewelry include both presentational and representational symbols, a religious DVD or music CD would be presentational.

Definition of traditional items of religious iconography. Religious Paintings: Scholars in the past have tended to underestimate the importance and relevance of religious paintings to the American culture.

The inclination to minimize the significance of religious visual culture has led to a kind of historical myopia in both art history and religious history. It would still, for example, come as a surprise to most art historians that a 'religious' painting, the Flagellants (1889), by Milwaukee artist Carl Marr, was one of two most frequently visited and energetically celebrated painters in the fine arts Palace at the 1893 World's Columbian Exhibition; that the only portrait for which agnostic Thomas Eakins received an official reward from the Pennsylvania Academy of fine arts depicted a Catholic priest (Eakins painted 17 priests among his 'heroes of modern life'); and that a group of well-known un-American painters competed in 1905 to provide the superior representation of a 'modern' Jesus, with the resulting paintings widely toured and published in the following year. Perhaps most startling, when registered against late-20th-century art historical expectations, Alfred H. Bar Jr., founding director of the Museum of modern Art, was also an observant Presbyterian who headed a commission on art for the national Council of Churches of Christ. This commission included among its leaders other prominent arts professionals like Perry T. Rathbone, Charles Rufus Morey, and George Heard Hamilton." (Morgan and Promey, 2001).

Religious Statuettes: Oddly, while Protestant Christians tend to have little difficulty accepting presentations of faith such as movies and paintings, they tend to object to the statues and statuettes that populate Catholic, Orthodox, and Episcopal churches as idolatrous.

The association of pictorial and sculpted figures with idolatry is undergirded by the biblical injunction to neither make nor worship images or likenesses of things; thus, Judaism, Islam and most of Protestant Christianity have been primarily traditions of holy Scripture (Torah, Qur'an, and Bible) inhospitable to or on comp Kabul with paintings and sculptures because of fear humans might confuse such creations with the creator and worship the former rather than the latter." (Schmidt, 1988).

Yet, while the Protestants consider that reading the Bible is enough to nourish their faith in salvation, the Catholics gain access to Scripture only by means of the tradition which created it and which has carried it down the ages, according to the church's living teaching and especially thanks to the liturgy." (Di Falco, 2000).

In other words, the Catholic faith sees no problem with displaying a wide variety of images employed to bolster faith.

Religious pendants: Pendants other than crosses, crucifixes, and rosaries include the fish symbol, as well as medals of saints such as St. Christopher. These pendants play an important role in religiosity. They have been used since ancient times. "Archeological finds have included a number of Tau Cross reliquaries, rings, and pendants, and woodcuts . . . (http://www. geocities.com/ Athens/Pantheon/7756/ anthony.html, May 16, 2005).

Holy Books: In the survey used in this study, Item 7 refers to "holy books (e.g., Bible, Book of Mormon, New Testament, and [sic] other Holy Books)," more specifically, "Christian Holy Books," as the focus of this study is Christian religious iconography. In the greater meaning of the word, holy books entail books considered sacred by any religion. For the purposes of this study, it was confined to "Christian Holy Books" that held collective sacred writings that symbolize the sacred conceptual beliefs within the traditions and or denominations that exist within Christianity as a whole.

The Bible serves as the heart of all Christians. It is believed that the New Testament is a historical history of early Christianity and, thus, provides a foundation for which Christianity holds sacred. The sacred is seen as "culminating with the Ministry of Christ." (Di Falco, 2000). In addition to the sacred revelation of God through Saint John, in the Book of Revelation that binds God and His believers.

Multiple regression analysis is used to identify the best predictors of traditional and non-traditional iconography ownership status. For each category, participants were asked if they owned the item. If not, they were asked if they would purchase the item or not. Finally, participants had the option to say that they were "unsure" of whether they would purchase religious iconography. The predictor variables include the Religiosity Index, Church Service Attendance, Religious Service Attendance, Social Vices, Social Virtues, and State Location.

While controlling for gender and age, the best model accounted for 20 percent of the variance in the prediction of Traditional Ownership. Using stepwise regression, the religiosity index entered the equation (accounting for 14.5 percent of the variance), followed by state location, social vices, and social virtues. These results suggest that church service attendance is not as a good predictor of iconography ownership. In contrast, the religiosity index was the primary predictor and, with a reliability value of .79, Cronbach's Alpha should be considered for future studies.

This study reinforces that in its "commercial product form" religious iconography, such as the cross, which was chosen as one of the 13 Icons (item 1, the traditional icon), provides a value to the consumer beyond the cost of the materials used in its manufacture, as described by distinguished scholar William C. Spohn, not only in spiritual meaning, but also in motivation both inside and outside the Christian community, since motivation:

> . . . cannot be so readily separated from moral content, since why we do something often enters into the very meaning of what we are doing. Often, different motivation changes the meaning of the action. Nonviolence understood as participating in the cross of the Christ has a meaning different from Gandhian nonviolence. They are not the same moral practice, outfitted in disposable rhetorical garments. (Spohn, 2007).

It is apparent that this study must first identify the distinction between religious iconography in the broader sense of the word and in its meaning within the confines of this study. This section defines Christian iconography within the parameters of the CAGS survey used in this study. Once this section has defined, the parameters of Christian iconography, insofar as the definitions relate from the broader sense to the confines of this study, it then defines the forms of symbolism and how they relate to the sacred within the confines of the study of religious iconography. The items included in the survey upon which this study is based have been divided into two categories: traditional and non-traditional.

While religious iconography in the broader sense can include a wide variety of objects, actions, and experience, this study is limited to 13 items that have some commercial value as consumer goods, i.e., items of mass production and marketing. Religious iconography can take many forms, and each individual form can change in meaning over time, "since their relationship to what is symbolized is conventional or intentional rather than necessary, shifts in usage are commonplace. For example, during the Vietnam War, the forming of the fingers in a V-shape was employed in the peace movement to symbolize peace; the same gesture during World War II represented victory." (Schmidt, 1988). Nevertheless, the individual items included in the survey retain their character as either traditional or non-traditional iconography.

Religious Statuettes: Just as doctrinal symbolism can take a visual form that is portrayed in paintings or prints, so can it manifest itself in religious statuettes (e.g., Sacred Heart), such as an item included in the survey used in this study. Beyond statuettes, the survey also dealt with religious pendants or medals (e.g., St. Christopher, Virgin Mary, others), as well as other forms of iconography, which have contributed to the mass-production stage that religious iconography has reached, as referenced within this study.

We have clearly defined the respondents' choices of religious iconography as presented in this study based primarily upon the survey of 494 students of California State University, Long Beach (CSULB), and 216 students of the University of Arkansas, both combined in the CAGS survey in predominantly general education courses. By restricting the survey to those students enrolled in predominantly general education courses, this study was broad-based and representative of the University's demographic populations. The 710 students who responded to the survey were more than sufficient to represent the general populations of both Universities, plus or minus 3 percent. In addition to the survey conducted at CSULB, the same survey was concurrently conducted at the University of Arkansas, with approximately 216 students responding to the survey. The administration of the survey at the University of Arkansas was delegated to resident graduate students who were supervised and coordinated by MBA director Dr. Alan Ellstrand and coordinated within the parameters of this study, as prescribed by CSULB graduate student Pete Madrid Jr. The smaller number of respondents at the University of Arkansas does not impair or reduce the number required to achieve a plus or minus 3 percent representation of the student body of the University of Arkansas, since the University of Arkansas population is substantially smaller than that of California State University.

Distinctions Between
Traditional and Non-Traditional Iconography

This study makes a distinction between "Traditional Christian Iconography" and "Non-traditional Christian Iconography." Traditional Christian Iconography is defined by its long historical and widespread use by predominantly "mainstream" Christian denominations. More concisely, this study accepts 7 of the 13 items as traditional and 6 of the items as non-traditional forms of religious iconography. Both traditional and non-traditional forms can be representational, Doctrinal, or Conceptual forms of Christian Religious Iconography.

The examples of traditional religious iconography used in this survey were selected on the basis of expert opinion, as reflected in the peer reviewed literature.

The description of "traditional iconography," as presented in the survey:

A religious painting or print (e.g., Last Supper, angels)

A religious statuette (e.g., Sacred Heart)

A religious pendant or medal (e.g., St. Christopher, Virgin Mary, and others)

A Holy Book (e.g., Bible, Book of Mormon, New Testament, other Holy Books)

A cross

A crucifix

A rosary

Traditional iconography as defined in this study includes both presentational and representational symbols.

Representational religious symbols are words, gestures, or things that by custom or stipulation stand for or represent something sacred. Depending on the context, the same symbol may function either representationally only or presentationally. (Schmidt, 1988).

For example, while a cross or rosary would be representational, a holy book such as the Bible is defined as presentational.

The description of "non-traditional iconography," as presented in the survey:

1. A religious DVD or VCR movie (e.g., Passion of Christ, Ten Commandments)

2. Any religious music CD
3. Any other religious jewelry
4. Any other religious iconography
5. A religious book (e.g., Billy Graham, Chuck Missler, Hal Lindsey)
6. A religious bumper sticker (e.g., fish)

Non-traditional iconography as defined in this study includes both representational and presentational symbols. For example, while other religious iconography and other religious jewelry include both presentational and representational symbols, a religious DVD or music CD would be presentational.

Definition of traditional items of religious iconography. Religious Paintings: Scholars in the past have tended to underestimate the importance and relevance of religious paintings to the American culture. "The inclination to minimize the significance of religious visual culture has led to a kind of historical myopia in both art history and religious history. It would still, for example, come as a surprise to most art historians that a 'religious' painting, the Flagellants (1889), by Milwaukee artist Carl Marr, was one of two most frequently visited and energetically celebrated painters in the fine arts Palace at the 1893 world's Columbian exhibition; that the only portrait for which agnostic Thomas Eakins received an official reward from the Pennsylvania Academy of fine arts depicted a Catholic priest (Eakins painted 17 priests among his 'heroes of modern life'); and that a group of well-known un-American painters competed in 1905 to provide the superior representation of a 'modern' Jesus, with the resulting paintings widely toured and published in the following year. Perhaps most startling, when registered against late-20th-century art historical expectations, Alfred H. Bar Jr., founding director of the Museum of modern Art, was also an observant Presbyterian who headed a commission on art for the national Council of Churches of Christ. This commission included among its leaders other prominent arts professionals like Perry T. Rathbone, Charles Rufus Morey, and George Heard Hamilton." (Morgan and Promey, 2001).

Religious Statuettes: Oddly, while Protestant Christians tend to have little difficulty accepting presentations of faith such as movies and paintings, they tend to object to the statues and statuettes that populate Catholic, Orthodox, and Episcopal churches as idolatrous.

The association of pictorial and sculpted figures with idolatry is undergirded by the biblical injunction to neither make nor worship images or likenesses of things; thus, Judaism, Islam and most of Protestant Christianity have been primarily traditions of holy Scripture (Torah, Qur'an, and Bible) inhospitable to or incompatible with paintings and sculptures because of fear that humans might confuse such creations with the creator and worship the former rather than the latter. (Schmidt, 1988).

The aforementioned quote emphasizes early fears in Christianity that Christians may mistake the idols for the deities themselves.

Yet, while the Protestants consider that reading the Bible is enough to nourish their faith in salvation, the Catholics gain access to Scripture only by means of the tradition which created it and which has carried it down the ages, according to the church's living teaching and especially thanks to the liturgy. (Di Falco, 2000).

In other words, the Catholic faith sees no problem with displaying a wide variety of images employed to bolster faith.

Religious pendants: Pendants other than crosses, crucifixes and rosaries include the fish symbol, as well as medals of saints such as St. Christopher. These pendants play an important role in religiosity. They have been used since ancient times.

Holy Books: In the survey used in this study, Item 7 refers to "holy books (e.g., Bible, Book of Mormon, New Testament, and [sic] other Holy Books)" and, more specifically, "Christian Holy Books," as the focus of this study is Christian religious iconography. In the wider meaning of the word, holy books entail books considered sacred by any religion. For the purposes of this study, it was confined to "Christian Holy Books" that hold collective sacred writings that symbolize the sacred conceptual beliefs within the traditions and or denominations that exist within Christianity as a whole.

The Bible serves as the heart of all Christians. It is believed that the New Testament is a historical account of early Christianity and, thus, provides a foundation for that which Christianity holds sacred. The sacred is seen as "culminating with the Ministry of Christ." (Di Falco, 2000). In addition to the sacred revelation of God through Saint John, it is the Book of Revelations that binds God and His believers.

Such "holy books" as the Bible are predominantly acknowledged as entailing both the Old and New Testaments. Traditional differences include, as a "holy book," specifically the Bible, with and without the New Testament and a few of the Old Testament apocrypha. In Catholicism both the New Testament and several Old Testament apocrypha books are often included in the Bible. To Catholics the scriptures are only part of traditional access to that which has been passed down through the Catholic Church's teaching and liturgy.

Outside mainline religions, sacred Christian holy books include the Book of Mormon, which is regarded as sacred to the Christian denomination known as the Church of Jesus Christ of Latter-Day Saints. Other denominations accept other "holy books" as sacred and authoritative as the Bible, such as Christian Scientist and other Christian denominations that hold other "holy books" in the same conceptual symbolized manner as the Bible, as perceived or declared sacred by religious use or authority by other Christian denominations.

Logistically, there are varying translations of the Bible both within Catholicism and Protestantism. Many varying translations within the Catholic Church include footnotes or explanations in regard to allegorical interpretation of the Catholic traditions. "During the last two decades, some marvelous ecumenical translations have been made, with notes which pour out, when necessary, the different churches' interpretations; this is an important step towards Christian unity." (Di Falco, 2000).

Crosses: Although the cross has roots that go back in time to an era before Christianity, for the purposes of this study the cross is a Christian symbol.

> As a representational symbol, the cross was, for Jung, a symbolic
> reminder of divine love, but as a presentational symbol, the cross
> was an emotionally charged symbol of the mysterious and
> transcendent. He insisted that such symbols are archetypal; they
> are effective symbols that surfaced in dreams and myths and point
> beyond themselves to something superhuman." (Schmidt, 1988).

The cross is at the center of the history of the Christian world. The motto of the Carthusian order, "an austere contemplative Roman Catholic order founded by St. Bruno in 1084," (Thinkmap Visual Thesaurus—http://carthusian) is even: Stat crux dum volvitur orbis,

> . . . the cross stands firm in the swirling of this world. That is why
> our universe is full of crosses. Most churches are built in the shape

of a cross: the nave and apse form the vertical axis, the transept (made up of two wings) the horizontal one. The fact that the choir is often off-center can be explained by the way the crucified Christ had leant to one side when he "gave up his spirit." Inside the church, the 12 crosses of consecration symbolized the "apostles of the land." (Rev. 21:14.). Christians often wear crosses around their necks, and the pectoral cross is the distinguishing mark of prelates. Christian tunes have, since antiquity, been marked by a cross." (Di Falco, 2000).

Crucifixes: The survey for this study draws a distinction between a cross in its broader religious meaning and a crucifix in its broader religious meaning. The distinction of a crucifix is not great; in simplistic terms, since it is a cross of any religious type, as stated above; however, it includes the image of Jesus. The symbolism of a crucifix (Item 11, A crucifix in the survey) evolved to what is submitted in this study as "massed-produced religious iconography." However, individuals exhibit different attitudes toward crosses, compared to crucifixes, i.e., while the cross is a more or less generalized symbol of Christianity, the crucifix is a more specific reference to the crucifixion of Christ. Aside from the modified representations, the meaning of each is slightly differentiated from the general significance of the cross to something different, while remaining in the same general meaning as recognized within varying religious traditions and purposes. But its development is in reference to its affordability to masses in its reproductive product forms. Examples of these works are now economically available.

> The cross: the cross [crucifix] on which Jesus died for our salvation remains a sign of complete self-sacrifice ... in its combination of the horizontal and vertical axis, which just embraced the whole symbolism of the cardinal points, the cross has established itself in every culture and in all religions.... Conversely, the cross also invokes images of torture, suffering and confrontation. (Di Falco, 2000).

Rosaries: Regarding rosaries, respondents to the survey were asked about the rosary. The significance of the rosary is more predominantly within the Catholic tradition, although Protestant denominations, such as some Episcopal and Orthodox churches, also hold the rosary as a significant "Christian religious iconography." The rosary can best symbolize the sacred conceptual belief in "the mysteries of Jesus through the maternal tenderness of the virgin." (Di Falco, 2000). Indeed, the rosary is held in great esteem by the Catholic and Orthodox churches; the rosary is rich with symbolism:

> The most widespread form of Marian devotion is without a doubt the rosary . . . This 'Rose-Garden' (from the Latin rosarium) is a crown intended to honor the virgin mother. It consists of 5 sets of 10 beads, separated by an individual bead, which are an invitation to 50 recitations of 'Hail Mary,' 5 of 'our Father,' and 5 of 'glory be to the father.' The rosary also has a sort of scale, finishing with a cross, which carries 3 successive beads with 2 individual beads, 1 at each end on the cross, which is, in fact, the starting point we recite the 'I believe in God'; on the first individual bead the 'our Father,' then 3 'Hail Mary's' and finally a 'glory be to the father.' The rosary thus honors the Trinity, the cross and the virgin at the same time, all fundamental Catholic truths." (Di Falco, 2000).

Outside of the Catholic and Orthodox traditions, the rosary is not considered sacred or significant to the Protestant traditions with the exception of Episcopalians, who may individually relish and hold the rosary to be sacred. Indeed, most "protestants consider that giving to the mother is to take away from the son, and that turning to Mary is an offense to Christ's Universal power as mediator, even though our lady is entirely dependent on our Lord." (Di Falco, 2000).

In conclusion "traditional variables" were confined to "traditional Christian iconography," the type which evolved into a "commercial product form." It was this type that was used in the survey, for the purpose of this study. More specifically the items were set as physical in nature. "Non-traditional variables" for the purposes of this study were limited to the most common non-traditional values that have religious and commercial value with an established market. The "non-traditional variables" as used in the survey for the purpose of this study, were set as items with both commercial and religious values to the consumer, but lacking a long tradition of use as religious symbols.

Definition of "non-traditional iconography," as presented in the survey:
A religious DVD or VCR movie (e.g., Passion of Christ, Ten
Commandments)
Any religious music CD
Any other religious jewelry
Any other religious iconography
A religious book (e.g., Billy Graham, Chuck Missler, Hal Lindsey)
A religious bumper sticker (e.g., fish)

Non-traditional religious iconography has little history or tradition, primarily because of its origination in the 20th century. In spite of that lack of history and tradition, these non-traditional items do have a spiritual value for some consumers. Iconography tends to be visual, even in music, since the introduction of music videos in the late 20th century.

A religious DVD or VCR movie (e.g., Passion of Christ, Ten Commandments). Religious movies for DVD and VCR are a product of the late 20th century, so they have little history or tradition. Unlike the historical morality plays of the Medieval and Renaissance eras, these movies can be taken into the home and played repeatedly.

Any religious music CD: Music from the church choir to the modern CD can inspire and affirm religiosity. Unlike the church music of past eras, these forms of religious music can be taken into the home and do not require participation by the listeners. In addition, many new songs have been composed in modern styles, such as rock and roll, jazz, and reggae. This music is far different from traditional liturgical music.

> The aesthetic and non-discursively symbolic dimensions of a
> religion—for example, its poetry, music, art, and rituals—are not,
> as propositional cognitivism suggests, mere external decorations
> designed to make the hard core of explicitly statable beliefs and
> precepts more appealing to the masses. Rather, it is through these
> that the basic patterns of religion are interiorized, exhibited, and
> transmitted. The proclamation of the gospel, as a Christian would
> put it, may be first of all the telling of this story, but this gains
> power and meaning insofar as it is embodied in the total gestalt of
> community life and action." (Lindbeck, 1984).

Any other religious jewelry: Although a cross of any religious type, as stated above, has dominated the jewelry industry, other forms are also marketed.

Nearly all forms of both crosses and crucifixes are available and in great demand, both as a religious form of Iconography and as a sign of social status, readily affordable to the masses in its mass-produced product forms.

The fish symbol, for example, does not have a long tradition as religious jewelry. Even though early Christians might have carved the fish symbol into a piece of wood or drawn it in the dirt, its use in jewelry lacks a long history and tradition.

Any other religious iconography: Iconography can take many forms, including tattoos, poetry, sidewalk art, and more.

"Western painting, sculpture, music, architecture and goldsmithery are all inextricably linked to the 'holy story' told in the Bible, which today is still the world's number one bestseller." (Di Falco, 2000).

A religious book (e.g., Billy Graham, Chuck Missler, Hal Lindsey): Authors of religious books for the popular audience arose primarily in the past two centuries. Religious books were not available to a wide audience until very recently, since the cost of books was prohibitive. Even after the invention of the printing press, the bulk of the population were illiterate and depended upon the priests to read for them. Moreover, it is only in recent years that authors have been able to earn a living with their writing, and many authors still must work at other jobs to make ends meet.

Chuck Missler stands out as an example of religious writing without tradition, since he discusses UFOs and other phenomena of the 20th century. Hal Lindsey's books focus primarily on the end times, as predicted in the Book of Revelation. Billy Graham and authors like him offer advice on how to lead a Christian life, advice which traditionally came by word of mouth from the priests.

A religious bumper sticker (e.g., fish): Bumper stickers did not exist before automobiles became common in the 20th century, after Henry Ford made the Model-T affordable for most working people. Thus, they lack history and tradition.

CHAPTER 9
CONSUMER MARKETING
BEHAVIOR VARIABLES

For the purposes of this study, a subset of Consumer Social Behavior variables was carefully chosen. Twenty consumer marketing behavior variables were chosen, based on psychographics that help motivate individual consumers' marketing behavior. Activities, interests and opinions provide data for analysis of a person's day-to-day pattern of living to help identify a responsive target market. Each social marketing behavior was analyzed and defined as either a vice or a virtue, based upon social and religious attitudes toward that behavior.

> Understanding the lifestyles of target customers has been especially helpful in providing ideas for advertising themes . . . For example, lifestyle analysis might show that the 38-year-old is also a community-oriented consumer with traditional values who especially enjoys spectator sports and spends much time in other family activities. An ad might show the Sable [a car] being used by a happy family at a ball game so the target market could really identify with the ad. And the ad might be placed [in] a magazine like Sports Illustrated whose readers match the target lifestyle profile." (Perreault and McCarthy, 2006).

For the purposes of this study, 20 consumer marketing behavior variables were selected from individual consumer Activities, Interests, and Opinion (AIO) lifestyles dimensions.

Social impact = Effect of an activity on the social fabric of the community and well-being of the individuals and families.

Definition of the social and religious impact of Cigarettes/Cigars: The social marketing behavior variable "Cigarettes/Cigars" has two relevant issues, society as a whole, and religious world views. "From a purely marketing perspective, the variable lifestyle dimension or AIO specifics denote 'Cigarettes/Cigars' as an Interest, just as food is referenced as an interest in Essentials of Marketing": A Global-Managerial Approach (Perreault and McCarthy, 2006). For social purposes, the variable "Cigarettes/Cigars" is seen as having a negative connotation or impact.

> Cigarette smoking among college students is a critical public health problem . . . Studies show that smoking by college students

is associated with being White, living in housing where smoking is permitted, using alcohol and other substances, and having a lower psychological sense of well-being. Depression, life satisfaction, and coping style are also related to college smoking, but the causal relationship remains unclear. Although a large proportion of college students have made an attempt to quit smoking, only a minority actually succeed." (Patterson, Lerman, Kaufmann, Neuner, and Audrain-McGovern, 2004).

From a religious perspective, the social marketing behavior variable smoking Cigarettes/Cigars is viewed as a taboo or tenet violation in many denominations. According to non-academic references, Orthodox affiliations consider "Excessive smoking as a kind of indirect suicide, and thus is morally wrong." Way to Religion.com. (n.d.). (Greek Orthodox Archdiocese of America.) The Lutherans believe it "Should be avoided … each of us has responsibility to be a good steward of his or her own health out of thankfulness for the gift of life and in order to serve God and the neighbor." (Way to Religion.com, n.d.). (Evangelical Lutheran Church in America [ELCA].) The Methodists/Wesleyans "Oppose it" (Way to Religion.com, n.d.). (The Wesleyan Church WC), and Mormonism states that "The founder of the Latter-Day Saint movement, Joseph Smith, Jr., recorded that on February 27, 1833 he received a revelation which addressed tobacco use." It is commonly known as the Word of Wisdom, and is found in section 89 of the Doctrine and Covenants, a book canonized as scripture by Mormons (Section 89). While initially viewed as a guideline, this was eventually accepted as a commandment; consequently, faithful Mormons do not smoke." (Way to Religion.com, n.d.).

Not all denominations are specifically represented that do believe smoking cigarettes or cigars is a negative, and not all denominations oppose smoking cigarettes or cigars. Since not all denominations support the negative weighting of this variable, the statistic could be slightly skewed more heavily on the negative impact than normally expected on this variable. However, a large number of denominations do perceive smoking as negative, and more importantly, it is viewed as a social taboo, which would counter the slightly over-weighted variable.

In conclusion, the social marketing behavior variable "Cigarettes / Cigars" or smoking is for the purposes of this study a social marketing behavioral variable "vice."

Dancing: The social marketing behavior variable "Dancing" presents two relevant issues, society as a whole and religious world views. From a purely marketing perspective, the variable lifestyle dimension or AIO specifics denote "Dancing" as an activity, just as social events or entertainment is referenced as an activity in Essentials of Marketing: A Global-Managerial Approach (Perreault and McCarthy, 2006). For social purposes, the variable "Dancing" is seen as having a negative connotation or impact.

For example, the currently popular hip-hop music and dancing is viewed as promoting sexual activity outside of marriage.

> Rap and hip-hop music is not just entertainment, it's exploiting black adolescent girls and promoting unhealthy lifestyles," a researcher says. "Black girls are not seeing positive images of who they are and what they can be," said Carolyn West, associate professor of psychology and the study of prevention of violence at the University of Washington. "Looking at the sexual imagery really impacts on the functioning of teenage girls." Hip-hop culture was created in the early 1970s by black and Latino youth ... As hip-hop turned into a global phenomenon, it began to influence language, fashion and ways that youth interacted with each other. "What's changed over time is the greater sexualization of hip-hop." (Sae Ngian, 2008).

This is only one researcher's findings, but many other social research studies find that today's music that youths dance to includes degrading lyrics, that they wear revealing clothes, employ sexually explicit dance moves and provide fertile ground for sexual encounters.

From a religious perspective, the social marketing behavior variable is viewed as a taboo or tenet violation in many denominations. Social dancing has long been viewed by many Christians as dangerous to spiritual health if not actually sinful.

> The Missouri Synod Lutherans, for instance, disapprove of what a special committee of their ministers defined as "the embrace of members of the opposite sexes who are not married to each other." But, meeting in Milwaukee last week, the Concordia College

conference, attended by 50 ministers of the Missouri synod (membership: 2,150,230), tentatively opened the door to the "party." "In the literature of our synod with respect to the question of the dance," said the committee in a resolution before the conference, "we found quotations of theologians and conferences as far back as Chrysostom and the Council of Laodicea [probably 4th century] with constant and consistent warnings against the dangers [of dancing]." But through the years, there has also been a minority report." (Religion: Christian Dancing Monday, 1959).

The committee conclusion: If, after consideration, a Lutheran group finds social dancing "in accord with its objectives and to the best Christian interests of its members . . . it may permit the same under careful supervision and guidance, always striving toward the goal that whatsoever we do in word or deed we do all to the glory of God and in the name of the Lord Jesus." (Religion: Christian Dancing, 1959).

In non-academic references, many Baptist affiliations forbid "Dancing . . . because of sensuality. Improper touching can occur and movements of the body can cause impure thoughts and desires leading to immorality." (Baptist views on dancing/About Us—Basic Beliefs/Baptists—Baptist Beliefs/Expert—6/8/2008). Not all denominations are specifically represented that do believe Dancing is negative, and not all denominations oppose dancing. Since not all denominations support the negative weighting of this variable, the statistic could be slightly skewed more heavily on the negative impact than normally expected on this variable. However, a large number of denominations do perceive dancing as a vice, and more importantly, it is viewed as a social taboo. In conclusion, the social marketing behavior variable "Dancing" is for the purposes of this study a social marketing behavioral variable "vice."

Beer, Wine, etc.: The social marketing behavior variable "Beer, Wine, etc.," or drinking alcohol has two relevant issues, society as a whole and religious world views. From a purely marketing perspective, the variable lifestyle dimension or AIO specifics denote "Beer, Wine, Etc.," or drinking alcohol as an activity, just as social events or entertainment is referenced as an activity in Essentials of Marketing: A Global-Managerial Approach (Perreault and

50

McCarthy, 2006). For social purposes, the variable "Beer, Wine, etc.," is seen as having a negative connotation or impact.

> The number-one student risk factor in the minds of most college administrators now is alcohol use, and to a certain extent, the use of other drugs. Alcohol has been a risk factor in a number of student deaths, including the untimely death of Scott Krueger at MIT. Alcohol is heavily associated with secondary risks, such as sexual assault and student riots over changes in alcohol policies." (Lake, 2002).

From a religious perspective, the social marketing behavior variable is viewed as a taboo or tenet violation in many denominations. In non-academic references, Orthodox affiliations conclude, "The use of stimulants, depressants, and hallucinogens for any purpose other than the restoration of health or the alleviation of abnormal pain, when properly and legitimately prescribed by a physician, is condemned" (Way to Religion.com, n.d.). (GOAA). They go on to say, "Excessive drinking is a kind of indirect suicide, and thus is morally wrong" (Greek Orthodox Archdiocese of America.) The Methodists/Wesleyans (The Wesleyan Church, WC) oppose it, as do the Mormons; faithful Mormons do not drink. Not all denominations are specifically represented that do believe that "Beer, Wine, etc.," or drinking alcohol is negative, and not all denominations oppose drinking alcohol. Since not all denominations support the negative weighting of this variable, the weighting of this variable could be slightly skewed more heavily on the negative impact than normally expected on this variable. However, a large number of denominations do perceive drinking alcohol as negative; more importantly, it is viewed as a social taboo, which would counter the slightly over-weighted variable.

In conclusion, the social marketing behavior variable "Beer, Wine, Etc.," or drinking alcohol is for the purposes of this study a social marketing behavior variable "vice."

Night Clubbing: The social marketing behavior variable "Night Clubbing" includes many aspects of the three previously covered variables: smoking "cigarettes/cigars," "Dancing" and drinking alcohol "Beer, Wine, Etc." Like the three previously covered variables, the "Night Clubbing" variable has two relevant issues, society as a whole and religious world views. From a purely marketing perspective, this variable, like the others, has a lifestyle dimension or

AIO specifics that denote "Night Clubbing" as an activity, just as social events or entertainment is referenced as an activity in Essentials of Marketing: A Global-Managerial Approach (Perreault and McCarthy, 2006). For social purposes, the variable "Night Clubbing" is seen as having a negative connotation or impact.

From a religious perspective, the social marketing behavior variable is viewed as a taboo or tenet violation in many denominations. Please refer to the social marketing behavior variables smoking "cigarettes/cigars," "Dancing," and drinking alcohol, "Beer, Wine, Etc." From a religious perspective, the social marketing behavior variable is viewed as a taboo or tenet violation in many denominations. For social purposes, the variable is seen as having a negative connotation or impact. In conclusion, the social marketing behavior variable "Night Clubbing" is for the purposes of this study a social marketing behavior variable "vice."

Video Games: The social marketing behavior variable "Video Games" has one relevant issue, a social aspect. Religious denominations have yet to update their doctrines to deal with new technology in general. From a purely marketing perspective, the variable lifestyle dimension or AIO specifics denote "Video Games" as an activity, just as entertainment is referenced as an activity in Essentials of Marketing: A Global-Managerial Approach (Perreault and McCarthy, 2006). For social purposes, the variable "Video Games" is seen as having a negative connotation or impact. To cite one academic research study:

> A new study shows the more young adults play video games, the poorer their relationships are with family and friends. The research was conducted by a Brigham Young University student and his faculty mentor. They collected data from more than 800 college students around the country and found as the amount of time playing video games went up, the quality of relationships went down. The research found young adults who play more video games tend to engage in riskier behavior including drinking and drug abuse." ABC news (2010, October 12).

The following paragraphs provide some insight into the thinking of today's news media:

"When I start playing videogames, I tell myself I am only going to play for an hour, and sometimes, that becomes four or five hours," LSA senior Brian O'Byrne commented on his compulsive videogame habit.

Without nagging parents to tell them to come to dinner, go to sleep, or start studying, college dorms become a playland for students. LSA senior Mark Kloporwitz experienced this videogame overload his freshman year: "All the guys in my hall at East Quad were obsessed with playing Quake and it began to grow on me. I ended up paying people to pick up food for me so I could keep playing," said Kloporwitz. (Grandstaff, 2001).

For social purposes, the variable is seen as having a negative connotation or impact. In conclusion, the social marketing behavior variable "Video Games" is for the purposes of this study a social marketing behavior variable "vice."

TV Shopping: The social marketing behavior variable "TV Shopping" has one relevant issue, a social aspect. Religious denominations have yet to develop solid doctrine regarding TV shopping. From a purely marketing perspective, the variable lifestyle dimension or AIO specifics denote "TV Shopping" as an "Activity," just as "Shopping" is referenced as an "Activity" in Essentials of Marketing: A Global-Managerial Approach (Perreault and McCarthy, 2006). For social purposes, the variable is seen as having a negative connotation or impact. While shopping is normally viewed as a normal activity, it can be regarded as a bad habit or addiction.

"While many of us are able to call shopping 'retail therapy,' for some 13 million American adults, shopping can become an addiction that requires therapy" (Pouliot, 2007).

Dr. Keith Ablow, a psychiatrist in private practice and Fox News contributor describes the negative aspects of shopping addiction:

As with other addictions, "shopaholism" can do a real number on a person's life—from destroying their finances to destroying relationships.

"They feel guilty about what they've done," said Ablow. "They lie to others just like an addict or an alcoholic would lie to family members about the use of a substance and they spend a lot of time thinking about shopping and how they will feel when they get it." (Pouliot, 2007).

For social purposes, the variable is regarded as having a negative connotation or impact. In conclusion, the social marketing behavior variable "TV Shopping" is for the purposes of this study a social marketing behavior variable "vice."

Computer/Internet: The social marketing behavior variable "Computer/Internet" has one relevant issue, a social aspect. Religious denominations have yet to develop solid doctrine to deal with new technology as a whole, and computers and Internet in particular. From a purely marketing perspective, the variable lifestyle dimension or AIO specifics denote "Computer/Internet" as an interest, just as media enjoyment is referenced as an activity in Essentials of Marketing: A Global-Managerial Approach (Perreault and McCarthy, 2006). For social purposes, the variable is seen as having a negative connotation or impact. The following references one academic research study:

> The popular media suggests that Internet usage decreases the amount of social interaction individuals have with the world outside of their computer and may be accompanied by social anxiety, loneliness, lowered self-esteem, or chronic depression, and the psychological literature's mixed findings on these topics have not helped clarify the issue. (DeRushia, 2010).

For social purposes, the variable is seen as having a negative connotation or impact. In conclusion, the social marketing behavior variable "Computer/Internet" is for the purposes of this study a social marketing behavior variable "vice."

Self-improvement: The social marketing behavior variable "Self-improvement" has two relevant issues, society as a whole and religious world views. From a purely marketing perspective, the variable lifestyle dimension or AIO specifics denote "Self-improvement" as an interest, just as "Achievements" is referenced as an interest in Essentials of Marketing: A Global-Managerial Approach (Perreault and McCarthy, 2006). For social purposes, the variable is seen as having a positive connotation or impact.

The social aspect as viewed by society demonstrates that "Self-improvement" is "designed to help people identify what they want from their life and career, and then enhance their motivation and skills so they achieve their goals." (New York College of Health Professions, n.d.).

According to market research:

> There is no shortage of demand for products and programs that will allow Americans, especially affluent female Baby Boomers, to make more money, lose weight, improve their relationships and business skills, cope with stress, or obtain a quick dose of

motivation. Now more than ever, Americans are turning to gurus for help in a variety of areas. They want to be more in control of their emotional and financial lives. An elite handful of multi-millionaire celebrities like Tony Robbins, Deepak Chopra and Suze Orman have leveraged their names to build multi-media empires consisting of websites, books, tapes, CDs/DVDs, public or corporate seminars, workshops, catalogs, infomercials, TV or radio shows and consulting, according to Marketdata's Research Director, John LaRosa. Self-improvement Market in U.S. Worth $9.6 Billion, (LaRosa, 2006). Retrieved from http://www.prweb.com/releases/2006/9/prweb 440011.htm.

From the Religious perspective, self-improvement is part of a large process:

A study of leadership development among religious people, mostly Christians, found that "Most, 68 percent of our participants were in a seminar on church leadership or a Bible course and thus had a significant interest in pursuing their continued education for self-improvement and/or the improvement of their church." (Krejcir and Schaeffer, 2009).

From a religious perspective, the social marketing behavior variable is viewed as a positive attribute; however, it is not specifically addressed. Please refer to the social marketing behavior variable "Self-improvement" referenced above. For social purposes, the variable is seen as having a positive connotation or impact. In conclusion, the social marketing behavior variable "Self-improvement" is for the purposes of this study a social marketing behavior variable "virtue."

Cultural Events: The social marketing behavior variable "Cultural Events" has two relevant issues, society as a whole and religious world views. From a purely marketing perspective, the variable lifestyle dimension or AIO specifics denote "Cultural Events" as an "Opinion," just as "Culture" is referenced as an "Opinion" in Essentials of Marketing: A Global-Managerial Approach (Perreault and McCarthy, 2006). For social purposes, the variable is seen as having a positive connotation or impact.

Regarding social effects and influences, cultural events such as the promotion of art, literature, or other media such as movies and theatre, the effort to enlighten and promote social values or specific cultural elements is viewed as having a positive impact on society.

When humans meet, they experience communicative events. These communicative events involve the exchange of culture. My Cognitive Culture is developed continually from my encounter with others. The Social Culture occurs when we engage in interpersonal encounters. The encounters in turn clarify, affirm or modify, the Cognitive Culture. The term Social Culture refers to the full range of informal and formal structures in these encounters and relationships, including group identification and social infrastructure." (Jenkins, 2004).

From a religious perspective, the social marketing behavior variable "Cultural Events" is viewed as a positive attribute; however, it is not specifically addressed. Please refer to the social marketing behavior variable "Cultural Events" reference above. For social purposes, the variable is seen as having a positive connotation or impact. In conclusion, the social marketing behavior variable "Cultural Events" is for the purposes of this study a social marketing behavior variable "virtue."

Casino Gambling: The social marketing behavior variable "Casino Gambling" has two relevant issues, society as a whole and religious world views. From a purely marketing perspective, the variable lifestyle dimension or AIO specifics denote "Casino Gambling" as an interest, just as recreation is referenced as an interest in Essentials of Marketing: A Global-Managerial Approach. (Perreault and McCarthy, 2006). For social purposes, the variable is seen as having a negative connotation or impact.

College students appear to be at particular risk for experiencing problem or pathological gambling disorders, with rates nearly double that of general population adults (Lesieur et al., 1991; Neighbors, Lostutter, Larimer & Takushi, 2001; Shaffer et al., 1999; Winters, Bengston, Dorr, & Stinchfield, 1998). Winters et al., (1998) found that approximately 87 percent of Minnesota college students reported gambling in the previous year, and although the prevalence of disordered gambling was relatively low, it was still more than twice the state estimate for older adults. (Larimer and Neighbors, 2003).

56

From a religious perspective, the social marketing behavior variable "Casino Gambling" is viewed as a taboo or tenet violation in many denominations. In non-academic references, Baptist affiliations predominate in holding to this point of view:

> . . . conservative Baptists oppose gambling, alcohol, tobacco, and some prohibit dancing and movies. Especially in areas where Southern Baptists form a majority of the population, the denomination has been successful in imposing its values on the general population—"dry counties" in the South or the ban on music and dancing in the film Footloose, are examples. (ReligionFacts, n.d.).
>
> The Methodists/Wesleyans (The Wesleyan Church, WC . . . ranked gambling alongside alcohol as a threat to the moral, financial and spiritual well-being of the poor. At a time when many people lived on the margins of poverty, an ill-advised or unlucky gamble could mean the difference for a family between food and starvation, survival and the workhouse. Gambling was a spiritual issue for nineteenth century Methodists. (The Methodist Church, n.d.).

The faithful "Mormons consider gambling immoral and unworthy of Christian behavior. We encourage everyone to support laws which repeal gambling as a legal activity." (Mormon Church, n.d.).

In spite of secular promotion of state-sponsored gambling, many denominations also oppose state lotteries on social and moral grounds:

> Public lotteries are advocated as a means of relieving the burden of taxation. It has been clearly demonstrated, however, that all too often lotteries only add to the problems of the financially disadvantaged by taking money from them and giving nothing of value in return. The poor and the elderly become victims of the inducements that are held out to purchase lottery tickets on the remote chance of winning a substantial prize. (Oaks and Ensign, June 1987, 69–75).
>
> The Lutheran Church holds to a strong position against gambling:
>
> In February 1996 our Synod's Commission on Theology and

Church Relations adopted a report titled "Gambling," a 14-page document that discusses the practice of gambling in light of six scriptural principles. These principles are as follows: Gambling encourages the sins of greed and covetousness. Gambling promotes mismanagement of possessions entrusted to us by God. Gambling undermines absolute reliance on God for His provision. Gambling works at cross purposes with a commitment to productive work. Gambling is a potentially addictive behavior. Gambling threatens the welfare of our neighbor and militates against the common good. The document stops short of saying that every form of gambling is in and of itself contrary to the Word of God and therefore sinful. Read Synod President Barry's statement on legalized gambling. (The Lutheran Church, n.d.).

The Presbyterians espouse a similar doctrine. They "enacted Calvin's Ecclesiastical Ordinances, which set forth regulations on everything from church order and religious education to gambling, dancing, and swearing. Strict disciplinary measures were put in place to deal with transgressors of these ordinances" (ReligionFacts, n.d.).

With regard to gambling, Jehovah's Witnesses teach that "Every form of gambling is tainted by greed. So Christians do not take part in any kind of gambling, such as lotteries, horse racing, and bingo." (Ephesians 5:3–5) (ReligionFacts, n.d.).

Not all denominations are specifically represented that do believe that gambling is negative, and not all denominations oppose gambling. Since not all denominations support the negative weighting of this variable, the weighting of the variable "Casino Gambling" could be slightly skewed more heavily on the negative impact than normally expected on this variable. However, a large number of denominations do perceive gambling as negative; more importantly, it is viewed as a social taboo, which would counter the slightly over-weighted variable. In conclusion, the social marketing behavior variable "Casino Gambling" is for the purposes of this study a social marketing behavior variable "vice."

Lottery/Sweepstakes: The social marketing behavior variable "Lottery / Sweepstakes" includes many aspects of the previous covered variable "Casino

58

Gambling." The "Lottery/Sweepstakes" variable has two relevant issues, society as a whole and religious world views. From a purely marketing perspective, this variable, like the others, has a lifestyle dimension or AIO specifics that denote "Lottery/Sweepstakes" as an interests, just as recreation is referenced as an activity in Essentials of Marketing: A Global-Managerial Approach (Perreault and McCarthy, 2006). For social purposes, the variable "Lottery/Sweepstakes" is seen as having a negative connotation or impact. The same social reference as previously quoted under "Casino Gambling" can be applied here:

"College students appear to be at particular risk for experiencing problem or pathological gambling disorders, with rates nearly double that of general population adults." Lesieur et al., (1991) . . . found that approximately 87 percent of Minnesota college students reported gambling in the previous year, and although the prevalence of disordered gambling was relatively low, it was still more than twice the state estimate for older adults. (Larimer and Neighbors, 2003).

From a religious perspective, the social marketing behavior variable "Lottery/Sweepstakes" is viewed as a taboo or tenet violation in many denominations. Please refer to the social marketing behavior variable "Casino Gambling." From a religious perspective, the social marketing behavior variable is viewed as a taboo or tenet violation in many denominations. For social purposes, the variable is seen as having a negative connotation or impact. In conclusion, the social marketing behavior variable "Lottery/Sweepstakes" is for the purposes of this study a social marketing behavior variable "vice."

The social marketing behavior variable "Astrology/Horoscope" has two relevant issues, society as a whole and religious world views. From a purely marketing perspective, the variable lifestyle dimension or AIO specifics denote "Astrology/Horoscope" as an activity, just as entertainment is referenced as an activity in Essentials of Marketing: A Global-Managerial Approach (Perreault and McCarthy, 2006).

For social purposes, the variable is seen as having a negative connotation or impact.

In spite of strong public expressions of skepticism from the scientific community, polls show that more than nine out to ten American adults profess belief in paranormal phenomena. Some scientist view this as a social problem, directing much blame (but little research) at a variety of sources including lack of critical thinking skills, fads, need for transcendent experiences, failure of the educational system, and cultural cycles. Social impact theory provides an alternative focus: it views paranormal beliefs as a natural consequence of social influence processes in interpersonal settings. (Markovsky and Thye, 2001).

For Religious purposes, the variable "Astrology/Horoscope" is also seen as having a negative connotation or impact. When religious respondents inquire about horoscopes or astrology and whether it is a Christian taboo or tenet violation, they turn to the Bible as a guide. The most common scripture and interpretation is that:

Astrology is the 'interpretation' of an assumed influence the stars (and planets) exert on human destiny. This is a false belief. The royal astrologers of the Babylonian court were put to shame by God's prophet Daniel (Daniel 1:20) and were powerless to interpret the king's dream (Daniel 2:27). God specifies astrologers as among those who will be burned as stubble in God's judgment (Isaiah 47:13–14). Astrology as a form of divination is expressly forbidden in Scripture (Deuteronomy 18:10–14). God forbade the children of Israel to worship or serve the "host of heaven" (Deuteronomy 4:19). Several times in their history, however, Israel fell into that very sin (2 Kings 17:16 is one example). Their worship of the stars brought God's judgment each time ..." [Recommended Resource: The Truth Behind Ghosts, Mediums, and Psychic Phenomena by Ron Rhodes.] GotQuestions.org. (n.d.).

Another common scriptural interpretation is that:
The Bible strongly condemns spiritism, mediums, the occult, and psychics (Leviticus 20:27; Deuteronomy 18:10–13). Horoscopes, tarot cards, astrology, fortune tellers, palm readings, and séances fall into this category as well. These practices are based on the concept that there are gods, spirits, or deceased loved ones that can give advice and guidance. These "gods" or "spirits" are demons (2 Corinthians 11:14–15). The Bible gives us no reason to believe that deceased loved ones can contact us ... Satan pretends to be

60

kind and helpful. He tries to appear as something good. Satan and his demons will give a psychic information about a person in order to get that person hooked into spiritism, something that God forbids. It appears innocent at first, but soon people can find themselves addicted to psychics and unwittingly allow Satan to control and destroy their lives. Peter proclaimed, "Be self-controlled and alert. Your enemy the devil prowls around like a roaring lion looking for someone to devour" (1 Peter 5:8). In some cases, the psychics themselves are deceived, not knowing the true source of the information they receive. Whatever the case and wherever the source of the information, nothing connected to spiritism, witchcraft, or astrology is a godly means of discovering information. How does God want us to discern His will for our life? God's plan is simple, yet powerful and effective: study the Bible (2 Timothy 3:16–17) and pray for wisdom (James 1:5). [Recommended Resource: The Truth Behind Ghosts, Mediums, and Psychic Phenomena by Ron Rhodes.]" GotQuestions.org. (n.d.).

Given the examples above, it seems clear that, from a religious perspective, the social marketing behavior variable "Astrology/Horoscope" is viewed as a taboo or tenet violation in many denominations. Since not all denominations support the negative weighting of this variable, it could be slightly skewed more heavily on the negative impact than normally expected on this variable. However, a large number of denominations do perceive "Astrology/Horoscope" as negative. More importantly, it is viewed as a social taboo, which would counter the slightly over-weighted variable. In conclusion, the social marketing behavior variable "Astrology/Horoscope" is for the purposes of this study a social marketing behavior variable "vice."

Tarot Cards: The social marketing behavior variable "Tarot Cards" has two relevant issues, social and religious, which are essentially the same as in terms of social relevance as the social marketing behavior variable "Astrology/Horoscope" previously covered. Thus, the references cited above are also relevant to "Tarot Cards." From a purely marketing perspective, this variable also has a lifestyle dimension or AIO specifics that denote "Tarot Cards" as an activity, just as entertainment is referenced as an activity in Essentials of

Marketing: A Global-Managerial Approach (Perreault and McCarthy, 2006). For social purposes, the variable is seen as having a negative connotation or impact.

From a religious perspective or religious world view, the social marketing behavior variable "Tarot Cards" is viewed as a taboo or tenet violation in many denominations. Please refer to the social marketing behavior variable "Astrology/Horoscope." For social purposes, the variable is seen as having a negative connotation or impact. In conclusion, the social marketing behavior variable "Tarot Cards" is for the purposes of this study a social marketing behavior variable "vice."

Psychic Readings: The social marketing behavior variable "Psychic Readings" includes many of the two previously covered variables, "Astrology/Horoscope," and "Tarot Cards." Like the two previously covered variables, the "Psychic Readings" variable has two relevant issues, society as a whole and religious world views. From a purely marketing perspective, this variable, like the others, has a lifestyle dimension or AIO specifics that denote "Psychic Readings" as an activity, just as entertainment is referenced as an activity in Essentials of Marketing: A Global-Managerial Approach (Perreault and McCarthy, 2006). For social purposes, the variable "Psychic Readings" is seen as having a negative connotation or impact.

From a religious perspective, the social marketing behavior variable "Psychic Readings" is viewed as a taboo or tenet violation in many denominations. Please refer to the social marketing behavior variables "Astrology/Horoscope," and "Tarot Cards" above. From a religious perspective, the social marketing behavior variable is viewed as a taboo or tenet violation in many denominations. For social purposes, the variable is seen as having a negative connotation or impact. In conclusion, the social marketing behavior variable "Psychic Readings" is for the purposes of this study a social marketing behavior variable "vice."

Worship/Bible: The social marketing behavior variable "Worship/Bible" has two relevant issues, society as a whole and religious world views. From a purely marketing perspective, the variable lifestyle dimension or AIO specifics denote "Worship/Bible" as an "Opinion," just as "Education," "Social Issues," or "Culture" is referenced as an "Opinion" in Essentials of Markcting: A Global-Managerial Approach (Perreault and McCarthy, 2006). For social purposes, this variable is seen as having a positive connotation or impact.

62

By commonly accepted conventions, religious worshiping or reading the Bible is seen by most of society as a pious act, although a small number see it as an overzealous act. In the religious world view, it is seen as an enlightening activity that helps in the promotion of religious beliefs and values in society.

From a religious perspective, the social marketing behavior variable "Worship/Bible" is viewed as a positive attribute, and it is encouraged. For social purposes, the variable is seen as having a positive connotation or impact. In conclusion, the social marketing behavior variable "Worship/Bible" is for the purposes of this study a social marketing behavior variable "virtue."

Politics: The social marketing behavior variable "Politics" has one relevant issue, a social aspect. Most religious denominations have yet to develop doctrines that deal with politics as a whole. From a purely marketing perspective, the variable lifestyle dimension or AIO specifics denote "Politics" as an Opinion, just as their sample of politics is referenced as an Opinion in Essentials of Marketing: A Global-Managerial Approach (Perreault and McCarthy, 2006). For social purposes, the variable is seen as having a negative connotation or impact. Politics is a complex issue embracing multiple elements which the following polls and research studies will address. Interestingly, the majority view politics as a negative influence on society.

The Social Element includes the general perception of government ineffectiveness due to politicians' personal agendas leading to obstructionism.

The effects of obstructionism are far reaching, empowering obstructionist senators to pursue personal agendas and block the majority party's proposals. According to Michael Coen of the New America Foundation, there's an increasing tendency for obstructionist senators to prioritize career longevity over passing needed legislation. Self-serving interests motivate obstructionism, earning today's minority party the notoriety of being referred to in the media, such as CNN and MSNBC, as "the party of No." (The Problem with Filibusters: The Negative Impact of Political Obstructionism, March 1, 2010, Melissa Ridenour. http://www. suite101 .com/content/the-problem-with-filibusters-a207870#ixzz1 26qNlf00)

Regarding the Social Element, politicians are seen to employ religion as an implement for control.

This article makes the point that politicians should not use religion as a tool for power but should instead promote religious values as a means to achieve the common good. A free church and religious society are necessary conditions for genuine peace, both for individuals and for society as a whole. Alexius, Patriarch (2007).

Moreover, when studying the Social Element, it becomes apparent that there is a negative perception among industrial nations about politics and people. "The new poll finds Canadians holding increasingly negative views of both the U.S. and the American people." Released: June 23, 2005 / American Character Gets Mixed Reviews / U.S. Image Up Slightly, But Still Negative.

In addition, politicians are observed to utilize negativity to gain control and mislead their constituents:

The problem is that negative campaigning can go south quickly and drift into the world of hearsay, innuendo and outright lies. Republican presidential candidate Senator John McCain's pronouncement that his campaign is about to go on the offensive against his Democratic rival, Senator Barack Obama should open up concern to voters. The overlay of race makes such negative campaigning potentially more toxic as McCain's handlers will likely seek to exploit divisions that are already evident in the electorate." (Green 2008, October 7).

There is also a negative perception about politicians among top business executives:

The perceptions that business executives have of our politically elected leaders form the basis of their attitudes, judgments, and behavior. This report on these perceptions draws from an extensive study made over a period of eight years. The great majority of the executives asked to describe their image of the politician expressed negative—often bitter—feelings, feelings molded by a variety of tensions and experiences. (Reed and Dalmas, 2004 November 10).

Another aspect of the Social Element involves eligible voters who don not vote due to mistrust of politics.

They are more likely to be bored with the political process and admit they often do not know enough about candidates to cast ballots. Intermittent voters also are more mistrustful of people compared with those who vote regularly . . . according to a survey conducted Sept. 21–Oct. 4 among 1,804 adults by the Pew Research Center for the People & the Press in collaboration with the Associated Press. (October 18, 2006). Who Votes, Who Doesn't, and Why: Regular Voters, Intermittent Voters, and Those Who Don't.

With regard to the Religious Element, government is expected to maintain a role that is separate from religion, due to the perceived negativity of politics. "The Government of the United States is not in any sense founded upon the Christian Religion." The Treaty of Tripoli (1797).

The United States has a long history of limiting the role of government with regard to religion. For example, over 150 years ago, Millard Fillmore stated while running for President, "I am tolerant of all creeds. Yet if any sect suffered itself to be used for political objects I would meet it by political opposition. In my view church and state should be separate, not only in form, but fact. Religion and politics should not be mingled." (Millard Fillmore (1809–1865) 13th U.S. President, address during the 1856 presidential election; from Albert Menendez and Edd Doerr, eds., Great Quotations on Religious Freedom, Amherst, New York: Prometheus Books, 2002, p. 70). From the same source, we have a quote from President James Polk, who said, "Thank God, under our Constitution there was no connection between Church and State, and that in my action as President of the United States I recognized no distinction of creeds in my appointments office." (Menendez and Doerr, 2002).

Also with regard to the Religious Element, most people wish to reduce the negativity of politics and religion, according to a recent survey.

Some Americans are having a change of heart about mixing religion and politics. A new survey finds a narrow majority of the public saying that churches and other houses of worship should keep out of political matters and not express their views on day-to-day social and political matters.

"In addition to somewhat greater worries about the way religious and non-religious groups are influencing the parties, the survey suggests that frustration and disillusionment among social conservatives may be a part of the reason why a greater number now think that religious institutions should keep out of politics" which is shown in a national survey by the Pew Research Center conducted by telephone—both landline phones and cell phones—from July 31-Aug. 10 among a national sample of 2,905 adults. (Pew Research Center, 2008, August 21).

Moreover, some Religious Denominations forbid or preach against voting or taking part in political activity.

Do you know why Jehovah's Witnesses tend not to vote? Passages like John 17:14 where Jesus says of those who follow him: "They are not of the world, just as I am not of the world." This other-worldliness is what Jehovah's Witnesses have interpreted as a directive to remain above terrestrial concerns like the election and neutral in all political matters.

Also relating to Religious Denominations that forbid or preach against voting or taking part in political activity:

Voting in political elections is not allowed by certain religious organizations. Members of these organizations, which are usually cult organizations, could be excommunicated or disenfranchised for voting. Members of these organizations are taught or brainwashed to think that our world is coming to an end anyway and there is no point in voting. When the world ceases to be, and the new world comes into being, there will be peace without war, no more crime, and no more of any of the corruption in the world. These non-voters really live in this world just biding their time and don't vote because they do not consider themselves part of this world. (Georgii 2008, March 8).

Youth often hold different values and beliefs from other generations. In fact, there is a growing tendency to reject or ignore religion entirely.

66

. . . among youth coming of age in the 1990s and just forming their views about religion. Some of that generation, to be sure, held deeply conservative moral and political views, and they felt very comfortable in the ranks of increasingly conservative churchgoers. But a majority of the Millennial generation was liberal on most social issues, and above all, on homosexuality. The fraction of twenty-somethings who said homosexual relations were "always" or "almost always" wrong plummeted from about 75% in 1990 to about 40% in 2008." (Ironically, in polling, Millennials are actually more uneasy about abortion than their parents.) Sociologists Michael Hout and Claude Fischer of UC Berkeley were among the first to call attention to the ensuing rise in young "nones," and in our recent book, "American Grace," we have extended their analysis, showing the association between religion and politics (and especially religion's intolerance of homosexuality) was the single strongest factor in this portentous shift. In religious affinities, as in taste in music and preference for colas, habits formed in early adulthood tend to harden over time. So if more than one-quarter of today's young people are setting off in adult life with no religious identification, compared with about one-twentieth of previous generations, the prospects for religious observance in the coming decades are substantially diminished. (Putnam and Campbell, 2010).

From both religious and social perspectives, the social marketing behavior variable "Politics" is viewed as a taboo or tenet violation in many denominations. Please refer to the social marketing behavior variables referenced above, which are clearly deduced as a negative or at the very least having a negative impact on society. In conclusion, the social marketing behavior variable "Politics" is for the purposes of this study a social marketing behavior variable "vice."

Donating to Charity: The social marketing behavior variable "Donating to Charity" has two relevant issues, society as a whole and religious world views. From a purely marketing perspective, the variable lifestyle dimension or AIO specifics denote "Donating to Charity" as an "Opinion," just as "Social Issues" or "Culture" is referenced as an "Opinion" in Essentials of Marketing: A Global-

67

Managerial Approach (Perreault and McCarthy, 2006). For social purposes, the variable "Donating to Charity" is seen as having a positive connotation or impact.

According to generally accepted conventions, donating to charity is seen by society as good deed or promotion of what is the positive in the culture. In the religious world view, it is also seen as a good deed.

From the Social standpoint, the "Donating to Charity" variable is widely viewed as a pro-social behavior. "Prosocial Behavior refers to the phenomenon of people helping each other with no thought of reward or compensation" (Psychology Glossary, 1998–2010).

Regarding the Religious aspect of the variable "Donating to Charity," a paper by Azim F. Shariff and Ara Norenzayan published in Psychological Science that suggests "that when individuals are primed about God, they behave more generously in the dictator game. For those of you who might be unfamiliar with this economic game, it works as follows: Individual A is given a fixed amount of money (say $20) and is asked to split the money with individual B, who has no veto power over the offer. In other words, if individual A decides to keep $18 and only offer $2 to individual B, this is the manner in which the money will be split. From a classical economic perspective, one should not offer anything to individual B although perhaps not surprisingly for all people other than economists, people do offer some amount greater than zero (e.g., because of reputational concerns)." (Shariff and Norenzayan, 2009). Moreover, the Abrahamic religions (Judaism, Christianity and Islam) actively promote charitable behavior:

> The ethical principles of monotheism recognize "that there is one Creative Source of the one creation, but that this very unity conveys a moral imperative concerning ethical treatment and conduct" in creation itself (Genesis 18:19). Study and practice of these ethical principles not only constitute individual worship, but lead to the establishment of just social systems and the promotion of the common good." (Kunkle, 2009).

From the religious perspective, the social marketing behavior variable is viewed as a positive attribute, although it is not specifically addressed. For social purposes, the variable is seen as having a positive connotation or impact. In conclusion, the social marketing behavior variable "Donating to Charity" is for the purposes of this study a social marketing behavior variable "virtue."

Hunting / Shooting: The social marketing behavior variable "Hunting/ Shooting" has two relevant issues, society as a whole and religious world views. From a purely marketing perspective, the variable lifestyle dimension or AIO specifics denote "Hunting/Shooting."   (Perreault and McCarthy, 2006).   For social purposes, the variable is seen as having a negative connotation or impact.

Regarding Social references, a number of negative aspects of "Hunting/ Shooting" have been studied:

Accidental shootings and gun thefts. Studies show that guns in the home are far more likely to be used in an unintentional shooting than in self-defense. In addition, even trained gun owners often do not realize that a gun is loaded. This often happens with pistols where the ammunition magazine is removed, but a hidden bullet remains in the chamber, ready to kill. Guns stolen from homes and cars fuel crime. College dorm rooms, by comparison, would be even easier targets for gun thieves. Guns are also often taken and used in suicides. (All facts herein have been sourced in our in-depth report No Gun Left Behind: The Gun Lobby's Campaign to Push Guns Into Colleges and Schools (Brady Center, 2007).

Hunting is sometimes viewed as animal abuse or cruelty:
If animal cruelty is a sign of psychopathic behavior and hunting for fun is animal cruelty, is hunting not a sign of psychopathic behavior? What I mean is that most modern psychology teaches that one distinct characteristic of dangerous criminals is abuse to animals. Logically, hunting down and killing an innocent animal for fun is construed as animal cruelty, so is it not safe to say that people who hunt are more likely, according to psychology, to commit dangerous crimes? (Sports1234.com, 2009).

From a religious standpoint, there seems to be no specific taboo or tenet violation in many Christian denominations. For social purposes, the variable is seen as having a negative connotation or impact. In conclusion, the social marketing behavior variable "Hunting/Shooting" is for the purposes of this study a social marketing behavior variable "vice."

Play Sports: The social marketing behavior variable "Play Sports" has two relevant issues, society as a whole and religious world views. From a purely marketing perspective, the variable lifestyle dimension or AIO specifics denote "Play Sports" as an "Activities," just as sport is referenced as an "Activity" in Essentials of Marketing: Perreault and McCarthy, 2006). Although often viewed as a means of building character and teamwork among youth, playing sports has increasingly taken on a negative connotation in recent years.

The trend for using performance enhancing drugs is especially troubling:

> The general public is becoming less tolerant of doping and is more aware of and concerned about its consequences. People understand that what happens at the elite level of sport often has a trickle-down effect on children, who want to emulate sports stars. (Office of National Drug Control Policy, n.d.).

For social purposes, the variable "Play Sports" is seen as having a negative connotation or impact. Sports can be misused to emphasize winning and to disregard sportsmanship and the values of team playing. When winning at any cost becomes the end goal performance drugs can become a major issue. This is a major concern in today's society. It is understood that playing sports also has a positive influence in encouraging participants to remain healthy and physically engaged. However, this research study has found that playing sports can be both a vice and a virtue. For the purposes of this research, playing sports is defined as a vice. This is not to say that it does not acknowledge that this may be seen as a bias.

For social purposes, the variable is seen as having a negative connotation or impact. In conclusion, the social marketing behavior variable "Play Sports" is for the purposes of this study a social marketing behavior variable "vice."

CHAPTER 10
MULTIDIMENSIONAL VERSUS
UNIDIMENSIONAL INDICATORS OF RELIGIOSITY

Many academic discourses and their subsequent analyses to measure a person's religiosity have been unidimensional with regard to a subject's depth of religiosity. "Like other researchers, psychologists and sociologists of religion do not agree about the factorial complexity of the object of their study. Some continue to assume that religiousness is a unidimensional quality that can be adequately assessed by any number of indicators." (Wulff, 1997).

Many references to religiosity use church attendance as the sole indicator of religiosity, but while this is common, it is not necessarily an accurate measure of a person's religiosity. Yet some noted academic scholars in the discipline of religious studies have used the sole indicator of attendance. As a case in point, a publication in Time magazine states that "in the study of religion, the modern faith fault line is not denomination but church attendance. Weekly attendance is the best, though still imperfect, indicator." (The Real Clear Politics Blog, 2009). This attendance factor or indicator has been used throughout academic journals to assess religiosity. In addition, church attendance has been used in widespread correlational studies that range from politics, drugs and brain chemistry to a number of other characteristics and/or issues. An example of the media using church attendance as an indicator of religiosity was published in an article in April 2009, employing a Gallup Poll that analyzes an unweighted survey of 4,087 Protestants and 1,837 Catholics in 2008 to assess "church attendance among American Christians." (April 9, 2009, "Churchgoing Among U.S. Catholics Slides to Tie Protestants. However, long-term decline may have leveled off in past decade," by Lydia Saad, Princeton, NJ.

It is problematic to measure concepts that are ambiguous such as "prejudice," "social integration" or "religiosity." The challenge is therefore how to measure the individual's level of religiousness or religiosity. A person truly believes in the existence of God may choose not to attend church services. Yet, what about someone who attends church services that does not believe in God? How can you rank these peoples level of religiosity? Can this person be religious? This strongly indicates that religion is a multi-dimensional concept encompassing behaviors, beliefs, experiences, and cultural or social conditions.

This analysis uses a multidimensional methodology to measure religiosity in conjunction with specifications distinctive to religiosity and the correlated plausible marketing segmentation. This approach provides an opportunity to attain a distinctive marketing mix for manufacturers of religious iconography.

This section discusses the survey sample/participants, the CAGS Religion and Marketing questionnaire, the definition and construction of the religiosity measurement, the hypotheses, and study analysis.

This study utilizes permutated comparable multidimensional indicators as used in four other academic studies which refer to Methods such as the May 2007 study of The Influence of Religiosity on Contraceptive Use among Roman Catholic Women in the United States by Jennifer Ohlendorf, M.S., R.N. and Richard J. Fehring, Ph.D., R.N.

Ms. Ohlendorf is Clinical Instructor, Marquette University College of Nursing. 2—(2005) study of Indicators of Child, Family and Community Connections: The Measurement of Family Religiosity and Spirituality By: Laura Lippman and Erik Michelsen, Child Trends and Eugene C. Roehlekepartain, Search Institute. Paper prepared for Office of the Assistant Secretary for Planning and Evaluation, HHS for the contract, Indicators of Child, Family, and Community Connections. 3—(2001). "Further, health education and health promotion efforts are increasingly attentive to spirituality and spiritual well-being as important components of an individual's overall health (Bensley, 1991; Diax, 1993; Waite, Hawks & Gast, 1999.) Advances in the Measurement of Religiosity Among Older African Americans: Implications for Health and Mental Health Researchers, Linda M. Chatters, Robert Joseph Taylor, Karen D. Lincoln. and 4— "the Barna Group has an interesting approach to the topic of commitment. They evaluate eight practices (e.g., church attendance, frequency of prayer, etc.), and ten beliefs (e.g., belief in the inerrancy of the Bible, whether Satan is a real living entity, etc.)" to measure a person's religiosity.

In addition, each indicator is evaluated and substantiated through past and present polls and/or surveys. The substantiation of indicators from polls and/or surveys allows uncertainty to be minimized on any single account or specification. The substantiation of the indicators through past and present polls and/or surveys includes in-depth explanation of each indicator's weight in the religiosity index employed to measure respondents of the CAGS survey indicator questions used to compile the religiosity index.

CHAPTER 11
DESCRIPTIVE STATISTICS

Sample Data Compared to University Population

In regard to the CSULB and U of A, the total University vs. Sample populations (Table 3) are very similar. When gender is reviewed (Tables B1–B2) with regard to sample populations and after weighting for differing academic levels, the U of A sample respondents reveal a significantly higher number of Graduate respondents (Tables B3–B4) that can validate the initial comments. Those comments included: A plausible but circumstantial conclusion may or may not be cultural the conservative nature of Arkansas, a "red" state[X], following a practice "of single-earner households . . . social conservatives guarantee that their children will get pregnant early and often (Palin, Bristol), leading to teen childbirth, shotgun marriages and high divorce rates" (Douthat 2010, May 9).

Refer to tables in Appendix B to clearly see the percentage distribution calculations between the California and Arkansas samples as they relate to the following narrative of Descriptive Statistics. One significant distinction in the ethnic variable subsets between the U of A general population and the Arkansas sample reveals a large variance, in that a 27.1 times greater number of respondents classified themselves as "U.S. only." The overt response is partly due to the disparity in the subset variable "Caucasian," where the U of A general population has a 5.5 times greater number of respondents than the Arkansas sample.

TABLE 3. University vs. Sample populations

61.1% CSULB Total Population compared to 54.2% CSULB sample population.
49.5% U of A Total Population compared to 35.9% U of A sample population.

Geographic Variable	Sample Total[a]		
		Count	Column N%
California	494	69.6	
Arkansas	216	30.4	

[a]$N = 710$. Percentages and totals are based on respondents.

The remaining disparity is dispersed among most of the other subset variables. The overall relevance continues to paint a picture of a homogeneous ethnic university population at the U of A. The remaining disparity between the Arkansas sample and the U of A general population shows an increased number, except for one subset variable, Hispanics, which revealed a 2.8 times increase in the U of A sample. A significant variance in California reveals that the CSULB general population shows a 2.6 times greater number of Caucasian respondents than the California sample. These disparities were corrected, since the statistical analysis of the survey results selected a representative sample compared to the University's general population.

All the academic level variable subsets are inconsistent between the university populations of both CSULB and U of A. In regard to the California sample and the CSULB general population, three variable subsets are underrepresented in the survey sample by Freshmen (12.1), Sophomores (2.0) and Graduates (3.8). Two variable subsets were over-represented: Juniors (1.5) and Seniors (1.7). In regard to the Arkansas sample and the U of A population, three variable subsets are underrepresented in the survey sample by Freshmen (24.7), Sophomores (16.9), and Seniors (1.2). Two variable subsets were over-represented: Juniors (2.8), and Graduates (1.8).

These disparities were corrected, since the statistical analysis of the survey results selected a representative sample compared to the University's general population.

The mathematical formula employed in determining frequencies is:

$$f = x / y$$

Where:

f = Frequency

x = Prominent significant number

y = Minor significant number

The formula uses the prominent significant number, depending on which variable subsets this study sought to compare with regard to frequencies, with the minor significant number, i.e., Health and Human Services majors are 5.7 times more frequent than U of A respondents = 5.1 (CSULB) / 0.9 (U of A).

The cultural differences between CSULB and U of A samples can best be demonstrated by Table 4. When comparing the universities, the religiosity index is significantly greater for U of A students than CSULB students. The mean difference is shown in the table, Group Statistics Religiosity 2 by State, Table 4. These results will be explored and shown throughout the Appendix Tables.

TABLE 4. Group Statistics Religiosity 2 by State

Group Statistics Religiosity 2	State	"N"	Mean	Standard Deviation	Standard Mean
CSULB	California	494	7.6579	4.44374	.19993
U of A	Arkansas	216	10.2500	4.42009	.30075

The cultural differences between CSULB and U of A samples can best be demonstrated by the above table. When comparing the universities, the religiosity index is significantly greater for U of A students than CSULB students (Appendix B Tables B1–B4). However, the U of A sample shows a statistically greater number of respondents participate in Social Vices ((Appendix B Tables B1–B4). This may seem counter intuitive but remains outside the scope of this study. Further study of this anomaly is warranted.

CHAPTER 12
THE SURVEY SAMPLE DEMOGRAPHICS

This research was supported by the CAGS survey sample, which consisted of respondents from California State University, Long Beach, aka CSULB ($n =$ 494), and the University of Arkansas, aka U of A, in Fayetteville (n = 216). All information pertaining to University population was retrieved from University Outreach and School Relations, Division of Student Services for CSULB and Office of Institutional Research, Student Data for U of A. However, this section is primarily a narrative of the sample comparison of data from both universities within the scope of the CAGS survey. When establishing both sample surveys against the Universities, a mathematical method is used to determine the percentage in relation to total student populations of the Universities. The California State University, Long Beach, sample size was 1.5 percent (494/33,479 = .0147555) of the CSULB population; in contrast, the University of Arkansas sample was 1.2 percent (216/17,328 = .012465) of the U of A population.

This portion of the demographic narrative will be explicated with the methods used and supported throughout the demographics. As the (Appendix B Tables B1–B4) displays, there is a greater percentage of males at the U of A than CSULB respondents, 64.1% versus 45.8%, respectively. A plausible but circumstantial conclusion may or may not be the cultural conservative nature of Arkansas, a red state[X], following a practice "of single-earner households . . . , social conservatives' guarantee that their children will get pregnant early and often (see Palin, Bristol), leading to teen childbirth, shotgun marriages . . ." (Douthat, 2010, May 9). In contrast, the California (a blue state[X]), university CSULB has a greater percentage of females 54.2 percent to 35.9 of males, Appendix B Tables B1–B4, within the survey sample itself. This disparity may or may not be attributable to California being a blue state[X] where the liberals "agree on how this happened. First, the sexual revolution overturned the old order of single-earner households, early marriages . . . In its aftermath, the professional classes found a new equilibrium. Today, couples with college and (especially) graduate degrees tend to cohabit early and marry late,

delaying childbirth and raising smaller families than their parents
. . ." (Douthat, 2010, May 9.)

In analyzing the marital status variables within the CAGS sample survey, we can see disparities between the CSULB and U of A samples. More than double the respondents in the U of A sample are married, compared to the CSULB respondents. More than three times the number of widows are in California, .4 percent at CSULB, and 1.4 percent at the U of A. There is a 42.9 percent higher frequency in the number of U of A respondents who were separated or divorced. CSULB has a 17.2 percent higher frequency in single or never married respondents than U of A. If Arkansas as a "red state nurtures a conservative culture, people would be more likely to marry at earlier ages and refrain from divorce because of strong societal and religious taboos." (Douthat, 2010, May 9) .

Education majors show a significant variance between CSULB in California and U of A in Arkansas. CSULB Art majors are 7.6 times more frequent than U of A respondents. U of A Business majors are 1.3 times more frequent than CSULB California respondents. CSULB Health and Human Services majors are 5.7 times more frequent than U of A respondents. Liberal Arts Majors at CSULB are 5.3 times more frequent than U of A respondents. All counts and percentages reference Appendix B Tables B1–B4.

The survey sample provides an all-inclusive number of ethnic parameters. When European parameters are compressed, the research shows a slight difference of 1.1 times greater ethnic variables, favoring the U of A. It is striking that CSULB is 4.5 times more likely to have Asian Pacific Islander than Arkansas. When all Hispanic subsets are compressed, all Hispanics are 4.8 times more frequent at CSULB than at the U of A. The largest variance is found in the variable subsets "U.S. only," where it shows that U of A students are 5 times more likely to classify themselves in that category than CSULB students. A plausible explanation could be that the U of A has little ethnic diversity and fosters a loss of ethnic identity.

In analyzing the academic level variables, the analysis found significant variances on three class standings: Junior, Senior and Graduate levels. The U of A is more likely to have juniors, 1.5 times more frequently than CSULB, while CSULB respondents are 3.3 times more likely to have Seniors than U of A participating in the CAGS survey study. U of A respondents are 7.3 times likely to have Graduate level respondents to participate in the survey. The possible explanation is that the U of A classes that administered the survey included more graduate-level classes, which skewed the weighting of the survey sample at the U of A, but this does not necessarily adversely affect other independent variables.

The CAGS survey includes variables that neither university compiles, such as religious affiliation, occupation, income, and age. This research includes those variables within the survey sample. Religious affiliation: Catholic respondents are 1.7 times more prevalent in California at CSULB than the U of A. The Disciples of Christ respondents are 7.2 times more prevalent at CSULB than at the U of A. Methodists are 7.6 times more prevalent at the U of A than at CSULB. Surprisingly, Southern Baptists are 35.5 times more dominant in Arkansas at the U of A.

The dominant religious affiliations at the U of A within the survey sample are comprised of Catholics at 19.3 percent, Methodists at 13.0 percent and Southern Baptists at 21.3 percent, which represent 53.6 percent when weighted with Non-Preference at 7.7 percent, Secular/Agnostic/Atheist at 4.3 and Other Non-Christian at 3.9, making a total of these three 15.9 percent.

Looking at these totals, we can see that the remaining religious affiliations total 30.5 percent and are dispersed among thirteen relevant affiliations, where greater than 0.1 = is a relevant variable. In California at CSULB, the survey reveals two dominant religious affiliations, with Catholics at 33.3 percent and the Disciples of Christ at 10.1 percent, representing a total of 43.4 percent of all denominations. When weighted with Non-Preference at 14.2 percent, Secular/Agnostic/Atheist at 6.2 and Other Non-Christian at 13.1, the total of these three reaches 33.5 percent. Using this, we can see that the remaining religious affiliations total 23.1 percent and are dispersed among 17 relevant variable affiliations, where greater than 0.1 = is a relevant variable.

The sample survey clearly reveals that the survey sample identifies the U of A as less diverse in religious affiliations and substantially less likely to have non-preference, secular/Agnostic/Atheists and Other Non-Christian religions. The sample discloses the dissimilarity between California's CSULB and Arkansas' U of A. In reviewing religious affiliation variables, there were some denominations that contained limited quantity. As a result, distribution percentage tables were condensed and displayed in Table B13, which is condensed to the "Roof and McKinney" denominational divisions and B15, displaying the "World Christian Encyclopedia" divisions. The aforementioned descriptive narrative contains a review of all original "Annual Income" categories, as incorporated in the survey questionnaire.

The survey sample provides an all-inclusive assortment of occupational parameters. Outstanding variances include 2.3 times greater in CSULB compared to the U of A in the occupation variable subsets "Other Not Listed." The largest variance is found in the variable subset, "Middle Management," where it shows that the U of A is 3.3 times more frequent to be in "Middle Management" than CSULB. A plausible explanation could be that the U of A includes a greater number of Graduate Students, which conceivably could result in a higher frequency of middle-management positions. . In reviewing "Employment Status" variables there were some employment categories that contained limited quantity. As a result, distribution percentage tables were condensed, and only statistically relevant categories were discussed in the aforementioned descriptive narrative. All condensed income categories are displayed in Table B3.

Relevant income variables reveal that respondents from the U of A are 1.2 times more likely to make less than $4,999 then CSULB. However, when the first two subsets[X] are compressed and compared, both CSULB and U of A's N% are equal. The significance of the compression of the two subsets is to evaluate a comparison with the 2004 poverty threshold for a family unit size of one, which is $9,310. The survey sample reveals that approximately 41.5 percent of all respondents are at or below the U.S. poverty level. If the income variables are weighted for a family unit size of two for those that are married, the percentage of respondents that are living at or below the poverty level of $12,490 increases for both universities. A significant number of variances were found when analyzing upper-income levels. The highest variance is in the subset $50,000 through $54,999, where the U of A has a frequency 11.8 times greater than that of CSULB.

When the last three subsets are reviewed, a marked variance is found, showing more upper-income respondents at the U of A than in CSULB. In the subset variable $60,000 through $64,999, the U of A has 4.7 times the number of respondents of CSULB. The subset variable $65,000 through $79,999 also shows that the U of A has 1.7 times the number of respondents at CSULB. An even more significant variance is in the subset variable $80,000 or greater income level, where the number at the U of A is 7.9 times higher than that of CSULB respondents. With age variables being very similar, this may be viewed as a paradox, but with a higher level of graduate respondents, it is plausible that many U of A respondents may be utilizing an employer-provided continuing education program. In reviewing "Annual Income" variables, there were some income categories that contained limited quantity. As a result, distribution percentage tables were condensed; however, the aforementioned descriptive narrative contains a review of all original "Annual Income" categories, as incorporated in the survey questionnaire. All condensed income categories are displayed in Table B3.

In regard to the CSULB and U of A, the respondents' age variables are very similar. The survey sample of both universities, CSULB and U of A, and those less than age 18, are .2 percent and .3 percent, respectively; ages 18 through 24, 68.0 percent and 64.9 percent; ages 25 through 29, 18.6 percent and 18.3 percent; and ages 30 through 34, 7.5 percent and 10.6. Under 18 through age 34 comprise approximately 94 percent, with a variance of no more than .1 percent combined. It is seemingly out of the ordinary to ostensibly find the age variable subsets so numerically identical when all other independent demographic variables are so distinctly dissimilar. In reviewing "Age" variables, there were some age categories that contained limited quantity. As a result, distribution percentage tables were condensed; however, the aforementioned descriptive narrative contains a review of all original "age" categories as incorporated in the survey questionnaire. All condensed income categories are displayed in Appendix B Tables B3–B4.

In short, these survey sample results can substantiate the plausibility of CSULB as an eclectic and diverse student population, and the U of A as a more homogeneous student population. Appendix B contain additional demographic data, such as "Marital Status," "Ethnicity," "College Grad Status," and "Class Status." Variable Categories that were limited in quantity were condensed, but displayed in Appendix B Tables B1–B4.

Appendix B Tables B1–B4 contains the variables for the "Religiosity Iconography Items" related to the study. Categorized "Owned," "Don't Own, Would Buy," "Don't Own, Won't Buy," "Unsure."

CHAPTER 13

INFERENTIAL STATISTICS

A chief and unique hypothesis (hypothesis #1) of this study regarding the discipline of Religious Studies is that church attendance only cannot be an precise indicator of a person's religiosity. Another primary hypothesis, an even more unique hypothesis (hypothesis #2) of this study regarding the discipline of Business Marketing, is that a person's religiosity correlates with the purchasing behavior of religious iconography. Hypotheses #3 includes the assertions that Consumer Social Behaviors labeled by certain churches as "vices and virtues" also correlate to purchasing behavior of religious iconography that current ownership affects this purchasing behavior, and that religiosity affects specific choices of iconography. Hypotheses #4 utilizes the results from Hypotheses numbers 1 to 3 in correlation to the purchase or potential purchase of the religious iconography variables in this study to provide a predictor of demand for the specific iconography items using an affinity analysis to specific vices and or virtues.

Hypothesis #1: Identifies the problem that most studies define a person's religiosity with church attendance only (unidimensional). It further hypothesis that church attendance only cannot be a precise indicator of a person's religiosity. This study first establishes a proper construct of elements be weighted and statistically reviewed. The hypothesis establishes a quantitative analysis of relevant elements to a person's religiosity that proves attendance only cannot be a precise indicator of a person's religiosity. The validation of elements (multidimensional) (See Introduction) consists of the constructs of eleven elements to use in a religiosity index (Table 2, E10, E13, G7, and G9). The only other multidimensional known to have been used is a three-element (multidimensional) group that appeared in the Journal for the Scientific Study of Religion (Collett and Lizardo, June 2009). However, the variables employed in that religiosity index produce a moderate Cronbach's Alpha (rating of .64). This study's multidimensional religiosity index contains a Cronbach Alpha rating of .797. This reliability Statistics (Cronbach Alpha) provides the criteria of adequacy to reveal the best explanation for a person's religiosity.

Hypothesis #2: Tables 4, 40–46, and B5–B12 indicates that Religiosity is significantly related to the four categories of purchasing behavior: "Owned,"

"Will Buy," Won't Buy," and "Unsure." The Religiosity Index has the strongest relationships when compared to its eleven individual components. The Religiosity Index is also the best overall predictor of these categories in all Appendix D tables. Refer to the regression analysis (Inferential Statistics starting with Tables 5–125), which provides quantitative support for Hypothesis #2.

Hypothesis #2: The detailed correlation Tables 8–37, 51–53, 118, C36–C51, and all tables listed under Appendix D provide consistent results for selected social vices and social virtues. In particular, dancing, drinking, and night clubbing suggest that these respondents will purchase both traditional and non-traditional iconography, in part, due to not owning such items.

Hypothesis #3: Quantitative analysis in Tables 8–37 and 118-120 supports the affirmation that Consumer Social Behaviors variables considered as "vices and virtues" by some churches correlate to purchasing behavior of religious iconography. Tables 8–37, 118–120 provide quantitative support that ownership impacts this purchasing behavior and that religiosity impacts precise selections of iconography.

Hypothesis #4: Using this study's Multidimensional Religiosity Index (Introduction), which has to be quantified with the Cronbach's Alpha reliability statistic of .797 (Table 38) with eleven components (Religiosity Index, Table 2), the study can then be used to correlate this study's social vices and social virtues (Appendix D tables). The result of the aforementioned correlation can then be applied to the sample purchase patterns of the 13 religious iconography items (Tables 8–37, 118–120, C36–C51, and all tables listed under Appendix D) to establish a marketing target group (Appendix I: Target Market Group Diagram). These results then become the most valuable predictor of demand for the specific religious iconography items and thus provide a Target Market Group for market basket analysis and a more precise advertising mix.

TABLE 5. Correlations, Religiosity Index Elements

		Own	Don't Own, Will Buy	Don't Own, Won't Buy	Unsure
Religiosity Index	Pearson Correlation	.394	.087	-.402	-.101
	Sig. (2-tailed)	.000	.021	.000	.007
	N	710	710	710	710
Church Service Attendance	Pearson Correlation	.368	.019	-.316	-.108
	Sig. (2-tailed)	.000	.622	.000	.004
	N	710	710	710	710
Religious Service Atten.	Pearson Correlation	.364	.024	-.340	-.094
	Sig. (2-tailed)	.000	.515	.000	.012
	N	710	710	710	710
Religiousness Level	Pearson Correlation	.270	.103	-.306	-.066
	Sig. (2-tailed)	.000	.006	.000	.080
	N	710	710	710	710
Enjoy Worship / Bible	Pearson Correlation	.124	.111	-.190	-.057
	Sig. (2-tailed)	.001	.003	.000	.127
	N	710	710	710	710
Spiritual Value	Pearson Correlation	.263	.081	-.260	-.123
	Sig. (2-tailed)	.000	.031	.000	.001
	N	710	710	710	710
Worship	Pearson Correlation	.225	.055	-.260	-.038
	Sig. (2-tailed)	.000	.142	.000	.313
	N	710	710	710	710
Church Education	Pearson Correlation	.199	.086	-.224	-.072
	Sig. (2-tailed)	.000	.023	.000	.056
	N	710	710	710	710
Do you believe there is life after death?	Pearson Correlation	.180	.080	-.234	.000
	Sig. (2-tailed)	.000	.034	.000	.995
	N	710	710	710	710
Special Enlightenment	Pearson Correlation	.148	.001	-.122	-.026
	Sig. (2-tailed)	.000	.983	.001	.481
	N	710	710	710	710
Clergy	Pearson Correlation	.143	-.002	-.116	-.022
	Sig. (2-tailed)	.000	.956	.002	.559
	N	710	710	710	710
Church Newsletters	Pearson Correlation	.107	.079	-.148	-.024
	Sig. (2-tailed)	.004	.036	.000	.522
	N	710	710	710	710

TABLE 6. Correlations, Religiosity Index Elements

		Own	Don't Own, Will Buy	Don't Own, Will Buy	Unsure
Religiosity Index	Pearson Correlation	.580	.190	-.553	-.122
	Sig. (2-tailed)	.000	.000	.000	.001
	N	710	710	710	710
Church Service Atten.	Pearson Correlation	.471	.132	-.419	-.119
	Sig. (2-tailed)	.000	.000	.000	.002
	N	710	710	710	710
Religious Service Atten.	Pearson Correlation	.469	.136	-.450	-.088
	Sig. (2-tailed)	.000	.000	.000	.020
	N	710	710	710	710
Religiousness Level	Pearson Correlation	.501	.157	-.461	-.122
	Sig. (2-tailed)	.000	.000	.000	.001
	N	710	710	710	710
Enjoy Worship/Bible	Pearson Correlation	.471	.126	-.449	-.079
	Sig. (2-tailed)	.000	.001	.000	.036
	N	710	710	710	710
Spiritual Value	Pearson Correlation	.426	.125	-.386	-.117
	Sig. (2-tailed)	.000	.001	.000	.002
	N	710	710	710	710
Worship	Pearson Correlation	.324	.106	-.333	-.046
	Sig. (2-tailed)	.000	.005	.000	.223
	N	710	710	710	710
Church Education	Pearson Correlation	.263	.174	-.306	-.061
	Sig. (2-tailed)	.000	.000	.000	.102
	N	710	710	710	710
Do you believe there is life after death?	Pearson Correlation	.213	.104	-.242	-.009
	Sig. (2-tailed)	.000	.005	.000	.820
	N	710	710	710	710
Special Enlightenment	Pearson Correlation	.221	.032	-.166	-.056
	Sig. (2-tailed)	.000	.402	.000	.138
	N	710	710	710	710
Clergy	Pearson Correlation	.121	.069	-.121	-.050
	Sig. (2-tailed)	.001	.065	.001	.179
	N	710	710	710	710
Church Newsletters	Pearson Correlation	.216	.101	-.215	-.051
	Sig. (2-tailed)	.000	.007	.000	.171
	N	710	710	710	710

TABLE 7. Correlations, Religiosity Index Elements

		Social Virtues	Social Vices
Religiosity Index	Pearson Correlation	.314	.010
	Sig. (2-tailed)	.000	.792
	N	710	710
Church Service Attendance	Pearson Correlation	.173	-.061
	Sig. (2-tailed)	.000	.104
	N	710	710
Religious Service Attendance	Pearson Correlation	.226	-.016
	Sig. (2-tailed)	.000	.679
	N	710	710
Religiousness Level	Pearson Correlation	.228	-.064
	Sig. (2-tailed)	.000	.089
	N	710	710
Enjoy Worship/Bible	Pearson Correlation	.497	.106
	Sig. (2-tailed)	.000	.005
	N	710	710
Spiritual Value	Pearson Correlation	.266	.057
	Sig. (2-tailed)	.000	.132
	N	710	710
Worship	Pearson Correlation	.199	.022
	Sig. (2-tailed)	.000	.550
	N	710	710
Church Education	Pearson Correlation	.136	.062
	Sig. (2-tailed)	.000	.097
	N	710	710
Do you believe there is life after death?	Pearson Correlation	.122	.081
	Sig. (2-tailed)	.001	.032
	N	710	710
Special Enlightenment	Pearson Correlation	.170	.027
	Sig. (2-tailed)	.000	.470
	N	710	710
Clergy	Pearson Correlation	.100	-.047
	Sig. (2-tailed)	.008	.215
	N	710	710
Church Newsletters	Pearson Correlation	.089	-.005
	Sig. (2-tailed)	.017	.902
	N	710	710

NOTE: Correlation Table

TABLE 7. Continued

Traditional Iconography Ownership Status.
CORRELATIONS Variables Q23_Bad_Behavior Q23_Good_Behavior with
RTradA RTradB RTradC RTradD.

TABLE 8. Correlations, Social Vices, Social Virtues

		Own	Don't Own, Will Buy	Don't Own, Will Buy	Unsure
Social Vices	Pearson Correlation	.095	.188	-.181	-.047
	Sig. (2-tailed)	.011	.000	.000	.208
	N	710	710	710	710
Social Virtues	Pearson Correlation	.156	.046	-.162	-.054
	Sig. (2-tailed)	.000	.225	.000	.152
	N	710	710	710	710

NOTE: CORRELATION TABLE FOR Social Behaviors Indices by Non-Traditional Iconography Ownership Status.
CORRELATIONS Variables Q23_Bad_Behavior Q23_Good_Behavior with
RNontradA RNontradB RNontradC RNontradD.

TABLE 9. Correlations, Social Vices, Social Virtues

		Own	Don't Own, Will Buy	Don't Own, Will Buy	Unsure
Social Vices	Pearson Correlation	-.008	.098	-.037	-.002
	Sig. (2-tailed)	.838	.009	.321	.952
	N	710	710	710	710
Social Virtues	Pearson Correlation	.291	.094	-.269	-.083
	Sig. (2-tailed)	.000	.013	.000	.027
	N	710	710	710	710

NOTE: VICES.
CORRELATION TABLE FOR Social Behaviors Indices by Traditional
Iconography Ownership Status.
CORRELATIONS: Variables RQ23_item71 RQ23_item72 RQ23_item73
RQ23_item74 RQ23_item75 RQ23_Item76, RQ23_item77 RQ23_item78
RQ23_item81 RQ23_item82 RQ23_item83 RQ23_item84, RQ23_item85
RQ23_item87 RQ23_item89 RQ23_item90 with RtradA RtradB RtradC RtradD.

TABLE 10. Correlations of 20 Social Vices and Virtues

		Own	Don't Own, Will Buy	Don't Own. Will Buy	Unsure
Cigarette/Cigars	Pearson Correlation	-.018	.117	-.053	-.044
	Sig. (2-tailed)	.641	.002	.156	.237
	N	710	710	710	710
Dancing	Pearson Correlation	.215	.033	-.155	-.089
	Sig. (2-tailed)	.000	.386	.000	.018
	N	710	710	710	710
Beer, wine, etc.	Pearson Correlation	-.012	.129	-.066	.016
	Sig. (2-tailed)	.750	.001	.078	.661
	N	710	710	710	710
Concerts	Pearson Correlation	.066	.121	-.108	-.026
	Sig. (2-tailed)	.078	.001	.004	.489
	N	710	710	710	710
Night clubbing	Pearson Correlation	.138	.145	-.189	-.066
	Sig. (2-tailed)	.000	.000	.000	.078
	N	710	710	710	710
Video Games	Pearson Correlation	-.063	.114	-.029	.029
	Sig. (2-tailed)	.094	.002	.445	.446
	N	710	710	710	710
TV Shopping	Pearson Correlation	.010	.064	-.067	.012
	Sig. (2-tailed)	.781	.086	.076	.741
	N	710	710	710	710

TABLE 10. Continued

		Own	Don't Own, Will Buy	Don't Own, Will Buy	Unsure
Computer / Internet	Pearson Correlation	-.020	.111	-.081	.047
	Sig. (2-tailed)	.588	.003	.030	.210
	N	710	710	710	710
Lottery / Sweepstakes	Pearson Correlation	.083	.037	-.080	-.025
	Sig. (2-tailed)	.027	.320	.034	.513
	N	710	710	710	710
Astrology / Horoscope	Pearson Correlation	.105	.048	-.081	-.097
	Sig. (2-tailed)	.005	.202	.031	.010
	N	710	710	710	710
Tarot Cards	Pearson Correlation	.062	.059	-.063	-.049
	Sig. (2-tailed)	.097	.117	.093	.189
	N	710	710	710	710
Psychic Readings	Pearson Correlation	.023	.013	-.001	-.042
	Sig. (2-tailed)	.548	.722	.969	.267
	N	710	710	710	710
Politics	Pearson Correlation	.040	.050	-.055	-.007
	Sig. (2-tailed)	.289	.186	.142	.860
	N	710	710	710	710
Hunting / Shooting	Pearson Correlation	.013	.078	-.049	-.042
	Sig. (2-tailed)	.720	.039	.192	.269
	N	710	710	710	710
Watch / play Sports	Pearson Correlation	.026	.122	-.113	-.006
	Sig. (2-tailed)	.482	.001	.003	.872
	N	710	710	710	710

NOTE: CORRELATION TABLE FOR Social Vices by Non Traditional Buys. CORRELATIONS Variables RQ23_item71 RQ23_item72 RQ23_item73 RQ23_item74 RQ23_item75 RQ23_Item76, RQ23_item77 RQ23_item78 RQ23_item81 RQ23_item82 RQ23_item83 RQ23_item84, RQ23_itcm85 RQ23_item87 RQ23_item89 RQ23_item90 with RNontradA RnontradB RnontradC RnontradD.

TABLE 11. Correlations of 20 Social Vices and Virtues

		Own	Don't Own, Will Buy	Don't Own, Will Buy	Unsure
Cigarette/Cigars	Pearson Correlation		.002	.002	-.008
	Sig. (2-tailed)	.733	.953	.953	.834
	N	710	710	710	710
Dancing	Pearson Correlation	.143	.043	-.089	-.083
	Sig. (2-tailed)	.000	.253	.018	.027
	N	710	710	710	710
Beer, wine, etc.	Pearson Correlation	-.124	.120	.027	.029
	Sig. (2-tailed)	.001	.001	.466	.439
	N	710	710	710	710
Concerts	Pearson Correlation	.130	.023	-.094	-.002
	Sig. (2-tailed)	.001	.542	.012	.967
	N	710	710	710	710
Night clubbing	Pearson Correlation	-.032	.137	-.034	-.054
	Sig. (2-tailed)	.394	.000	.372	.152
	N	710	710	710	710
Video Games	Pearson Correlation	-.093	.008	.038	.095
	Sig. (2-tailed)	.013	.825	.313	.011
	N	710	710	710	710
TV Shopping	Pearson Correlation	-.012	.017	-.008	.015
	Sig. (2-tailed)	.757	.650	.832	.690
	N	710	710	710	710
Computer/Internet	Pearson Correlation	.010	-.007	-.029	.069
	Sig. (2-tailed)	.797	.851	.434	.065
	N	710	710	710	710
Casino Gambling	Pearson Correlation	-.117	.042	.061	.023
	Sig. (2-tailed)	.002	.259	.107	.546
	N	710	710	710	710
Lottery/Sweepstakes	Pearson Correlation	-.012	.026	.011	-.008
	Sig. (2-tailed)	.757	.482	.767	.836
	N	710	710	710	710
Astrology/Horoscope	Pearson Correlation	-.019	.052	.007	-.046
	Sig. (2-tailed)	.611	.166	.851	.222
	N	710	710	710	710
Tarot Cards	Pearson Correlation	.003	-.002	.025	-.018
	Sig. (2-tailed)	.940	.947	.505	.631
	N	710	710	710	710

TABLE 11. Continued

		Own	Don't Own, Will Buy	Don't Own, Will Buy	Unsure
Psychic Readings	Pearson Correlation	-.039	-.001	.055	-.011
	Sig. (2-tailed)	.302	.985	.143	.774
	N	710	710	710	710
Politics	Pearson Correlation	.047	.060	-.063	-.002
	Sig. (2-tailed)	.208	.113	.096	.966
	N	710	710	710	710
Hunting / Shooting	Pearson Correlation	-.014	.044	-.014	.000
	Sig. (2-tailed)	.718	.241	.701	.995
	N	710	710	710	710
Watch / Play sports	Pearson Correlation	.057	.078	-.089	-.031
	Sig. (2-tailed)	.131	.039	.018	.411
	N	710	710	710	710

NOTE: VIRTUES.
CORRELATION TABLE FOR Social Virtues by Traditional Buys.
CORRELATIONS Variables RQ23_Item79 RQ23_Item80 RQ23_Item86
RQ23_Item88 with Rtrad[A] Rtrad[B] Rtrad[C] Rtrad[D].

TABLE 12. Correlations of Social Virtues

		Own	Don't Own, Will Buy	Don't Own, Will Buy	Unsure
Self-improvement	Pearson Correlation	.066	.060	-.096	-.034
	Sig. (2-tailed)	.080	.113	.010	.363
	N	710	710	710	710
Cultural Events	Pearson Correlation	.114	-.046	-.046	-.049
	Sig. (2-tailed)	.002	.216	.219	.194
	N	710	710	710	710
Enjoy Worship/Bible	Pearson Correlation	.124	.111	-.190	-.057
	Sig. (2-tailed)	.001	.003	.000	.127
	N	710	710	710	710
Donating to charity	Pearson Correlation	.112	-.006	-.097	.001
	Sig. (2-tailed)	.003	.863	.010	.982
	N	710	710	710	710

NOTE: CORRELATION TABLE FOR Social Virtues by Non Traditional Buys. CORRELATIONS Variables RQ23_Item79 RQ23_Item80 RQ23_Item86 RQ23_Item88 with RNontradA RNontradB RNontradC RNontradD.

TABLE 13. Correlations of Virtues

		Own	Don't Own, Will Buy	Don't Own, Will Buy	Unsure
Self-improvement	Pearson Correlation	.055	.061	-.080	-.041
	Sig. (2-tailed)	.141	.106	.033	.280
	N	710	710	710	710
Cultural Events	Pearson Correlation	.101	.029	-.076	-.051
	Sig. (2-tailed)	.007	.440	.044	.178
	N	710	710	710	710
Enjoy Worship/Bible	Pearson Correlation	.471	.126	-.449	-.079
	Sig. (2-tailed)	.000	.001	.000	.036
	N	710	710	710	710
Donating to charity	Pearson Correlation	.150	.030	-.112	-.050
	Sig. (2-tailed)	.000	.423	.003	.183
	N	710	710	710	710

NOTE: What variables are used for Traditional and Non-Traditional Iconography. Traditional items ($n = 7$): Painting or Print, Statuette, Pendant or Medal, Holy Book, Cross, Crucifix, Rosary.

Ownership RQ1A_item3 RQ1A_item4 RQ1A_item5 RQ1A_item7
RQ1A_item10 RQ1A_item11 RQ1A_item12 .
B C D rep the Don't Own will buy, won't buy and unsure.
Non-Traditional items ($n = 5$): DVD or VCR Movie, Music CD, Jewelry Other,
Religious Books, Bumper Sticker.
RQ1A_item1 RQ1A_item2 RQ1A_item6 RQ1A_item8 RQ1A_item9 .
OWN THE ITEM.
VICES.
CORRELATION TABLE FOR Social Behaviors Indices by Traditional
Iconography Ownership Status.
CORRELATIONS Variables RQ23_item71 RQ23_item72 RQ23_item73
RQ23_item74 RQ23_item75 RQ23_Item76, RQ23_item77 RQ23_item78
RQ23_item81 RQ23_item82 RQ23_item83 RQ23_item84, RQ23_item85
RQ23_item87 RQ23_item89 RQ23_item90 with RQ1A_item3 RQ1A_item4
RQ1A_item5 RQ1A_item7 RQ1A_item10, RQ1A_item 11 RQ1A_item12.

TABLE 14. Correlations of 16 Vices

		Painting or print	Statuette	Pendant or medal	Holy Book	Cross	Crucifix	Rosary
Cigarette / Cigars	Pearson Correlation	-.022	-.018	-.027	.059	-.035	-.029	-.006
	Sig. (2-tailed)	.554	.624	.473	.114	.358	.448	.863
	N	710	710	710	710	710	710	710
Dancing	Pearson Correlation	.175	.176	.154	.094	.176	.133	.146
	Sig. (2-tailed)	.000	.000	.000	.013	.000	.000	.000
	N	710	710	710	710	710	710	710
Beer, wine, etc.	Pearson Correlation	-.102	-.069	-.030	.022	.074	.008	.035
	Sig. (2-tailed)	.007	.068	.420	.562	.050	.829	.351
	N	710	710	710	710	710	710	710
Concerts	Pearson Correlation	.025	-.021	.032	.115	.139	.020	.010
	Sig. (2-tailed)	.504	.585	.399	.002	.000	.591	.791
	N	710	710	710	710	710	710	710
Night clubbing	Pearson Correlation	.043	.065	.106	.043	.172	.107	.132
	Sig. (2-tailed)	.256	.086	.005	.257	.000	.004	.000
	N	710	710	710	710	710	710	710

TABLE 14. Continued

		Painting or print	Statuette	Pendant or medal	Holy Book	Cross	Crucifix	Rosary
Video Games	Pearson Correlation	-.086	-.054	-.045	-.031	-.052	.014	-.053
	Sig. (2-tailed)	.021	.152	.227	.411	.169	.715	.162
	N	710	710	710	710	710	710	710
TV Shopping	Pearson Correlation	.021	.015	-.020	-.022	.018	.005	.034
	Sig. (2-tailed)	.584	.700	.596	.558	.627	.895	.363
	N	710	710	710	710	710	710	710
Computer/Internet	Pearson Correlation	-.029	-.013	-.012	.023	-.002	-.015	-.051
	Sig. (2-tailed)	.434	.727	.744	.533	.953	.691	.176
	N	710	710	710	710	710	710	710

TABLE 14. Continued

		Painting or print	Statuette	Pendant or medal	Holy Book	Cross	Cruci-fix	Rosary
Casino Gambling	Pearson Correlation	-.061	-.011	-.038	-.003	.005	.072	.067
	Sig. (2-tailed)	.107	.772	.314	.936	.904	.055	.073
	N	710	710	710	710	710	710	710
Lottery / Sweepstakes	Pearson Correlation	.045	.036	.074	.003	.061	.089	.094
	Sig. (2-tailed)	.228	.334	.050	.930	.105	.018	.012
	N	710	710	710	710	710	710	710
Astrology / Horoscope	Pearson Correlation	.034	.022	.106	.012	.085	.134	.116
	Sig. (2-tailed)	.362	.561	.005	.757	.024	.000	.002
	N	710	710	710	710	710	710	710
Tarot Cards	Pearson Correlation	.060	.066	.059	-.044	.018	.084	.059
	Sig. (2-tailed)	.112	.077	.115	.243	.637	.026	.114
	N	710	710	710	710	710	710	710
Psychic Readings	Pearson Correlation	.016	.061	.013	-.057	-.017	.039	.055
	Sig. (2-tailed)	.675	.102	.723	.129	.644	.302	.140
	N	710	710	710	710	710	710	710
Politics	Pearson Correlation	.037	.001	.012	.082	.043	.030	-.007
	Sig. (2-tailed)	.320	.983	.746	.029	.247	.427	.850
	N	710	710	710	710	710	710	710
Hunting / Shooting	Pearson Correlation	-.051	.019	.019	.043	-.007	.025	.022
	Sig. (2-tailed)	.176	.605	.615	.256	.862	.507	.561
	N	710	710	710	710	710	710	710
Watch / play Sports	Pearson Correlation	.013	-.005	-.013	.094	.045	.025	-.024
	Sig. (2-tailed)	.731	.888	.729	.012	.236	.508	.525
	N	710	710	710	710	710	710	710

NOTE: CORRELATION TABLE FOR Social Vices by Non Traditional Buys.

RQ23_item75 RQ23_Item76, RQ23_item77 RQ23_item78 RQ23_item81
RQ23_item82 RQ23_item83 RQ23_item84, RQ23_item85 RQ23_item87
RQ23_item89 RQ23_item90 with RQ1A_item1 RQ1A_item2 RQ1A_item6
RQ1A_item8 RQ1A_item9.

TABLE 15. Correlations

		DVD or VHS	Music CD	Jewelry Other	Book Other	Bumper sticker
Cigarette / Cigars	Pearson Correlation	.011	-.016	-.044	.030	-.035
	Sig. (2-tailed)	.763	.677	.243	.430	.355
	N	710	710	710	710	710
Dancing	Pearson Correlation	.037	.080	.197	.089	.009
	Sig. (2-tailed)	.322	.034	.000	.017	.817
	N	710	710	710	710	710
Beer, wine, etc.	Pearson Correlation	-.140	-.090	-.070	-.038	-.065
	Sig. (2-tailed)	.000	.016	.062	.316	.085
	N	710	710	710	710	710
Concerts	Pearson Correlation	.038	.104	.136	.099	-.009
	Sig. (2-tailed)	.311	.006	.000	.008	.814
	N	710	710	710	710	710
Night clubbing	Pearson Correlation	-.074	-.051	.088	-.029	-.077
	Sig. (2-tailed)	.050	.175	.019	.436	.041
	N	710	710	710	710	710
Video Games	Pearson Correlation	-.028	-.115	-.080	-.024	-.046
	Sig. (2-tailed)	.462	.002	.034	.530	.219
	N	710	710	710	710	710
TV Shopping	Pearson Correlation	-.040	-.030	.034	.014	-.036
	Sig. (2-tailed)	.288	.420	.368	.702	.336
	N	710	710	710	710	710
Computer / Internet	Pearson Correlation	.025	.013	-.017	.023	-.027
	Sig. (2-tailed)	.501	.739	.649	.548	.471
	N	710	710	710	710	710

TABLE 15. Continued

		DVD or VHS	Music CD	Jewelry Other	Book Other	Bumper sticker
Casino Gambling	Pearson Correlation	-.088	-.100	-.070	-.068	-.037
	Sig. (2-tailed)	.019	.008	.063	.071	.327
	N	710	710	710	710	710
Lottery / Sweepstakes	Pearson Correlation	.016	-.066	.075	-.052	-.013
	Sig. (2-tailed)	.680	.077	.047	.169	.720
	N	710	710	710	710	710
Astrology / Horoscope	Pearson Correlation	-.017	-.077	.096	-.049	-.029
	Sig. (2-tailed)	.658	.040	.010	.195	.435
	N	710	710	710	710	710
Tarot Cards	Pearson Correlation	-.022	-.086	.079	.031	-.002
	Sig. (2-tailed)	.565	.021	.035	.406	.949
	N	710	710	710	710	710
Psychic Readings	Pearson Correlation	-.048	-.086	.032	-.001	-.034
	Sig. (2-tailed)	.203	.022	.391	.987	.364
	N	710	710	710	710	710
Politics	Pearson Correlation	.026	.015	.014	.083	-.002
	Sig. (2-tailed)	.496	.695	.705	.027	.953
	N	710	710	710	710	710
Hunting / Shooting	Pearson Correlation	.036	-.039	-.037	.013	-.016
	Sig. (2-tailed)	.342	.305	.321	.738	.666
	N	710	710	710	710	710
Watch / play Sports	Pearson Correlation	.053	.057	-.010	.061	.017
	Sig. (2-tailed)	.160	.132	.786	.106	.643
	N	710	710	710	710	710

NOTE: VIRTUES.
CORRELATION TABLE FOR Social Virtues by Traditional Buys.
CORRELATIONS Variables RQ23_Item79 RQ23_Item80 RQ23_Item86
RQ23_Item88 with RQ1A_item3 RQ1A_item4 RQ1A_item5 RQ1A_item7
RQ1A_item10 RQ1A_item11 RQ1A_item12.

TABLE 16. Correlations of 4 Virtues

		Painting or print	Statuette	Pendant or Medal
Self-improvement	Pearson Correlation	.043	.024	.059
	Sig. (2-tailed)	.247	.529	.119
	N	710	710	710
Cultural Events	Pearson Correlation	.119	.067	.121
	Sig. (2-tailed)	.001	.072	.001
	N	710	710	710
Enjoy Worship/Bible	Pearson Correlation	.182	.069	.040
	Sig. (2-tailed)	.000	.066	.293
	N	710	710	710
Donating to charity	Pearson Correlation	.124	.018	.068
	Sig. (2-tailed)	.001	.629	.070
	N	710	710	710

TABLE 17. 1 of 4 Virtues

		Holy Book	Cross	Crucifix	Rosary
Self-improvement	Pearson Correlation	.046	.082	.036	.029
	Sig. (2-tailed)	.218	.029	.343	.445
	N	710	710	710	710
Cultural Events	Pearson Correlation	.005	.077	.097	.067
	Sig. (2-tailed)	.901	.040	.010	.073
	N	710	710	710	710
Enjoy Worship/Bible	Pearson Correlation	.283	.145	-.009	-.094
	Sig. (2-tailed)	.000	.000	.817	.012
	N	710	710	710	710
Donating to charity	Pearson Correlation	.112	.145	.076	.004
	Sig. (2-tailed)	.003	.000	.043	.913
	N	710	710	710	710

NOTE: CORRELATION TABLE FOR Social Virtues by Non Traditional Buys. CORRELATIONS Variables RQ23_Item79 RQ23_Item80 RQ23_Item86 RQ23_Item88 with RQ1A_item1 RQ1A_item2 RQ1A_item6 RQ1A_item8 RQ1A_item9.

TABLE 18. Correlations of 4 Virtues

		DVD or VHS	Music CD	Jewelry Other
Self-improvement	Pearson Correlation	.025	.025	.028
	Sig. (2-tailed)	.500	.513	.457
	N	710	710	710
Cultural Events	Pearson Correlation	.062	.053	.106
	Sig. (2-tailed)	.097	.158	.005
	N	710	710	710
Enjoy Worship/Bible	Pearson Correlation	.267	.419	.178
	Sig. (2-tailed)	.000	.000	.000
	N	710	710	710
Donating to charity	Pearson Correlation	.054	.105	.109
	Sig. (2-tailed)	.152	.005	.004
	N	710	710	710

TABLE 19. Correlations of 4 Virtues

		Book Other	Bumper sticker
Self-improvement	Pearson Correlation	.092	-.023
	Sig. (2-tailed)	.015	.543
	N	710	710
Cultural Events	Pearson Correlation	.080	-.021
	Sig. (2-tailed)	.033	.580
	N	710	710

TABLE 19. Continued

		Book Other	Bumper sticker
Enjoy Worship/Bible	Pearson Correlation	.428	.167
	Sig. (2-tailed)	.000	.000
	N	710	710
Donating to charity	Pearson Correlation	.153	.020
	Sig. (2-tailed)	.000	.601
	N	710	710

NOTE: Don't Own, Will Buy.
  Vices.

NOTE: CORRELATION TABLE FOR Social Behaviors Indices by Traditional
Iconography Ownership Status.
CORRELATIONS Variables RQ23_item71 RQ23_item72 RQ23_item73
RQ23_item74 RQ23_item75 RQ23_Item76, RQ23_item77 RQ23_item78
RQ23_item81 RQ23_item82 RQ23_item83 RQ23_item84, RQ23_item85
RQ23_item87 RQ23_item89 RQ23_item90 with RQ1B_item3 RQ1B_item4
RQ1B_item5 RQ1B_item7 RQ1B_item10, RQ1B_item
11 RQ1B_item12.

TABLE 20. Correlations of 16 Vices

		Painting or print	Statuette	Pendant or medal	Holy Book	Cross	Cruci- fix	Rosary
Cigarette / Cigars	Pearson Correlation	.084	.036	.045	.011	.098	.145	.084
	Sig. (2-tailed)	.024	.332	.232	.776	.009	.000	.025
	N	710	710	710	710	710	710	710
Dancing	Pearson Correlation	.018	.037	.054	.082	-.031	-.010	.015
	Sig. (2-tailed)	.641	.322	.154	.028	.407	.780	.693
	N	710	710	710	710	710	710	710
Beer, wine, etc.	Pearson Correlation	.154	.091	.060	.075	.041	.080	.052
	Sig. (2-tailed)	.000	.015	.108	.045	.280	.032	.167
	N	710	710	710	710	710	710	710
Concerts	Pearson Correlation	.132	.158	.061	.031	-.005	.062	.060
	Sig. (2-tailed)	.000	.000	.105	.409	.897	.097	.110
	N	710	710	710	710	710	710	710
Night clubbing	Pearson Correlation	.116	.159	.116	.105	.031	.077	.031
	Sig. (2-tailed)	.002	.000	.002	.005	.405	.040	.414
	N	710	710	710	710	710	710	710
Video Games	Pearson Correlation	.091	.059	.100	.089	.102	.023	.048
	Sig. (2-tailed)	.015	.116	.008	.018	.006	.532	.198
	N	710	710	710	710	710	710	710

TABLE 20. Continued

		Painting or print	Statuette	Pendant or medal	Holy Book	Cross	Cruci- fix	Rosary
TV Shopping	Pearson Correlation	.007	.041	.052	.112	.016	.033	.061
	Sig. (2-tailed)	.846	.277	.170	.003	.664	.381	.105
	N	710	710	710	710	710	710	710
Computer / Internet	Pearson Correlation	.087	.124	.095	.017	.051	.019	.074
	Sig. (2-tailed)	.020	.001	.012	.643	.173	.605	.047
	N	710	710	710	710	710	710	710
Casino Gambling	Pearson Correlation	.045	.033	.048	.023	.068	.019	-.034
	Sig. (2-tailed)	.228	.381	.205	.546	.072	.618	.370
	N	710	710	710	710	710	710	710
Lottery / Sweepstakes	Pearson Correlation	.008	.035	.028	.083	.051	.010	-.029
	Sig. (2-tailed)	.833	.346	.457	.027	.178	.797	.434
	N	710	710	710	710	710	710	710
Astrology / Horoscope	Pearson Correlation	.074	.026	-.004	.032	-.013	.049	.043
	Sig. (2-tailed)	.049	.487	.909	.389	.727	.189	.248
	N	710	710	710	710	710	710	710
Tarot Cards	Pearson Correlation	.035	-.007	.028	.129	.002	.007	.116
	Sig. (2-tailed)	.358	.847	.449	.001	.954	.862	.002
	N	710	710	710	710	710	710	710
Psychic Readings	Pearson Correlation	.041	-.048	.030	.047	-.040	-.020	.067
	Sig. (2-tailed)	.277	.203	.431	.208	.289	.590	.075
	N	710	710	710	710	710	710	710
Politics	Pearson Correlation	.017	.049	.043	.042	-.001	.015	.065
	Sig. (2-tailed)	.648	.196	.248	.269	.981	.696	.081
	N	710	710	710	710	710	710	710
Hunting / Shooting	Pearson Correlation	.123	.036	.008	-.041	.106	.043	.026
	Sig. (2-tailed)	.001	.342	.827	.279	.005	.248	.483
	N	710	710	710	710	710	710	710
Watch / play Sports	Pearson Correlation	.101	.135	.108	-.021	.068	.040	.068
	Sig. (2-tailed)	.007	.000	.004	.574	.068	.284	.068
	N	710	710	710	710	710	710	710

NOTE: CORRELATION TABLE FOR Social Vices by Non Traditional Buys.

TABLE 20. Continued

CORRELATIONS Variables RQ23_item71 RQ23_item72 RQ23_item73, RQ23_item
74 RQ23_item75 RQ23_Item76, RQ23_item77 RQ23_item78, RQ23_item81, RQ23_
item82 RQ23_item83 RQ23_item84, RQ23_item85 RQ23_item87 RQ23_item89, RQ23_item90 with RQ1B_item1 RQ1B_item2 RQ1B_item6 RQ1B_item8 RQ1B_
item9.

TABLE 21. Correlations of 16 Vices

		DVD or VHS	Music CD	Jewelry Other	Book Other	Bumper sticker
Cigarette/Cigars	Pearson Correlation	-.012	.006	.061	-.017	-.031
	Sig. (2-tailed)	.746	.880	.107	.655	.410
	N	710	710	710	710	710
Dancing	Pearson Correlation	.078	.036	-.035	.039	-.003
	Sig. (2-tailed)	.038	.338	.346	.297	.934
	N	710	710	710	710	710
Beer, wine, etc.	Pearson Correlation	.145	.087	.071	.051	-.028
	Sig. (2-tailed)	.000	.021	.059	.173	.461
	N	710	710	710	710	710
Concerts	Pearson Correlation	.065	-.004	.000	-.002	-.004
	Sig. (2-tailed)	.083	.911	.995	.961	.907
	N	710	710	710	710	710
Night clubbing	Pearson Correlation	.106	.111	.076	.073	.020
	Sig. (2-tailed)	.005	.003	.044	.052	.588
	N	710	710	710	710	710
Video Games	Pearson Correlation	.041	.017	.074	-.044	-.076
	Sig. (2-tailed)	.281	.655	.049	.246	.043
	N	710	710	710	710	710
TV Shopping	Pearson Correlation	.016	-.003	-.025	.030	.031
	Sig. (2-tailed)	.672	.942	.511	.418	.411
	N	710	710	710	710	710

TABLE 21. Continued

		DVD or VHS	Music CD	Jewelry Other	Book Other	Bumper sticker
Computer/Internet	Pearson Correlation	.000	-.032	.034	-.034	.009
	Sig. (2-tailed)	.997	.395	.370	.370	.813
	N	710	710	710	710	710
Casino Gambling	Pearson Correlation	.075	-.005	.085	.001	-.047
	Sig. (2-tailed)	.046	.884	.023	.977	.207
	N	710	710	710	710	710
Lottery/Sweepstakes	Pearson Correlation	.048	.011	-.011	.027	-.004
	Sig. (2-tailed)	.203	.772	.764	.478	.920
	N	710	710	710	710	710
Astrology/Horoscope	Pearson Correlation	.076	.019	-.014	.014	.046
	Sig. (2-tailed)	.044	.617	.714	.708	.223
	N	710	710	710	710	710
Tarot Cards	Pearson Correlation	.020	-.045	.008	-.015	.020
	Sig. (2-tailed)	.597	.226	.829	.692	.588
	N	710	710	710	710	710
Psychic Readings	Pearson Correlation	.025	-.011	-.005	-.025	.008
	Sig. (2-tailed)	.500	.761	.901	.502	.837
	N	710	710	710	710	710
Politics	Pearson Correlation	.086	.033	.055	-.029	.011
	Sig. (2-tailed)	.021	.375	.142	.443	.778
	N	710	710	710	710	710
Hunting/Shooting	Pearson Correlation	.007	.051	.018	.054	.001
	Sig. (2-tailed)	.850	.172	.630	.152	.977
	N	710	710	710	710	710
Watch/Play Sports	Pearson Correlation	.026	.050	.086	.025	.038
	Sig. (2-tailed)	.491	.182	.022	.512	.314
	N	710	710	710	710	710

NOTE: VIRTUES.
CORRELATION TABLE FOR Social Virtues by Traditional Buys.
CORRELATIONS Variables RQ23_Item79 RQ23_Item80 RQ23_Item86
RQ23_Item88 with RQ1B_item3 RQ1B_item4 RQ1B_item5 RQ1B_item7
RQ1B_item10, RQ1B_item
11 RQ1B_item12.

TABLE 22. Correlations of 4 Virtues

		Painting or print	Statuette	Pendant or Medal
Self-improvement	Pearson Correlation	.083	.111	.018
	Sig. (2-tailed)	.026	.003	.633
	N	710	710	710
Cultural Events	Pearson Correlation	-.006	.008	-.065
	Sig. (2-tailed)	.878	.840	.085
	N	710	710	710
Enjoy Worship/Bible	Pearson Correlation	.090	.064	.070
	Sig. (2-tailed)	.016	.086	.064
	N	710	710	710
Donating to charity	Pearson Correlation	-.011	.039	-.028
	Sig. (2-tailed)	.771	.302	.455
	N	710	710	710

TABLE 23. Correlations of 4 Virtues

		Holy Book	Cross	Cruci-fix	Rosary
Self-improvement	Pearson Correlation	.056	-.012	-.027	.025
	Sig. (2-tailed)	.137	.748	.480	.504
	N	710	710	710	710
Cultural Events	Pearson Correlation	.017	-.090	-.047	-.015
	Sig. (2-tailed)	.650	.016	.208	.690
	N	710	710	710	710
Enjoy Worship/Bible	Pearson Correlation	-.119	.126	.112	.088
	Sig. (2-tailed)	.001	.001	.003	.019
	N	710	710	710	710
Donating to charity	Pearson Correlation	-.005	-.057	.000	.034
	Sig. (2-tailed)	.886	.130	.998	.366
	N	710	710	710	710

NOTE: CORRELATION TABLE FOR Social Virtues by Non Traditional Buys. CORRELATIONS Variables RQ23_Item79 RQ23_Item80 RQ23_Item86 RQ23_Item88 with RQ1B_item1 RQ1B_item2 RQ1B_item6 RQ1B_item8 RQ1B_item9.

TABLE 24. Correlations of 4 Virtues

		DVD or VHS	Music CD	Jewelry Other
Self-improvement	Pearson Correlation	.033	.028	.040
	Sig. (2-tailed)	.380	.457	.293
	N	710	710	710
Cultural Events	Pearson Correlation	.024	.037	-.043
	Sig. (2-tailed)	.527	.320	.248
	N	710	710	710
Enjoy Worship/Bible	Pearson Correlation	.135	-.042	.047
	Sig. (2-tailed)	.000	.269	.211
	N	710	710	710
Donating to charity	Pearson Correlation	.069	-.030	.015
	Sig. (2-tailed)	.065	.422	.682
	N	710	710	710

TABLE 25. Correlations of 4 Virtues

		Book Other	Bumper sticker
Self-improvement	Pearson Correlation	.036	.038
	Sig. (2-tailed)	.335	.314
	N	710	710
Cultural Events	Pearson Correlation	.022	.044
	Sig. (2-tailed)	.550	.245
	N	710	710
Enjoy Worship/Bible	Pearson Correlation	-.011	.219
	Sig. (2-tailed)	.778	.000
	N	710	710
Donating to charity	Pearson Correlation	.000	.020
	Sig. (2-tailed)	.990	.587
	N	710	710

NOTE: INFERENTIAL STATISTICS.
DON'T OWN, WONT BUY.
VICES.
CORRELATION TABLE FOR Social Behaviors Indices by Traditional Iconography Ownership Status.

CORRELATIONS Variables RQ23_item71 RQ23_item72 RQ23_item73
RQ23_item74 RQ23_item75 RQ23_Item76, RQ23_item77 RQ23_item78
RQ23_item81 RQ23_item82
TABLE 25. Continued

RQ23_item83 RQ23_item84, RQ23_item85 RQ23_item87 RQ23_item89
RQ23_item90 with RQ1C_item3 RQ1C_item4 RQ1C_item5 RQ1C_item7
RQ1C_item10, RQ1C_item
11 RQ1C_item12.

TABLE 26. Correlations of 16 Vices

		Painting or print	Statuette	Pendant or medal	Holy Book	Cross	Cruci-fix	Rosary
Cigarette / Cigars	Pearson Correlation	-.031	-.030	.003	-.063	-.051	-.076	-.036
	Sig. (2-tailed)	.415	.423	.930	.091	.179	.043	.334
	N	710	710	710	710	710	710	710
Dancing	Pearson Correlation	-.120	-.136	-.151	-.131	-.124	-.079	-.078
	Sig. (2-tailed)	.001	.000	.000	.000	.001	.036	.037
	N	710	710	710	710	710	710	710
Beer, wine, etc.	Pearson Correlation	-.054	-.015	-.010	-.046	-.107	-.042	-.073
	Sig. (2-tailed)	.150	.690	.791	.224	.004	.267	.053
	N	710	710	710	710	710	710	710
Concerts	Pearson Correlation	-.143	-.100	-.046	-.112	-.121	-.029	-.031
	Sig. (2-tailed)	.000	.007	.219	.003	.001	.438	.403
	N	710	710	710	710	710	710	710
Night clubbing	Pearson Correlation	-.089	-.169	-.160	-.098	-.181	-.143	-.132
	Sig. (2-tailed)	.017	.000	.000	.009	.000	.000	.000
	N	710	710	710	710	710	710	710
Video Games	Pearson Correlation	-.024	-.020	-.040	-.028	-.032	-.020	.009
	Sig. (2-tailed)	.523	.587	.287	.457	.395	.593	.803
	N	710	710	710	710	710	710	710
TV Shopping	Pearson Correlation	-.035	-.046	-.033	-.023	-.054	-.062	-.083
	Sig. (2-tailed)	.350	.223	.379	.546	.149	.100	.027
	N	710	710	710	710	710	710	710

TABLE 26. Continued

		Painting or print	Statuette	Pendant or medal	Holy Book	Cross	Crucifix	Rosary
Computer / Internet	Pearson Correlation	-.069	-.098	-.080	-.064	-.037	-.026	-.052
	Sig. (2-tailed)	.067	.009	.032	.087	.325	.497	.163
	N	710	710	710	710	710	710	710
Casino Gambling	Pearson Correlation	.002	-.050	.005	-.015	-.063	-.080	-.067
	Sig. (2-tailed)	.964	.184	.904	.686	.092	.034	.073
	N	710	710	710	710	710	710	710
Lottery / Sweepstakes	Pearson Correlation	-.027	-.070	-.062	-.057	-.085	-.058	-.055
	Sig. (2-tailed)	.467	.061	.100	.129	.024	.121	.145
	N	710	710	710	710	710	710	710
Astrology / Horoscope	Pearson Correlation	-.058	-.035	-.044	-.021	-.044	-.101	-.101
	Sig. (2-tailed)	.123	.352	.245	.574	.239	.007	.007
	N	710	710	710	710	710	710	710
Tarot Cards	Pearson Correlation	-.058	-.048	-.038	-.030	-.008	-.035	-.103
	Sig. (2-tailed)	.123	.205	.314	.425	.840	.345	.006
	N	710	710	710	710	710	710	710
Psychic Readings	Pearson Correlation	-.015	.011	.000	.036	.045	.007	-.074
	Sig. (2-tailed)	.682	.762	.994	.335	.233	.858	.050
	N	710	710	710	710	710	710	710
Politics	Pearson Correlation	-.040	-.055	-.027	-.113	-.054	-.009	-.016
	Sig. (2-tailed)	.288	.143	.471	.003	.153	.808	.668
	N	710	710	710	710	710	710	710
Hunting / Shooting	Pearson Correlation	-.051	-.040	-.022	.000	-.087	-.024	-.025
	Sig. (2-tailed)	.174	.287	.557	.994	.020	.525	.506
	N	710	710	710	710	710	710	710
Watch / play Sports	Pearson Correlation	-.104	-.122	-.081	-.118	-.091	-.048	-.041
	Sig. (2-tailed)	.005	.001	.031	.002	.016	.201	.280
	N	710	710	710	710	710	710	710

NOTE: CORRELATION TABLE FOR Social Vices by Non Traditional Buys.
CORRELATIONS Variables RQ23_item71 RQ23_item72 RQ23_item73
RQ23_item74 RQ23_item75 RQ23_Item76 RQ23_item77 RQ23_item78
RQ23_item81 RQ23_item82 RQ23_item83 RQ23_item84 RQ23_item85
RQ23_item87 RQ23_item89 RQ23_item90
with RQ1C_item1 RQ1C_item2 RQ1C_item6 RQ1C_item8 RQ1C_item9.

TABLE 27. Correlations of 16 Vices

		DVD or VHS	Music CD	Jewelry Other	Book Other	Bumper sticker
Cigarette / Cigars	Pearson Correlation	.005	.023	-.007	-.016	.004
	Sig. (2-tailed)	.899	.549	.842	.663	.922
	N	710	710	710	710	710
Dancing	Pearson Correlation	-.074	-.064	-.155	-.088	.060
	Sig. (2-tailed)	.048	.088	.000	.019	.110
	N	710	710	710	710	710
Beer, wine, etc.	Pearson Correlation	.000	.024	.014	.012	.048
	Sig. (2-tailed)	.993	.529	.716	.754	.198
	N	710	710	710	710	710
Concerts	Pearson Correlation	-.118	-.075	-.109	-.058	.018
	Sig. (2-tailed)	.002	.047	.004	.120	.637
	N	710	710	710	710	710
Night clubbing	Pearson Correlation	-.003	-.011	-.126	-.014	.029
	Sig. (2-tailed)	.944	.763	.001	.708	.439
	N	710	710	710	710	710
Video Games	Pearson Correlation	-.056	.083	.015	.033	.055
	Sig. (2-tailed)	.135	.026	.693	.378	.142
	N	710	710	710	710	710
TV Shopping	Pearson Correlation	-.007	.018	-.022	-.010	-.009
	Sig. (2-tailed)	.850	.627	.553	.785	.814
	N	710	710	710	710	710
Computer / Internet	Pearson Correlation	-.036	-.001	-.024	-.019	-.026
	Sig. (2-tailed)	.335	.975	.521	.608	.492
	N	710	710	710	710	710
Casino Gambling	Pearson Correlation	.020	.113	-.020	.069	.028
	Sig. (2-tailed)	.597	.003	.589	.066	.457
	N	710	710	710	710	710
Lottery / Sweepstakes	Pearson Correlation	-.042	.078	-.056	.044	.008
	Sig. (2-tailed)	.262	.039	.135	.237	.834
	N	710	710	710	710	710

TABLE 27. Continued

		DVD or VHS	Music CD	Jewelry Other	Book Other	Bumper sticker
Astrology / Horoscope	Pearson Correlation	-.026	.082	-.081	.049	-.007
	Sig. (2-tailed)	.485	.029	.031	.195	.854
	N	710	710	710	710	710
Tarot Cards	Pearson Correlation	.017	.138	-.069	.005	-.010
	Sig. (2-tailed)	.655	.000	.065	.895	.791
	N	710	710	710	710	710
Psychic Readings	Pearson Correlation	.039	.113	-.015	.047	.007
	Sig. (2-tailed)	.298	.003	.683	.207	.843
	N	710	710	710	710	710
Politics	Pearson Correlation	-.119	-.034	-.025	-.041	-.007
	Sig. (2-tailed)	.002	.365	.507	.272	.860
	N	710	710	710	710	710
Hunting / Shooting	Pearson Correlation	-.029	-.012	.039	-.029	-.019
	Sig. (2-tailed)	.437	.754	.295	.445	.613
	N	710	710	710	710	710
Watch / play Sports	Pearson Correlation	-.038	-.078	-.075	-.071	-.053
	Sig. (2-tailed)	.309	.038	.045	.057	.157
	N	710	710	710	710	710

NOTE: VIRTUES.

CORRELATION TABLE FOR Social Virtues by Traditional Buys.
CORRELATIONS Variables RQ23_Item79 RQ23_Item80 RQ23_Item86
RQ23_Item88 with RQ1C_item3 RQ1C_item4 RQ1C_item5 RQ1C_item7
RQ1C_item10 RQ1C_item11 RQ1C_item12.

TABLE 28. Correlations of 4 Virtues

		Painting or print	Statuette	Pendant or medal
Self-improvement	Pearson Correlation	-.099	-.105	-.067
	Sig. (2-tailed)	.009	.005	.076
	N	710	710	710
Cultural Events	Pearson Correlation	-.066	-.068	-.038
	Sig. (2-tailed)	.079	.069	.314
	N	710	710	710
Enjoy Worship/Bible	Pearson Correlation	-.256	-.130	-.082
	Sig. (2-tailed)	.000	.001	.029
	N	710	710	710
Donating to charity	Pearson Correlation	-.079	-.062	-.053
	Sig. (2-tailed)	.036	.099	.159
	N	710	710	710

TABLE 29. Correlations of 4 Virtues

		Holy Book	Cross	Crucifix	Rosary
Self-improvement	Pearson Correlation	-.078	-.077	-.041	-.043
	Sig. (2-tailed)	.037	.041	.279	.250
	N	710	710	710	710
Cultural Events	Pearson Correlation	-.015	-.011	-.018	-.021
	Sig. (2-tailed)	.680	.767	.629	.585
	N	710	710	710	710
Enjoy Worship/Bible	Pearson Correlation	-.236	-.250	-.101	.008
	Sig. (2-tailed)	.000	.000	.007	.824
	N	710	710	710	710
Donating to charity	Pearson Correlation	-.101	-.107	-.092	-.024
	Sig. (2-tailed)	.007	.004	.014	.526
	N	710	710	710	710

NOTE: CORRELATION TABLE FOR Social Virtues by Non Traditional Buys.
CORRELATIONS Variables RQ23_Item79 RQ23_Item80 RQ23_Item86
RQ23_Item88 with RQ1C_item1 RQ1C_item2 RQ1C_item6 RQ1C_item8
RQ1C_item9.

TABLE 30. Correlations of 4 Virtues

		DVD or VHS	Music CD	Jewelry Other
Self-improvement	Pearson Correlation	-.033	-.054	-.083
	Sig. (2-tailed)	.380	.147	.027
	N	710	710	710
Cultural Events	Pearson Correlation	-.042	-.072	-.065
	Sig. (2-tailed)	.264	.054	.085
	N	710	710	710
Enjoy Worship/Bible	Pearson Correlation	-.354	-.351	-.226
	Sig. (2-tailed)	.000	.000	.000
	N	710	710	710
Donating to charity	Pearson Correlation	-.115	-.071	-.107
	Sig. (2-tailed)	.002	.059	.004
	N	710	710	710

TABLE 31. Correlations of 4 Virtues

		Book Other	Bumper sticker
Self-improvement	Pearson Correlation	-.098	-.018
	Sig. (2-tailed)	.009	.638
	N	710	710
Cultural Events	Pearson Correlation	-.080	-.011
	Sig. (2-tailed)	.033	.769
	N	710	710
Enjoy Worship/Bible	Pearson Correlation	-.367	-.304
	Sig. (2-tailed)	.000	.000
	N	710	710
Donating to charity	Pearson Correlation	-.097	-.013
	Sig. (2-tailed)	.010	.729
	N	710	710

NOTE: UNSURE.
VICES.
CORRELATION TABLE FOR Social Behaviors Indices by Traditional
Iconography Ownership Status.
RQ23_item90 with RQ1D_item3 RQ1D_item4 RQ1D_item5 RQ1D_item7,
Q1D_item10 RQ1D_item11 RQ1D_item12.

TABLE 32. Correlations of 16 Vices

		Painting or print	Statuette	Pendant or medal	Holy Book	Cross	Crucifix	Rosary
Cigarette / Cigars	Pearson Correlation	-.059	.029	-.032	-.052	-.033	-.047	-.034
	Sig. (2-tailed)	.116	.436	.396	.166	.386	.209	.359
	N	710	710	710	710	710	710	710
Dancing	Pearson Correlation	-.090	-.059	-.073	-.022	-.068	-.029	-.079
	Sig. (2-tailed)	.017	.119	.051	.560	.070	.447	.036
	N	710	710	710	710	710	710	710
Beer, wine, etc.	Pearson Correlation	.036	.025	.008	-.027	-.003	-.025	.045
	Sig. (2-tailed)	.337	.503	.826	.472	.928	.505	.228
	N	710	710	710	710	710	710	710
Concerts	Pearson Correlation	.002	.020	-.037	-.078	-.035	-.041	.010
	Sig. (2-tailed)	.965	.593	.325	.038	.347	.276	.792
	N	710	710	710	710	710	710	710
Night clubbing	Pearson Correlation	-.099	-.032	-.075	-.041	-.071	-.022	.008
	Sig. (2-tailed)	.009	.390	.045	.279	.058	.555	.829
	N	710	710	710	710	710	710	710
Video Games	Pearson Correlation	.036	.056	.010	.000	-.010	-.005	.036
	Sig. (2-tailed)	.336	.138	.799	.997	.780	.893	.345
	N	710	710	710	710	710	710	710
TV Shopping	Pearson Correlation	.011	-.019	.020	-.041	.001	.042	.022
	Sig. (2-tailed)	.767	.613	.587	.278	.979	.259	.560
	N	710	710	710	710	710	710	710

TABLE 32. Continued

		Painting or print	Statuette	Pendant or medal	Holy Book	Cross	Crucifix	Rosary
Computer / Internet	Pearson Correlation	.015	-.005	.017	.047	.012	.049	.092
	Sig. (2-tailed)	.683	.900	.643	.212	.758	.193	.014
	N	710	710	710	710	710	710	710
Casino Gambling	Pearson Correlation	.023	.042	-.013	-.025	-.023	-.023	.063
	Sig. (2-tailed)	.537	.265	.721	.509	.535	.542	.091
	N	710	710	710	710	710	710	710
Lottery / Sweepstakes	Pearson Correlation	-.013	-.010	-.052	-.003	-.018	-.026	.005
	Sig. (2-tailed)	.728	.783	.168	.937	.639	.497	.899
	N	710	710	710	710	710	710	710
Astrology / Horoscope	Pearson Correlation	-.080	-.014	-.113	-.049	-.064	-.092	-.053
	Sig. (2-tailed)	.032	.706	.003	.192	.090	.014	.156
	N	710	710	710	710	710	710	710
Tarot Cards	Pearson Correlation	-.047	-.009	-.066	.003	-.021	-.053	-.031
	Sig. (2-tailed)	.214	.813	.080	.943	.572	.161	.413
	N	710	710	710	710	710	710	710
Psychic Readings	Pearson Correlation	-.051	-.037	-.069	.037	.004	-.037	-.016
	Sig. (2-tailed)	.171	.329	.066	.319	.925	.329	.674
	N	710	710	710	710	710	710	710
Politics	Pearson Correlation	-.003	.047	-.023	-.024	.009	-.034	-.011
	Sig. (2-tailed)	.936	.207	.533	.530	.819	.363	.772
	N	710	710	710	710	710	710	710
Hunting / Shooting	Pearson Correlation	-.038	-.037	-.025	-.042	-.016	-.037	-.010
	Sig. (2-tailed)	.316	.325	.499	.263	.669	.325	.800
	N	710	710	710	710	710	710	710
Watch / play Sports	Pearson Correlation	-.030	-.003	.002	-.001	-.016	-.013	.029
	Sig. (2-tailed)	.426	.943	.954	.984	.665	.727	.445
	N	710	710	710	710	710	710	710

NOTE: CORRELATION TABLE FOR Social Vices by Non Traditional Buys.
CORRELATIONS: Variables RQ23_item71 RQ23_item72 RQ23_item73,
Q23_item 74, RQ23_item75 RQ23_Item76, RQ23_item77 RQ23_item78
RQ23_item81 RQ23_item82 RQ23_item83 RQ23_item84, RQ23_item85
RQ23_item87 RQ23_item89 RQ23_item90
with RQ1D_item1, RQ1D_item2 RQ1D_item6 RQ1D_item8 RQ1D_item9.

TABLE 33. Correlations of 16 Vices

		DVD or VHS	Music CD	Jewelry Other	Book Other	Bumper sticker
Cigarette / Cigars	Pearson Correlation	-.015	-.024	-.032	-.027	.067
	Sig. (2-tailed)	.686	.527	.396	.478	.076
	N	710	710	710	710	710
Dancing	Pearson Correlation	-.057	-.051	-.040	-.037	-.089
	Sig. (2-tailed)	.126	.179	.286	.322	.018
	N	710	710	710	710	710
Beer, wine, etc.	Pearson Correlation	-.008	.035	.019	.007	.046
	Sig. (2-tailed)	.832	.348	.605	.854	.220
	N	710	710	710	710	710
Concerts	Pearson Correlation	.038	-.011	-.026	-.038	.025
	Sig. (2-tailed)	.310	.777	.495	.306	.505
	N	710	710	710	710	710
Night clubbing	Pearson Correlation	-.060	-.041	-.064	-.010	.000
	Sig. (2-tailed)	.110	.270	.088	.782	.997
	N	710	710	710	710	710
Video Games	Pearson Correlation	.071	.037	.043	.074	.088
	Sig. (2-tailed)	.057	.331	.248	.048	.019
	N	710	710	710	710	710
TV Shopping	Pearson Correlation	.045	.036	.020	-.059	.004
	Sig. (2-tailed)	.230	.333	.587	.115	.926
	N	710	710	710	710	710
Computer / Internet	Pearson Correlation	.038	.044	.029	.057	.065
	Sig. (2-tailed)	.313	.240	.434	.132	.085
	N	710	710	710	710	710
Casino Gambling	Pearson Correlation	-.010	-.010	.035	-.011	.064
	Sig. (2-tailed)	.795	.791	.356	.766	.088
	N	710	710	710	710	710
Lottery / Sweepstakes	Pearson Correlation	-.016	-.010	-.018	-.007	.025
	Sig. (2-tailed)	.667	.783	.630	.859	.507
	N	710	710	710	710	710
Astrology / Horoscope	Pearson Correlation	-.038	-.038	-.026	-.021	-.031
	Sig. (2-tailed)	.314	.313	.496	.569	.411
	N	710	710	710	710	710

TABLE 33. Continued

		DVD or VHS	Music CD	Jewelry Other	Book Other	Bumper sticker
Tarot Cards	Pearson Correlation	-.016	-.017	-.017	-.026	.013
	Sig. (2-tailed)	.677	.649	.654	.483	.722
	N	710	710	710	710	710
Psychic Readings	Pearson Correlation	-.021	-.021	.001	-.031	.031
	Sig. (2-tailed)	.570	.574	.984	.416	.411
	N	710	710	710	710	710
Politics	Pearson Correlation	.019	.021	-.049	-.022	.029
	Sig. (2-tailed)	.615	.572	.189	.563	.437
	N	710	710	710	710	710
Hunting/Shooting	Pearson Correlation	-.008	.012	-.025	-.044	.063
	Sig. (2-tailed)	.836	.741	.499	.239	.093
	N	710	710	710	710	710
Watch/play Sports	Pearson Correlation	-.061	-.048	.002	-.024	.022
	Sig. (2-tailed)	.106	.199	.954	.531	.566
	N	710	710	710	710	710

NOTE: VIRTUES.
CORRELATION TABLE FOR Social Virtues by Traditional Buys.
CORRELATIONS Variables RQ23_Item79 RQ23_Item80 RQ23_Item86,
RQ23_Item88 with RQ1D_item3 RQ1D_item4 RQ1D_item5 RQ1D_item7,
RQ1D_item10, RQ1D_item 11 RQ1D_item12.

TABLE 34. Correlations of 4 Virtues

		Painting or print	Statuette	Pendant or medal
Self-improvement	Pearson Correlation	-.061	-.031	-.033
	Sig. (2-tailed)	.103	.413	.377
	N	710	710	710
Cultural Events	Pearson Correlation	-.073	.009	-.053
	Sig. (2-tailed)	.051	.820	.162
	N	710	710	710
Enjoy Worship/Bible	Pearson Correlation	-.068	-.025	-.072
	Sig. (2-tailed)	.071	.507	.055
	N	710	710	710
Donating to charity	Pearson Correlation	-.048	.026	.007
	Sig. (2-tailed)	.204	.486	.844
	N	710	710	710

TABLE 35. Correlations of 4 Virtues

		Holy Book	Cross	Crucifix	Rosary
Self-improvement	Pearson Correlation	-.055	-.021	.029	-.011
	Sig. (2-tailed)	.144	.572	.437	.774
	N	710	710	710	710
Cultural Events	Pearson Correlation	-.002	-.001	-.054	-.044
	Sig. (2-tailed)	.967	.972	.151	.247
	N	710	710	710	710
Enjoy Worship/Bible	Pearson Correlation	-.109	-.076	.018	.007
	Sig. (2-tailed)	.003	.043	.640	.853
	N	710	710	710	710
Donating to charity	Pearson Correlation	-.070	-.014	.049	.015
	Sig. (2-tailed)	.062	.717	.191	.696
	N	710	710	710	710

NOTE: CORRELATION TABLE FOR Social Virtues by Non Traditional Buys. CORRELATIONS Variables RQ23_Item79 RQ23_Item80 RQ23_Item86 RQ23_Item88 with RQ1D_item1 RQ1D_item2 RQ1D_item6 RQ1D_item8 RQ1D_item9.

TABLE 36. Correlations of 4 Virtues

		DVD or VHS	Music CD	Jewelry Other
Self-improvement	Pearson Correlation	-.051	-.002	.011
	Sig. (2-tailed)	.177	.959	.763
	N	710	710	710
Cultural Events	Pearson Correlation	-.084	-.015	-.018
	Sig. (2-tailed)	.025	.683	.637
	N	710	710	710
Enjoy Worship/Bible	Pearson Correlation	-.081	-.065	-.048
	Sig. (2-tailed)	.032	.086	.199
	N	710	710	710
Donating to charity	Pearson Correlation	-.002	-.018	-.044
	Sig. (2-tailed)	.954	.627	.245
	N	710	710	710

TABLE 37. Correlations of 4 Virtues

		Book Other	Bumper sticker
Self-improvement	Pearson Correlation	-.071	-.024
	Sig. (2-tailed)	.060	.516
	N	710	710
Cultural Events	Pearson Correlation	-.021	-.025
	Sig. (2-tailed)	.583	.501
	N	710	710
Enjoy Worship/Bible	Pearson Correlation	-.131	.052
	Sig. (2-tailed)	.000	.165
	N	710	710
Donating to charity	Pearson Correlation	-.103	-.005
	Sig. (2-tailed)	.006	.885
	N	710	710

The general null hypothesis for this study states that there are no significant relationships between the religiosity index and the individual Consumer Social Behaviors and religious iconographic ownership variables. This study utilized SPSS software to conduct the statistical analysis.

Interestingly, Social Vices are not significant related to the Religiosity Index nor its components with the exception of "Enjoy Worship/Bible" and "Do you believe there is life after death?" In contrast, Social Virtues is significantly correlated with the Religiosity Index and each its components.

While the Religiosity Index accounts for the most of the explained variance, the state location impacts the equation with a negative beta coefficient. The California sample indeed owns more traditional iconography than their Arkansas counterparts. All other coefficients have positive values.

Consistent with earlier analyses, as the Religiosity Index and Social Vices increase, the frequency of those who "Won't Buy" decreases.

There is only two relationships that are not significant (Do you belief there is life after death with Clergy and Church Newsletter). The Cronbach's Alpha also supports the Religiosity Index with a value of .797 ($n = 710$) (Table 167).

TABLE 38. Cronbach's Alpha

Cronbach's Alpha	N of Items
.797	11

Regression tables

TABLE 39. Final Multiple Regression Step for Traditional Iconography—Owned

		Coefficients[a]				
		Unstandardized Coefficients		Standardized Coefficients		
Model		B	Std. Error	Beta	t	Sig.
Final Mode	(Constant)	.574	.290		1.975	.049
	Gender	.516	.158	.115	3.258	.001
	Age	.052	.090	.020	.580	.562
	Religiosity Index	.090	.037	.185	2.428	.015
	State Location	-.755	.180	-.155	-4.189	.000
	Social Vices	.092	.028	.120	3.324	.001
	Church Attendance	.308	.106	.177	2.900	.004
	Religious Attendance	.251	.123	.122	2.053	.041

a. Dependent Variable: Count: How many traditional items do you own?
Gender and Age are entered as control variables in step 1.

TABLE 40. Final Multiple Regression Step for Traditional Iconography—Don't Own, Would Buy

| Model | | Coefficients[a] | | | | |
| | | Unstandardized Coefficients | | Standardized Coefficients | | |
		B	Std. Error	Beta	t	Sig.
Final	(Constant)	1.242	.211		5.875	.000
Step	Gender	-.289	.130	-.084	-2.224	.026
	Age	-.234	.075	-.119	-3.126	.002
	Social Vices	.100	.023	.170	4.409	.000
	State Location	.360	.142	.097	2.537	.011

a. Dependent Variable: Count: How many traditional items don't you own, but would buy? Gender and Age are entered as control variables in step 1.

TABLE 41. Final Multiple Regression Step for Traditional Iconography—Don't Own, Won't Buy

| Model | | Coefficients[a] | | | | |
| | | Unstandardized Coefficients | | Standardized Coefficients | | |
		B	Std. Error	Beta	t	Sig.
Final	(Constant)	4.787	.309		15.486	.000
Step	Gender	-.255	.168	-.054	-1.522	.128
	Age	.061	.095	.023	.648	.517
	Religiosity Index	-.225	.019	-.443	-11.851	.000
	Social Vices	-.182	.032	-.227	-5.688	.000
	Social Virtues	.232	.080	.122	2.886	.004

a. Dependent Variable: Count: How many traditional items don't you own, but won't buy? Gender and Age are entered as control variables in step 1.

TABLE 42. Final Multiple Regression Step for Traditional Iconography—Unsure

		Coefficients[a]				
		Unstandardized Coefficients		Standardized Coefficients		
Model		B	Std. Error	Beta	t	Sig.
Final	(Constant)	.573	.116		4.924	.000
Step	Gender	-.101	.089	-.044	-1.134	.257
	Age	.055	.051	.042	1.084	.279
	Church Attendance	-.097	.035	-.107	-2.796	.005

a. Dependent Variable: Count: How many traditional items are you unsure about buying? Gender and Age are entered as control variables in step 1.

TABLE 43. Final Multiple Regression Step for Non-Traditional Iconography—Owned

		Coefficients[a]				
		Unstandardized Coefficients		Standardized Coefficients		
Model		B	Std. Error	Beta	t	Sig.
Final	(Constant)	-.488	.129		-3.782	.000
Step	Gender	.315	.086	.114	3.650	.000
	Age	.139	.049	.089	2.852	.004
	Religiosity Index	.165	.010	.554	16.718	.000
	Social Virtues	.077	.037	.069	2.044	.041

a. Dependent Variable: Count: How many non-traditional items do you own? Gender and Age are entered as control variables in step 1.

TABLE 44. Final Multiple Regression Step for Non-Traditional Iconography—
Don't Own, Would Buy

		Coefficients[a]				
		Unstandardized Coefficients			Standardized Coefficients	
Model		B	Std. Error	Beta	t	Sig.
Final Step	(Constant)	.907	.169		5.366	.000
	Gender	-.043	.090	-.018	-.472	.637
	Age	-.161	.053	-.118	-3.054	.002
	Religiosity Index	.043	.010	.166	4.399	.000
	Social Vices	.031	.016	.076	1.967	.050

a. Dependent Variable: Count: How many non-traditional items don't you own, but would buy? Gender and Age are entered as control variables in step 1.

TABLE 45. Final Multiple Regression Step for Non-Traditional Iconography—
Don't Own, Won't Buy

		Coefficients[a]				
		Unstandardized Coefficients			Standardized Coefficients	
Model		B	Std. Error	Beta	t	Sig.
Final Step	(Constant)	3.907	.161		24.272	.000
	Gender	-.205	.108	-.061	-1.901	.058
	Age	-.004	.062	-.002	-.060	.952
	Religiosity Index	-.206	.012	-.561	-17.620	.000

a. Dependent Variable: Count: How many non-traditional items don't you own, but won't buy? Gender and Age are entered as control variables in step 1.

TABLE 46. Final Multiple Regression Step for Non-Traditional Iconography—Unsure

Model		Unstandardized Coefficients		Standardized Coefficients		
		B	Std. Error	Beta	t	Sig.
Final (Constant)		.431	.075		5.770	.000
Step	Gender	-.091	.057	-.061	-1.598	.111
	Age	-.003	.033	-.004	-.101	.919
	Church Attendance	-.068	.022	-.117	-3.060	.002

Coefficients[a]

a. Dependent Variable: Count: How many non-traditional items are you unsure about buying? Gender and Age are entered as control variables in step 1.

TABLE 47. Relationship between Religiosity Indicators and Traditional Iconography Status

		Own	Don't Own, Will Buy	Don't Own, Won't Buy	Unsure
Religiosity Index	Pearson Correlation	.394*	.087*	-.402*	-.101*
Church Service Atten.	Pearson Correlation	.368*	.019	-.316*	-.108*
Relig. Service Atten.	Pearson Correlation	.364*	.024	-.340*	-.094*
Religiousness Level	Pearson Correlation	.270*	.103*	-.306*	-.066
Enjoy Worship/Bible	Pearson Correlation	.124*	.111*	-.190*	-.057
Spiritual Value	Pearson Correlation	.263*	.081*	-.260*	-.123*
Worship	Pearson Correlation	.225*	.055	-.260*	-.038
Church Education	Pearson Correlation	.199*	.086*	-.224*	-.072
Do you believe there is life after death?	Pearson Correlation	.180*	.080*	-.234*	.000
Special Enlightenment	Pearson Correlation	.148*	.001	-.122*	-.026
Clergy	Pearson Correlation	.143*	-.002	-.116*	-.022
Church Newsletters	Pearson Correlation	.107*	.079*	-.148*	-.024

NOTE: $p <= .05$ ($N = 710$)

123

TABLE 48. Relationship between Religiosity Indicators and Non-Traditional Iconography Status

		Own	Don't Own, Will Buy	Don't Own, Won't Buy	Unsure
Religiosity Index	Pearson Correlation	.580*	.190*	-.553*	-.122*
Church Service Atten.	Pearson Correlation	.471*	.132*	-.419*	-.119*
Religious Service Atten.	Pearson Correlation	.469*	.136*	-.450*	-.088*
Religiousness Level	Pearson Correlation	.501*	.157*	-.461*	-.122*
Enjoy Worship/Bible	Pearson Correlation	.471*	.126*	-.449*	-.079*
Spiritual Value	Pearson Correlation	.426*	.125*	-.386*	-.117*
Worship	Pearson Correlation	.324*	.106*	-.333*	-.046
Church Education	Pearson Correlation	.263*	.174*	-.306*	-.061
Do you believe there is life after death?	Pearson Correlation	.213*	.104*	-.242*	-.009
Special Enlightenment	Pearson Correlation	.221*	.032	-.166*	-.056
Clergy	Pearson Correlation	.121*	.069	-.121*	-.050
Church Newsletters	Pearson Correlation	.216*	.101*	-.215*	-.051

NOTE: $p <= .05$ ($N = 710$)

124

TABLE 49. Relationship between Religiosity Indicators and Social Consumer Behaviors

		Social Virtues	Social Vices
Religiosity Index	Pearson Correlation	.314*	.010
Church Service Attendance	Pearson Correlation	.173*	-.061
Religious Service Attendance	Pearson Correlation	.226*	-.016
Religiousness Level	Pearson Correlation	.228*	-.064
Enjoy Worship/Bible	Pearson Correlation	.497*	.106*
Spiritual Value	Pearson Correlation	.266*	.057
Worship	Pearson Correlation	.199*	.022
Church Education	Pearson Correlation	.136*	.062
Do you believe there is life after death?	Pearson Correlation	.122*	.081*
Special Enlightenment	Pearson Correlation	.170*	.027
Clergy	Pearson Correlation	.100*	-.047
Church Newsletters	Pearson Correlation	.089*	-.005

NOTE: $p <= .05$ ($N = 710$)

REGRESSION

NOTE: We want to predict the purchasing of Iconography.
Dependent measures will be TradA TradB TradC NonTradA NonTradB NonTradC.
Independent Covariant will be State.
Independent Predictor variables will be Q23_Bad_Behavior Q23_Good_Behavior

RELIGIOSITY2 RQ27_item103a

DEPENDENT VARIABLE TradA.
COVARIANTS RQ14_Item52 (gender) abd RQ24 (age).
INDEPENDENT VARIABLE Q23_Bad_Behavior Q23_Good_Behavior State
RQ27_item103b RQ34_item127 RELIGIOSITY2.

TABLE 49. Continued

REGRESSION
/DESCRIPTIVES MEAN STDDEV CORR SIG N
/MISSING LISTWISE
/STATISTICS COEFF OUTS R ANOVA CHANGE
/CRITERIA = PIN(.05) POUT(.10)
/NOORIGIN
/DEPENDENT TradA
/METHOD = ENTER RQ14_Item52 RQ24
/METHOD = STEPWISE Q23_Bad_Behavior Q23_Good_Behavior
RQ27_item103b RQ34_item127 State RELIGIOSITY2.

TABLE 50. Descriptive Statistics

	Mean	Std. Deviation	N
Count: How many traditional items do you own?	2.7684	2.23793	678
Gender	.4882	.50023	678
Age	1.5265	.87390	678
Social Vices	5.2198	2.92149	678
Social Virtues	1.4130	1.23487	678
Church Service Attendance	1.5133	1.28586	678
Religious Service Attendance	1.5147	1.08389	678
State Location	.30	.459	678
Religiosity Index	8.5059	4.61061	678

TABLE 51. Traditionally Owned Correlations

		Count: How many traditional items do you own?	Gender	Age	Social Vices
Pearson Correlation	Count: How many traditional items do you own?	1.000	.155	-.053	.074
	Gender	.155	1.000	-.089	-.103
	Age	-.053	-.089	1.000	-.207
	Social Vices	.074	-.103	-.207	1.000
	Social Virtues	.135	.178	-.103	.426
	Church Service Attendance	.381	.030	-.054	-.066
	Religious Service Attendance	.368	.070	-.079	.008
	State Location	-.044	-.171	.028	.161
	Religiosity Index	.396	.075	-.081	.030
Sig. (1-tailed)	Count: How many traditional items do you own?		.000	.084	.028
	Gender	.000	.	.010	.004
	Age	.084	.010	.	.000
	Social Vices	.028	.004	.000	.
	Social Virtues	.000	.000	.004	.000
	Church Service Attendance	.000	.217	.079	.042
	Religious Service Attendance	.000	.035	.020	.417
	State Location	.125	.000	.234	.000
	Religiosity Index	.000	.026	.017	.219

TABLE 51. Continued

Count: How many traditional items do you own?	Gender	Age	Social Vices	678
Gender	678	678	678	678
Age	678	678	678	678
Social Vices	678	678	678	678
Social Virtues	678	678	678	678
Church Service Atten.	678	678	678	678
Religious Service Atten.	678	678	678	678
State Location	678	678	678	678
Religiosity Index	678	678	678	678

TABLE 52. Traditionally Owned Correlations

		Social Virtues	Church Service Atten.	Religious Service Atten.
Pearson Correlation	Count: How many traditional items do you own?	.135	.381	.368
	Gender	.178	.030	.070
	Age	-.103	-.054	-.079
	Social Vices	.426	-.066	.008
	Social Virtues	1.000	.208	.233
	Church Service Atten.	.208	1.000	.698
	Religious Service Atten.	.233	.698	1.000
	State Location	.166	.173	.229
	Religiosity Index	.368	.819	.816

128

TABLE 52. Continued

		Social Virtues	Church Service Atten.	Religious Service Atten.
Sig. (1-tailed)	Count: How many traditional items do you own?	.000	.000	.000
	Gender	.000	.217	.035
	Age	.004	.079	.020
	Social Vices	.000	.042	.417
	Social Virtues	.	.000	.000
	Church Service Atten.	.000	.	.000
	Religious Service Atten.	.000	.000	.
	State Location	.000	.000	.000
	Religiosity Index	.000	.000	.000
N	Count: How many traditional items do you own?	678	678	678
	Gender	678	678	678
	Age	678	678	678
	Social Vices	678	678	678
	Social Virtues	678	678	678
	Church Service Atten.	678	678	678
	Religious Service Atten.	678	678	678
	State Location	678	678	678
	Religiosity index	678	678	678

TABLE 53. Traditionally Owned Correlations

		State Location	Religiosity Scale
Pearson Correlation	Count: How many traditional items do you own?	-.044	.396
	Gender	-.171	.075
	Age	.028	-.081
	Social Vices	.161	.030
	Social Virtues	.166	.368
	Church Service Attendance	.173	.819
	Religious Service Attendance	.229	.816
	State Location	1.000	.280
	Religiosity Index	.280	1.000
Sig. (1-tailed)	Count: How many traditional items do you own?	.125	.000
	Gender	.000	.026
	Age	.234	.017
	Social Vices	.000	.219
	Social Virtues	.000	.000
	Church Service Attendance	.000	.000
	Religious Service Attendance	.000	.000
	State Location		.000
	Religiosity Index	.000	
N	Count: How many traditional items do you own?	678	678
	Gender	678	678
	Age	678	678
	Social Vices	678	678
	Social Virtues	678	678
	Church Service Attendance	678	678
	Religious Service Attendance	678	678
	State Location	678	678
	Religiosity Index	678	678

TABLE 54. Model/Method

Model	Variables Entered	Variables Removed	Method
1	Age, Gender	.	Enter
2	Religiosity Index	.	Stepwise (Criteria: Probability-of-F-to-enter < = .050, Probability-of-F-to-remove > = .100).
3	State Location	.	Stepwise (Criteria: Probability-of-F-to-enter < = .050, Probability-of-F-to-remove > = .100).
4	Social Vices	.	Stepwise (Criteria: Probability-of-F-to-enter < = .050, Probability-of-F-to-remove > = .100).
5	Church Service Attendance	.	Stepwise (Criteria: Probability-of-F-to-enter < = .050, Probability-of-F-to-remove > = .100).
6	Religious Service Attendance	.	Stepwise (Criteria: Probability-of-F-to-enter < = .050, Probability-of-F-to-remove > = .100).

a. All requested variables entered.
b. Dependent Variable: Count: How many traditional items do you own?

TABLE 55. Model Summary

Model	R	R Square	Adjusted R Square	Std. Error of the Estimate
1	.160a	.026	.023	2.21231
2	.439c	.173	.169	2.03949
3	.449d	.193	.188	2.01695
4	.462e	.202	.196	2.00655
5	.467f	.213	.206	1.99392
6		.218	.210	1.98916

131

TABLE 56. Model Summary

	Change Statistics				
Model	R Square Change	F Change	df1	df2	Sig. F Change
1	.026	8.887	2	675	.000
2	.148	120.240	1	674	.000
3	.019	16.147	1	673	.000
4	.009	7.998	1	672	.005
5	.011	9.538	1	671	.002
6	.005	4.213	1	670	.002

a. Predictors: (Constant), Age, Gender
b. Predictors: (Constant), Age, Gender, Religiosity Index
c. Predictors: (Constant), Age, Gender, Religiosity Index, State Location
d. Predictors: (Constant), Age, Gender, Religiosity Index, State Location, Social Vices
e. Predictors: (Constant), Age, Gender, Religiosity Index, State Location, Social Vices, Church Service Attendance
f. Predictors: (Constant), Age, Gender, Religiosity Index, State Location, Social Vices, Church Service Attendance, Religious Service Attendance

TABLE 57. ANOVA[g]

Model		Sum of Squares	df	Mean Square	F	Sig.
1	Regression	86.990	2	43.495	8.887	.000a
	Residual	3303.655	675	4.894		
	Total	3390.645	677			.000b
2	Regression	587.132	3	195.711	47.051	
	Residual	2803.513	674	4.160		
	Total	3390.645	677			.000c
3	Regression	652.820	4	163.205	40.118	
	Residual	2737.825	673	4.068		
	Total	3390.645	677			.000d

132

TABLE 57. Continued

Model		Sum of Squares	df	Mean Square	F	Sig.
4	Regression	685.021	5	137.004	34.028	
	Residual	2705.624	672	4.026		
	Total	3390.645	677			.000e
5	Regression	722.941	6	120.490	30.307	
	Residual	2667.703	671	3.976		
	Total	3390.645	677			.000f
6	Regression	739.612	7	105.659	26.703	
	Residual	2651.033	670	3.957		
	Total	3390.645	677			

a. Predictors: (Constant), Age, Gender

b. Predictors: (Constant), Age, Gender, Religiosity Index

c. Predictors: (Constant), Age, Gender, Religiosity Index, State Location

d. Predictors: (Constant), Age, Gender, Religiosity Index, State Location, Social Vices

e. Predictors: (Constant), Age, Gender, Religiosity Index, State Location, Social Vices, Church Service Attendance

f. Predictors: (Constant), Age, Gender, Religiosity Index, State Location, Social Vices, Church Service Attendance, Religious Service Attendance

g. Dependent Variable: Count: How many traditional items do you own?

TABLE 58. Coefficients[a]

Model		Unstandardized Coefficients		Standardized Coefficients		
		B	Std. Error	Beta	t	Sig.
1	(Constant)	2.592	.196		13.193	.000
	Gender	.679	.171	.152	3.977	.000
	Age	-.102	.098	-.040	-1.039	.299
2	(Constant)	.941	.236		3.996	.000
	Gender	.561	.158	.125	3.560	.000
	Age	-.027	.090	-.011	-.301	.764
	Religiosity Index	.187	.017	.386	10.965	.000

TABLE 58. Continued

Model		Unstandardized Coefficients		Standardized Coefficients		
		B	Std. Error	Beta	t	Sig.
3	(Constant)	1.018	.234		4.355	.000
	Gender	.435	.159	.097	2.736	.006
	Age	-.014	.089	-.005	-.154	.877
	Religiosity Index	.209	.018	.430	11.783	.000
	State Location	-.722	.180	-.148	-4.018	.000
4	(Constant)	.516	.293		1.762	.079
	Gender	.478	.159	.107	3.006	.003
	Age	.044	.091	.017	.481	.631
	Religiosity Index	.210	.018	.433	11.912	.000
	State Location	-.801	.181	-.164	-4.425	.000
	Social Vices	.078	.028	.102	2.828	.005
5	(Constant)	.564	.291		1.936	.053
	Gender	.522	.159	.117	3.290	.001
	Age	.047	.091	.019	.523	.601
	Religiosity Index	.133	.030	.275	4.383	.000
	State Location	-.749	.181	-.154	-4.145	.000
	Social Vices	.091	.028	.118	3.277	.001
	Church Service Atten.	.327	.106	.188	3.088	.002
6	(Constant)	.574	.290		1.975	.049
	Gender	.516	.158	.115	3.258	.001
	Age	.052	.090	.020	.580	.562
	Religiosity Index	.090	.037	.185	2.428	.015
	State Location	-.755	.180	-.155	-4.189	.000
	Social Vices	.092	.028	.120	3.324	.001
	Church Service Atten.	.308	.106	.177	2.900	.004
	Religious Service Atten.	.251	.123	.122	2.053	.041

a. Dependent Variable: Count: How many traditional items do you own?

134

TABLE 59. Excluded Variables

Model		Beta In	t	Sig.	Partial Correlation	Collinearity Statistics Tolerance
1	Social Vices	.086[a]	2.201	.028	.084	.942
	Social Virtues	.376[a]	2.795	.005	.107	.961
	Church Service Attendance	.358[a]	10.666	.000	.380	.996
	Religious Service Attendance	-.018[a]	10.052	.000	.361	.990
	State Location	.386[a]	-.459	.647	-.018	.971
	Religiosity Index	.077[b]	10.965	.000	.389	.989
2	Social Vices	-.037[b]	2.146	.032	.082	.942
	Social Virtues	.184[b]	-.967	.334	-.037	.838
	Church Service Attendance	.131[b]	3.031	.003	.116	.328
	Religious Service Attendance	-.148[b]	2.162	.031	.083	.335
	State Location	.102[c]	-4.018	.000	-.153	.883
3	Social Vices	-.021[c]	2.828	.005	.108	.920
	Social Virtues	.158[c]	-.542	.588	-.021	.828
	Church Service Attendance	.131[c]	2.607	.009	.100	.323
	Religious Service Attendance	-.089[d]	2.202	.028	.085	.335
4	Social Virtues	.188[d]	-2.089	.037	-.080	.652
	Church Service Attendance	.137[d]	3.088	.002	.118	.316
	Religious Service Attendance	-.076[e]	2.308	.021	.089	.334
5	Social Virtues	.122[e]	-1.795	.073	-.069	.645
	Religious Service Attendance	-.067[f]	2.053	.041	.079	.331
6	Social Virtues		-1.554	.121	-.060	.635

a. Predictors in the Model: (Constant), Age, Gender
b. Predictors in the Model: (Constant), Age, Gender, Religiosity Index
c. Predictors in the Model: (Constant), Age, Gender, Religiosity Index, State Location
d. Predictors in the Model: (Constant), Age, Gender, Religiosity Index, State Location, Social Vices
e. Predictors in the Model: (Constant), Age, Gender, Religiosity Index, State Location, Social Vices, Church Service Attendance
f. Predictors in the Model: (Constant), Age, Gender, Religiosity Index, State Location, Social Vices, Church Service Attendance, Religious Service Attendance
g. Dependent Variable: Count: How many traditional items do you own?

NOTE: DEPENDENT VARIABLE TradB.
COVARIANTS RQ14_Item52 (gender) and RQ24 (age).

135

TABLE 59. Continued

INDEPENDENT VARIABLE Q23_Bad_Behavior Q23_Good_Behavior State
RQ27_item103b RQ34_item127 RELIGIOSITY2.

REGRESSION
/DESCRIPTIVES MEAN STDDEV CORR SIG N/MISSING LISTWISE
/STATISTICS COEFF OUTS R ANOVA CHANGE/CRITERIA = PIN(.05)
POUT(.10)
/NOORIGIN/DEPENDENT TradB/METHOD = ENTER RQ14_Item52 RQ24
/METHOD = STEPWISE Q23_Bad_Behavior Q23_Good_Behavior
RQ27_item103b RQ34_item127 State RELIGIOSITY2 .

Regression

TABLE 60. Descriptive Statistics

	Mean	Standard Deviation	N
Count: How many traditional items don't own, but would buy?	1.3732	1.71301	678
Gender	.4882	.50023	678
Age	1.5265	.87390	678
Social Vices	5.2198	2.92149	678
Social Virtues	1.4130	1.23487	678
Church Service Attendance	1.5133	1.28586	678
Religious Service Attendance	1.5147	1.08389	678
State Location	.30	.459	678
Religiosity Index	8.5059	4.61061	678

TABLE 61. Correlations

		Count: How many traditional items don't you own, but would buy?	Gender	Age	Social Vices	Social Virtues
Pearson Correlation	Count: How many traditional items don't you own, but would buy?	1.000	-.108	-.144	.219	.058
	Gender	-.108	1.000	-.089	-.103	.178
	Age	-.144	-.089	1.000	-.207	-.103
	Social Vices	.219	-.103	-.207	1.000	.426
	Social Virtues	.058	.178	-.103	.426	1.000
	Church Service Atten.	.000	.030	-.054	-.066	.208
	Religious Service Atten.	.032	.070	-.079	.008	.233
	State Location	.135	-.171	.028	.161	.166
	Religiosity Index	.079	.075	-.081	.030	.368
Sig. (1-tailed)	Count: How many traditional items don't you own, but would buy?		.002	.000	.000	.067
	Gender	.002		.010	.004	.000
	Age	.000	.010		.000	.004
	Social Vices	.000	.004	.000		.000
	Social Virtues	.067	.000	.004	.000	
	Church Service Atten.	.499	.217	.079	.042	.000
	Religious Service Atten.	.205	.035	.020	.417	.000
	State Location	.000	.000	.234	.000	.000
	Religiosity Index	.020	.026	.017	.219	.000

TABLE 61. Continued

		Count: How many traditional items don't you own, but would buy?	Gender	Age	Social Vices	Social Virtues
N	Count: How many traditional items don't you own, but would buy?	678	678	678	678	678
	Gender	678	678	678	678	678
	Age	678	678	678	678	678
	Social Vices	678	678	678	678	678
	Social Virtues	678	678	678	678	678
	Church Service Attendance	678	678	678	678	678
	Religious Service Atten.	678	678	678	678	678
	State Location	678	678	678	678	678
	Religiosity Index	678	678	678	678	678

TABLE 62. Correlations

		Church Service Attendance	Religious Service Attendance	State Location	Religiosity Scale
Pearson Correlation	Count: How many traditional items don't you own, but would buy?	.000	.032	.135	.079
	Gender	.030	.070	-.171	.075
	Age	-.054	-.079	.028	-.081
	Social Vices	-.066	.008	.161	.030
	Social Virtues	.208	.233	.166	.368
	Church Service Atten.	1.000	.698	.173	.819
	Religious Service Atten.	.698	1.000	.229	.816
	State Location	.173	.229	1.000	.280
	Religiosity Index	.819	.816	.280	1.000

TABLE 62. Continued

		Church Service Attendance	Religious Service Attendance	State Location	Relig-iosity Scale
Sig. (1-tailed)	Count: How many traditional items don't you own, but would buy?	.499	.205	.000	.020
	Gender	.217	.035	.000	.026
	Age	.079	.020	.234	.017
	Social Vices	.042	.417	.000	.219
	Social Virtues	.000	.000	.000	.000
	Church Service Atten.		.000	.000	.000
	Religious Service Attendance	.000		.000	.000
	State Location	.000	.000		.000
	Religiosity Index	.000	.000	.000	
N	Count: How many traditional items don't you own, but would buy?	678	678	678	678
	Gender	678	678	678	678
	Age	678	678	678	678
	Social Vices	678	678	678	678
	Social Virtues	678	678	678	678
	Church Service Atten.	678	678	678	678
	Religious Service Atten.	678	678	678	678
	State Location	678	678	678	678
	Religiosity Index	678	678	678	678

TABLE 63. Variables Entered/Removed[b]

Model	Variables Entered	Variables Removed	Method
1	Age, Gender	.	Enter
2	Social Vices	.	Stepwise (Criteria: Probability-of-F-to-enter < = .050, Probability-of-F-to-remove > = .100).
3	State Location	.	Stepwise (Criteria: Probability-of-F-to-enter < = .050, Probability-of-F-to-remove > = .100).

a. All requested variables entered.

b. Dependent Variable: Count: How many traditional items don't you own, but would buy?

TABLE 64. Model Summary

Model	R	R Square	Adjusted R Square	Std. Error of the Estimate
1	.188[a]	.035	.033	1.68485
2	.277[c]	.068	.064	1.65760
3		.077	.071	1.65095

TABLE 65. Model Summary

Model	Change Statistics				
	R Square Change	F Change	df1	df2	Sig. F Change
1	.035	12.411	2	675	.000
2	.032	23.376	1	674	.000
3	.009	6.437	1	673	.011

a. Predictors: (Constant), Age, Gender

b. Predictors: (Constant), Age, Gender, Social Vices

c. Predictors: (Constant), Age, Gender, Social Vices, State Location

TABLE 66. ANOVA[d]

Model		Sum of Squares	df	Mean Square	F	Sig.
1	Regression	70.463	2	35.232	12.411	.000[a]
	Residual	1916.128	675	2.839		
	Total	1986.591	677			.000[b]
2	Regression	134.691	3	44.897	16.340	
	Residual	1851.901	674	2.748		
	Total	1986.591	677			.000[c]
3	Regression	152.235	4	38.059	13.963	
	Residual	1834.356	673	2.726		
	Total	1986.591	677			

a. Predictors: (Constant), Age, Gender
b. Predictors: (Constant), Age, Gender, Social Vices
c. Predictors: (Constant), Age, Gender, Social Vices, State Location
d. Dependent Variable: Count: How many traditional items don't you own, but would buy?

TABLE 67. Coefficients[a]

Model		B	Std. Error	Standardized Coefficients Beta	t	Sig.
1	(Constant)	2.040	.150		13.636	.000
	Gender	-.416	.130	-.122	-3.202	.001
	Age	-.304	.074	-.155	-4.086	.000
2	(Constant)	1.315	.210		6.256	.000
	Gender	-.339	.129	-.099	-2.628	.009
	Age	-.225	.075	-.115	-3.000	.003
	Social Vices	.109	.022	.185	4.835	.000
3	(Constant)	1.242	.211		5.875	.000
	Gender	-.289	.130	-.084	-2.224	.026
	Age	-.234	.075	-.119	-3.126	.002
	Social Vices	.100	.023	.170	4.409	.000
	State Location	.360	.142	.097	2.537	.011

a. Dependent Variable: Count: How many traditional items don't you own, but would buy?

TABLE 68. Excluded Variables[d]

Model		Beta In	t	Sig.	Partial Correlation	Collinearity Statistics Tolerance
1	Social Vices	.185[a]	4.835	.000	.183	.942
	Social Virtues	-.005[a]	1.708	.088	.066	.961
	Church Service Atten.	.028[a]	-.123	.902	-.005	.996
	Religious Service Atten.	.122[a]	.740	.459	.028	.990
	State Location	.076[a]	3.206	.001	.123	.971
	Religiosity Index	-.020[b]	2.005	.045	.077	.989
2	Social Virtues	.009[b]	-.474	.635	-.018	.769
	Church Service Atten.	.028[b]	.246	.806	.009	.991
	Religious Service Atten.	.097[b]	.755	.450	.029	.990
	State Location	.072[b]	2.537	.011	.097	.948
	Religiosity Index	-.038[c]	1.932	.054	.074	.988
3	Social Virtues	-.010[c]	-.878	.380	-.034	.751
	Church Service Atten.	.005[c]	-.257	.797	-.010	.952
	Religious Service Atten.	.048[c]	.130	.897	.005	.928
	Religiosity Index		1.231	.219	.047	.899

a. Predictors in the Model: (Constant), Age, Gender

b. Predictors in the Model: (Constant), Age, Gender, Social Vices

c. Predictors in the Model: (Constant), Age, Gender, Social Vices, State Location

d. Dependent Variable: Count: How many traditional items don't you own, but would buy?

NOTE: DEPENDENT VARIABLE TradC.
COVARIANTS RQ14_Item52 (gender) abd RQ24 (age).
INDEPENDENT VARIABLE Q23_Bad_Behavior Q23_Good_Behavior State
RQ27_item103b RQ34_item127 RELIGIOSITY2.
REGRESSION
/DESCRIPTIVES MEAN STDDEV CORR SIG N
/MISSING LISTWISE
/STATISTICS COEFF OUTS R ANOVA CHANGE
/CRITERIA = PIN(.05) POUT(.10)
/NOORIGIN
/DEPENDENT TradC
/METHOD = ENTER RQ14_Item52 RQ24
/METHOD = STEPWISE Q23_Bad_Behavior Q23_Good_Behavior
RQ27_item103b RQ34_item127 State RELIGIOSITY2 .

Regression

TABLE 69. Descriptive Statistics

	Mean	Standard Deviation	N
Count: How many traditional items don't you own, but won't buy?	2.2153	2.34365	678
Gender	.4882	.50023	678
Age	1.5265	.87390	678
Social Vices	5.2198	2.92149	678
Social Virtues	1.4130	1.23487	678
Church Service Attendance	1.5133	1.28586	678
Religious Service Attendance	1.5147	1.08389	678
State Location	.30	.459	678
Religiosity Index	8.5059	4.61061	678

TABLE 70. Correlations

		Count: How many traditional items don't you own, but won't buy?	Gender	Age	Social Vices	Social Virtues
Pearson Correlation	Count: How many traditional items don't you own, but won't buy?	1.000	-.044	.098	-.188	-.150
	Gender	-.044	1.000	-.089	-.103	.178
	Age	.098	-.089	1.000	-.207	-.103
	Social Vices	-.188	-.103	-.207	1.000	.426
	Social Virtues	-.150	.178	-.103	.426	1.000
	Church Service Atten.	-.320	.030	-.054	-.066	.208
	Religious Service Attendance	-.354	.070	-.079	.008	.233
	State Location	-.085	-.171	.028	.161	.166
	Religiosity Index	-.411	.075	-.081	.030	.368
Sig. (1-tailed)	Count: How many traditional items don't you own, but won't buy?	.				
			.124	.005	.000	.000
	Gender	.124	.	.010	.004	.000
	Age	.005	.010	.	.000	.004
	Social Vices	.000	.004	.000	.	.000
	Social Virtues	.000	.000	.004	.000	.
	Church Service Atten.	.000	.217	.079	.042	.000
	Religious Service Attendance	.000	.035	.020	.417	.000
	State Location	.013	.000	.234	.000	.000
	Religiosity Index	.000	.026	.017	.219	.000

144

TABLE 70. Continued

		Count: How many traditional items don't you own, but won't buy?	Gender	Age	Social Vices	Social Virtues
N	Count: How many traditional items don't you own, but won't buy?	678	678	678	678	678
	Gender	678	678	678	678	678
	Age	678	678	678	678	678
	Social Vices	678	678	678	678	678
	Social Virtues	678	678	678	678	678
	Church Service Atten.	678	678	678	678	678
	Religious Service Atten.	678	678	678	678	678
	State Location	678	678	678	678	678
	Religiosity Index	678	678	678	678	678

TABLE 71. Correlations

		Church Service Atten.	Religious Service Atten.	State Location	Religiosity Scale
Pearson Correlation	Count: How many traditional items don't you own, but won't buy?	-.320	-.354	-.085	-.411
	Gender	.030	.070	-.171	.075
	Age	-.054	-.079	.028	-.081
	Social Vices	-.066	.008	.161	.030
	Social Virtues	.208	.233	.166	.368
	Church Service Attendance	1.000	.698	.173	.819
	Religious Service Atten.	.698	1.000	.229	.816
	State Location	.173	.229	1.000	.280
	Religiosity Index	.819	.816	.280	1.000

		Church Service Atten.	Religious Service Atten.	State Location	Religiosity Scale
Sig. (1-tailed)	Count: How many traditional items don't you own, but won't buy?	.000	.000	.013	.000
	Gender	.217	.035	.000	.026
	Age	.079	.020	.234	.017
	Social Vices	.042	.417	.000	.219
	Social Virtucs	.000	.000	.000	.000
	Church Service Atten.		.000	.000	.000
	Religious Service Atten.	.000		.000	.000
	State Location	.000	.000		.000
	Religiosity Index	.000	.000	.000	

146

TABLE 71. Continued

N					
	Count: How many traditional items don't you own, but won't buy?	678	678	678	678
	Gender	678	678	678	678
	Age	678	678	678	678
	Social Vices	678	678	678	678
	Social Virtues	678	678	678	678
	Church Service Atten.	678	678	678	678
	Religious Service Atten.	678	678	678	678
	State Location	678	678	678	678
	Religiosity Index	678	678	678	678

TABLE 72. Variables Entered/Removed[b]

Model	Variables Entered	Variables Removed	Method
1	Age, Gender		Enter
2	Religiosity Index		Stepwise (Criteria: Probability-of-F-to-enter < = .050, Probability-of-F-to-remove > = .100).
3	Social Vices		Stepwise (Criteria: Probability-of-F-to-enter < = .050, Probability-of-F-to-remove > = .100).
4	Social Virtues		Stepwise (Criteria: Probability-of-F-to-enter < = .050, Probability-of-F-to-remove > = .100).

a. All requested variables entered.

b. Dependent Variable: Count: How many traditional items don't you own, but won't buy?

TABLE 73. Model Summary

Model	R	R Square	Adjusted R Square	Standard Error of the Estimate
1	.105[a]	.011	.008	2.33427
2	.449[c]	.173	.169	2.13588
3	.460[d]	.201	.197	2.10061
4		.211	.205	2.08926

TABLE 74. Model Summary

		Change Statistics			
Model	R Square Change	F Change	df1	df2	Sig. F Change
1	.011	3.728	2	675	.025
2	.162	132.217	1	674	.000
3	.028	23.820	1	673	.000
4	.010	8.330	1	672	.004

a. Predictors: (Constant), Age, Gender
b. Predictors: (Constant), Age, Gender, Religiosity Index
c. Predictors: (Constant), Age, Gender, Religiosity Index, Social Vices
d. Predictors: (Constant), Age, Gender, Religiosity Index, Social Vices, Social Virtues

TABLE 75. ANOVA[e]

Model		Sum of Squares	df	Mean Square	F	Sig.
1	Regression	40.623	2	20.312	3.728	.025[a]
	Residual	3677.937	675	5.449		
	Total	3718.560	677			.000[b]
2	Regression	643.795	3	214.598	47.041	
	Residual	3074.766	674	4.562		
	Total	3718.560	677			.000[c]
3	Regression	748.901	4	187.225	42.430	
	Residual	2969.660	673	4.413		
	Total	3718.560	677			.000[d]
4	Regression	785.262	5	157.052	35.980	
	Residual	2933.299	672	4.365		
	Total	3718.560	677			

149

TABLE 76. Coefficients[a]

Model		Unstandardized Coefficient		Standardized Coefficients		
		B	Std. Error	Beta	t	Sig.
1	(Constant)	1.909	.207		9.208	.000
	Gender	-.169	.180	-.036	-.937	.349
	Age	.255	.103	.095	2.471	.014
2	(Constant)	3.722	.247		15.089	.000
	Gender	-.040	.165	-.008	-.241	.810
	Age	.173	.095	.065	1.829	.068
	Religiosity Index	-.206	.018	-.405	-11.499	.000
3	(Constant)	4.633	.306		15.134	.000
	Gender	-.140	.164	-.030	-.856	.392
	Age	.073	.095	.027	.763	.446
	Religiosity Index	-.204	.018	-.401	-11.581	.000
	Social Vices	-.139	.028	-.173	-4.881	.000
4	(Constant)	4.787	.309		15.486	.000
	Gender	-.255	.168	-.054	-1.522	.128
	Age	.061	.095	.023	.648	.517
	Religiosity Index	-.225	.019	-.443	-11.851	.000
	Social Vices	-.182	.032	-.227	-5.688	.000
	Social Virtues	.232	.080	.122	2.886	.004

a. Dependent Variable: Count: How many traditional items don't you own, but won't buy?

150

TABLE 77. Excluded Variables[e]

Model		Beta In	t	Sig.	Partial Correlation	Collinearity Statistics Tolerance
1	Social Vices	-.182[a]	-4.694	.000	-.178	.942
	Social Virtues	-.314[a]	-3.589	.000	-.137	.961
	Church Service Attendance	-.348[a]	-8.635	.000	-.316	.996
	Religious Service Attendance	-.097[a]	-9.632	.000	-.348	.990
	State Location	-.405[a]	-2.498	.013	-.096	.971
	Religiosity Index	-.173[b]	-11.499	.000	-.405	.989
2	Social Vices	.009[b]	-4.881	.000	-.185	.942
	Social Virtues	.049[b]	.237	.812	.009	.838
	Church Service Attendance	-.054[b]	.797	.426	.031	.328
	Religious Service Attendance	.029[b]	-.897	.370	-.035	.335
	State Location	.122[c]	.768	.443	.030	.883
3	Social Virtues	.000[c]	2.886	.004	.111	.653
	Church Service Attendance	-.064[c]	.005	.996	.000	.319
	Religious Service Attendance	.057[c]	-1.068	.286	-.041	.334
	State Location	.019[d]	1.550	.122	.060	.862
4	Church Service Attendance	-.042[d]	.310	.757	.012	.315
	Religious Service Attendance	.053[d]	-.698	.485	-.027	.328
	State Location		1.436	.151	.055	.861

a. Predictors in the Model: (Constant), Age, Gender
b. Predictors in the Model: (Constant), Age, Gender, Religiosity Index
c. Predictors in the Model: (Constant), Age, Gender, Religiosity Index, Social Vices
d. Predictors in the Model: (Constant), Age, Gender, Religiosity Index, Social Vices, Social Virtues
e. Dependent Variable: Count: How many traditional items don't you own, but won't buy?

NOTE: DEPENDENT VARIABLE Traditional D.
COVARIANTS RQ14_Item52 (gender) abd RQ24 (age).

151

INDEPENDENT VARIABLE Q23_Bad_Behavior Q23_Good_Behavior State
RQ27_item103b RQ34_item127 RELIGIOSITY2.
REGRESSION
/DESCRIPTIVES MEAN STDDEV CORR SIG N, /MISSING LISTWISE,
/STATISTICS COEFF OUTS R ANOVA CHANGE, /CRITERIA = PIN(.05)
POUT(.10), /NOORIGIN
/DEPENDENT Traditional D, /METHOD = ENTER RQ14_Item52 RQ24,
/METHOD = STEPWISE Q23_Bad_Behavior Q23_Good_Behavior
RQ27_item103b, RQ34_item127 State RELIGIOSITY2.

Regression

TABLE 78. Descriptive Statistics

	Mean	Standard Deviation	N
Count: How many traditional items are you unsure about buying?	.4617	1.15970	678
Gender	.4882	.50023	678
Age	1.5265	.87390	678
Social Vices	5.2198	2.92149	678
Social Virtues	1.4130	1.23487	678
Church Service Attendance	1.5133	1.28586	678
Religious Service Attendance	1.5147	1.08389	678
State Location	.30	.459	678
Religiosity Index	8.5059	4.61061	678

153

TABLE 79. Correlations

		Count: How many traditional items are you unsure about buying?	Gender	Age	Social Vices	Social Virtues
Pearson Correlation	Count: How many traditional items are you unsure about buying?	1.000	-.050	.051	-.053	-.055
	Gender	-.050	1.000	-.089	-.103	.178
	Age	.051	-.089	1.000	-.207	-.103
	Social Vices	-.053	-.103	-.207	1.000	.426
	Social Virtues	-.055	.178	-.103	.426	1.000
	Church Service Atten.	-.111	.030	-.054	-.066	.208
	Religious Service Atten.	-.092	.070	-.079	.008	.233
	State Location	.058	-.171	.028	.161	.166
	Religiosity Index	-.090	.075	-.081	.030	.368
Sig. (1-tailed)	Count: How many traditional items are you unsure about buying?		.095	.091	.084	.077
	Gender	.095		.010	.004	.000
	Age	.091	.010		.000	.004
	Social Vices	.084	.004	.000		.000
	Social Virtues	.077	.000	.004	.000	
	Church Service Atten.	.002	.217	.079	.042	.000
	Religious Service Atten.	.008	.035	.020	.417	.000
	State Location	.066	.000	.234	.000	.000
	Religiosity Index	.010	.026	.017	.219	.000

154

TABLE 79. Continued

N						
	Count: How many traditional items are you unsure about buying?	678	678	678	678	678
	Gender	678	678	678	678	678
	Age	678	678	678	678	678
	Social Vices	678	678	678	678	678
	Social Virtues	678	678	678	678	678
	Church Service Atten.	678	678	678	678	678
	Religious Service Atten.	678	678	678	678	678
	State Location	678	678	678	678	678
	Religiosity Index	678	678	678	678	678

TABLE 80. Correlations

		Church Service Atten.	Religious Service Atten.	State Location	Religiosity Scale
Pearson Correlation	Count: How many traditional items are you unsure about buying?	-.111	-.092	.058	-.090
	Gender	.030	.070	-.171	.075
	Age	-.054	-.079	.028	-.081
	Social Vices	-.066	.008	.161	.030
	Social Virtues	.208	.233	.166	.368
	Church Service Atten.	1.000	.698	.173	.819
	Religious Service Atten.	.698	1.000	.229	.816
	State Location	.173	.229	1.000	.280
	Religiosity Index	.819	.816	.280	1.000

TABLE 80. Continued

		Church Service Atten.	Religious Service Atten.	State Location	Religiosity Scale
Sig. (1-tailed)	Count: How many traditional items are you unsure about buying?	.002	.008	.066	.010
	Gender	.217	.035	.000	.026
	Age	.079	.020	.234	.017
	Social Vices	.042	.417	.000	.219
	Social Virtues	.000	.000	.000	.000
	Church Service Atten.		.000	.000	.000
	Religious Service Atten.	.000		.000	.000
	State Location	.000	.000		.000
	Religiosity Index	.000	.000	.000	
N	Count: How many traditional items are you unsure about buying?	678	678	678	678
	Gender	678	678	678	678
	Age	678	678	678	678
	Social Vices	678	678	678	678
	Social Virtues	678	678	678	678
	Church Service Atten.	678	678	678	678
	Religious Service Atten.	678	678	678	678
	State Location	678	678	678	678
	Religiosity Index	678	678	678	678

TABLE 81. Variables Entered/Removed[b]

Model	Variables Entered	Variables Removed	Method
1	Age, Gender		Enter
2	Church Service Attendance		Stepwise (Criteria: Probability-of-F-to-enter < = .050, Probability-of-F-to-remove > = .100).

a. All requested variables entered.
b. Dependent Variable: Count: How many traditional items are you unsure about buying?

TABLE 82. Model Summary

Model	R	R Square	Adjusted R Square	Std. Error of the Estimate
1	.069[a]	.005	.002	1.15866
2		.016	.012	1.15285

TABLE 83. Model Summary

Model	Change Statistics				
	R Square Change	F Change	df1	df2	Sig. F Change
1	.005	1.611	2	675	.200
2	.011	7.820	1	674	.005

a. Predictors: (Constant), Age, Gender
b. Predictors: (Constant), Age, Gender, Church Service Attendance

157

TABLE 84. ANOVA[c]

Model		Sum of Squares	df	Mean Square	F	Sig.
1	Regression	4.327	2	2.163	1.611	.200[a]
	Residual	906.176	675	1.342		
	Total	910.503	677			.012[b]
2	Regression	14.720	3	4.907	3.692	
	Residual	895.783	674	1.329		
	Total	910.503	677			

a. Predictors: (Constant), Age, Gender
b. Predictors: (Constant), Age, Gender, Church Service Attendance
c. Dependent Variable: Count: How many traditional items are you unsure about buying?

TABLE 85. Coefficients[a]

Model		Unstandardized Coefficients	
		B	Std. Error
1	(Constant)	.418	.103
	Gender	-.107	.089
	Age	.063	.051
2	(Constant)	.573	.116
	Gender	-.101	.089
	Age	.055	.051
	Church Service Attendance	-.097	.035

158

TABLE 86. Coefficients[a]

Model		Standardized Coefficients Beta	t	Sig.
1	(Constant)		4.066	.000
	Gender	-.046	1.199	.231
	Age	.047	1.224	.221
2	(Constant)		4.924	.000
	Gender	-.044	1.134	.257
	Age	.042	1.084	.279
	Church Service Attendance	-.107	2.796	.005

a. Dependent Variable: Count: How many traditional items are you unsure about buying?

TABLE 87. Excluded Variables[c]

Model		Beta In	t	Sig.	Partial Correlation	Collinearity Statistics Tolerance
1	Social Vices	-.051[a]	-1.291	.197	-.050	.942
	Social Virtues	-.107[a]	-1.112	.266	-.043	.961
	Church Service Atten.	-.086[a]	-2.796	.005	-.107	.996
	Relig. Service Atten.	.050[a]	-2.227	.026	-.085	.990
	State Location	-.083[a]	1.284	.200	.049	.971
	Religiosity Index	-.060[b]	-2.162	.031	-.083	.989
2	Social Vices	-.022[b]	-1.517	.130	-.058	.937
	Social Virtues	-.021[b]	-.564	.573	-.022	.921
	Relig. Service Atten.	.072[b]	-.393	.694	-.015	.509
	State Location	.014[b]	1.834	.067	.071	.938
	Religiosity Index		.216	.829	.008	.325

a. Predictors in the Model: (Constant), Age, Gender
b. Predictors in the Model: (Constant), Age, Gender, Church Service Attendance
c. Dependent Variable: Count: How many traditional items are you unsure about buying?

159

TABLE 87. Continued

NOTE: DEPENDENT VARIABLE NonTradA.
COVARIANTS RQ14_Item52 (gender) abd RQ24 (age).
INDEPENDENT VARIABLE Q23_Bad_Behavior Q23_Good_Behavior State
RQ27_item103b RQ34_item127 RELIGIOSITY2.

REGRESSION
/DESCRIPTIVES MEAN STDDEV CORR SIG N, /MISSING LISTWISE,
/STATISTICS COEFF OUTS R ANOVA CHANGE, /CRITERIA = PIN(.05)
POUT(.10)
/NOORIGIN, /DEPENDENT NonTradA, /METHOD = ENTER RQ14_Item52
RQ24
/METHOD = STEPWISE Q23_Bad_Behavior Q23_Good_Behavior
RQ27_item103b RQ34_item127 State RELIGIOSITY2 .

Regression

TABLE 88. Descriptive Statistics

	Mean	Standard Deviation	N
Count: How many non-traditional items do you own?	1.3938	1.37602	678
Gender	.4882	.50023	678
Age	1.5265	.87390	678
Social Vices	5.2198	2.92149	678
Social Virtues	1.4130	1.23487	678
Church Service Attendance	1.5133	1.28586	678
Religious Service Attendance	1.5147	1.08389	678
State Location	.30	.459	678
Religiosity Index	8.5059	4.61061	678

TABLE 89. Correlations

		Count: How many non-traditional items do you own?	Gender	Age	Social Vices	Social Virtues
Pearson Correlation	Count: How many non- traditional items do you own?	1.000	.160	.026	-.026	.284
	Gender	.160	1.000	-.089	-.103	.178
	Age	.026	-.089	1.000	-.207	-.103
	Social Vices	-.026	-.103	-.207	1.000	.426
	Social Virtues	.284	.178	-.103	.426	1.000
	Church Service Atten.	.472	.030	-.054	-.066	.208
	Religious Service Atten.	.478	.070	-.079	.008	.233
	State Location	.123	-.171	.028	.161	.166
	Religiosity Index	.581	.075	-.081	.030	.368
Sig. (1-tailed)	Count: How many non- traditional items do you own?		.000	.247	.250	.000
	Gender	.000		.010	.004	.000
	Age	.247	.010		.000	.004
	Social Vices	.250	.004	.000		.000
	Social Virtues	.000	.000	.004	.000	
	Church Service Atten.	.000	.217	.079	.042	.000
	Religious Service Atten.	.000	.035	.020	.417	.000
	State Location	.001	.000	.234	.000	.000
	Religiosity Index	.000	.026	.017	.219	.000

TABLE 89. Continued

		Count: How many non-traditional items do you own?	Gender	Age	Social Vices	Social Virtues
N	Count: How many non-traditional items do you own?	678	678	678	678	678
	Gender	678	678	678	678	678
	Age	678	678	678	678	678
	Social Vices	678	678	678	678	678
	Social Virtues	678	678	678	678	678
	Church Service Atten.	678	678	678	678	678
	Religious Service Atten.	678	678	678	678	678
	State Location	678	678	678	678	678
	Religiosity Index	678	678	678	678	678

TABLE 90. Correlations

		Church Service Atten.	Religious Service Atten.	State Location	Religiosity Scale
Pearson Correlation	Count: How many non-traditional items do you own?	.472	.478	.123	.581
	Gender	.030	.070	-.171	.075
	Age	-.054	-.079	.028	-.081
	Social Vices	-.066	.008	.161	.030
	Social Virtues	.208	.233	.166	.368
	Church Service Attendance	1.000	.698	.173	.819
	Religious Service Attendance	.698	1.000	.229	.816
	State Location	.173	.229	1.000	.280
	Religiosity Index	.819	.816	.280	1.000

TABLE 90. Continued

		Church Service Atten.	Religious Service Atten.	State Location	Religi-osity Scale
Sig. (1-tailed)	Count: How many non-traditional items do you own?	.000	.000	.001	.000
	Gender	.217	.035	.000	.026
	Age	.079	.020	.234	.017
	Social Vices	.042	.417	.000	.219
	Social Virtues	.000	.000	.000	.000
	Church Service Attendance		.000	.000	.000
	Religious Service Attendance	.000		.000	.000
	State Location	.000	.000		.000
	Religiosity Index	.000	.000	.000	
N	Count: How many non-traditional items do you own?	678	678	678	678
	Gender	678	678	678	678
	Age	678	678	678	678
	Social Vices	678	678	678	678
	Social Virtues	678	678	678	678
	Church Service Attendance	678	678	678	678
	Religious Service Attendance	678	678	678	678
	State Location	678	678	678	678
	Religiosity Index	678	678	678	678

TABLE 91. Variables Entered/Removed[b]

Model	Variables Entered	Variables Removed	Method
1	Age, Gender		Enter
2	Religiosity Scale		Stepwise (Criteria: Probability-of-F-to-enter < = .050, Probability-of-F-to-remove > = .100
3	Social Virtues		Stepwise (Criteria: Probability-of-F-to-enter < = .050, Probability-of-F-to-remove > = .100)

a. All requested variables entered.

b. Dependent Variable: Count: How many non-traditional items do you own?

TABLE 92. Model Summary

Model	R	R Square	Adjusted R Square	Std. Error of the Estimate
1	.165[a]	.027	.024	1.35910
2	.602[c]	.358	.355	1.10484
3		.362	.358	1.10225

TABLE 93. Model Summary

Model	Change Statistics				
	R Square Change	F Change	df1	df2	Sig. F Change
1	.027	9.479	2	675	.000
2	.331	347.430	1	674	.000
3	.004	4.179	1	673	.041

a. Predictors: (Constant), Age, Gender

b. Predictors: (Constant), Age, Gender, Religiosity Index

c. Predictors: (Constant), Age, Gender, Religiosity Index, Social Virtues

TABLE 94. ANOVA[d]

Model		Sum of Squares	df	Mean Square	F	Sig.
1	Regression	35.018	2	17.509	9.479	.000[a]
	Residual	1246.836	675	1.847		
	Total	1281.854	677			.000[b]
2	Regression	459.118	3	153.039	125.372	
	Residual	822.736	674	1.221		
	Total	1281.854	677			.000[c]
3	Regression	464.196	4	116.049	95.518	
	Residual	817.658	673	1.215		
	Total	1281.854	677			

a. Predictors: (Constant), Age, Gender

b. Predictors: (Constant), Age, Gender, Religiosity Index

c. Predictors: (Constant), Age, Gender, Religiosity Index, Social Virtues

d. Dependent Variable: Count: How many non-traditional items do you own?

TABLE 95. Coefficients[a]

Model		Standardized Coefficients			t	Sig.
		B	Std.Error	Beta		
1	(Constant)	1.076	.121		8.911	.000
	Gender	.451	.105	.164	4.299	.000
	Age	.064	.060	.041	1.072	.284
2	(Constant)	-.445	.128		-3.484	.001
	Gender	.343	.085	.125	4.010	.000
	Age	.133	.049	.084	2.715	.007
	Religiosity Index	.173	.009	.578	18.639	.000
3	(Constant)	-.488	.129		-3.782	.000
	Gender	.315	.086	.114	3.650	.000
	Age	.139	.049	.089	2.852	.004
	Religiosity Index	.165	.010	.554	16.718	.000
	Social Virtues	.077	.037	.069	2.044	.041

a. Dependent Variable: Count: How many non-traditional items do you own?

TABLE 96. Excluded Variables[d]

Model		Beta In	t	Sig.	Partial Corre-lation	Collinearity Statistics Tolerance
1	Social Vices	-.001[a]	-.018	.985	-.001	.942
	Social Virtues	.471[a]	7.224	.000	.268	.961
	Church Service Atten.	.475[a]	14.064	.000	.476	.996
	Religious Service Atten.	.155[a]	14.156	.000	.479	.990
	State Location	.578[a]	4.058	.000	.154	.971
	Religiosity Index	-.014[b]	18.639	.000	.583	.989
2	Social Vices	.069[b]	-.432	.666	-.017	.942
	Social Virtues	-.004[b]	2.044	.041	.079	.838
	Church Service Atten.	.012[b]	-.079	.937	-.003	.328
	Religious Service Atten.	-.023[b]	.231	.818	.009	.335
	State Location	-.057[c]	-.693	.488	-.027	.883

TABLE 97. Model Summary

Model		Beta In	t	Sig.	Partial Corre-lation	Collinearity Statistics
	Church Service Atten.	.027[c]	.271	.787	.010	Tolerance
	Religious Service Atten.	-.030[c]	.505	.614	.019	.329
	State Location		-.924	.356	-.036	.872

a. Predictors in the Model: (Constant), Age, Gender

b. Predictors in the Model: (Constant), Age, Gender, Religiosity Index

c. Predictors in the Model: (Constant), Age, Gender, Religiosity Index, Social Virtues

d. Dependent Variable: Count: How many non-traditional items do you own?

NOTE: DEPENDENT VARIABLE NonTradB.
COVARIANTS RQ14_Item52 (gender) abd RQ24 (age).
INDEPENDENT VARIABLE Q23_Bad_Behavior Q23_Good_Behavior State RQ27_item103b RQ34_item127 RELIGIOSITY2.

TABLE 97. Continued

REGRESSION
/DESCRIPTIVES MEAN STDDEV CORR SIG N
/MISSING LISTWISE
/STATISTICS COEFF OUTS R ANOVA CHANGE
/CRITERIA = PIN(.05) POUT(.10)
/NOORIGIN
/DEPENDENT NonTradB

/METHOD = ENTER RQ14_Item52 RQ24
/METHOD = STEPWISE Q23_Bad_Behavior Q23_Good_Behavior
RQ27_item103b RQ34_item127 State RELIGIOSITY2 .

Regression

TABLE 98. Descriptive Statistics

	Mean	Standard Deviation	N
Count: How many non-traditional items don't you own, but would buy?	1.1667	1.18967	678
Gender	.4882	.50023	678
Age	1.5265	.87390	678
Social Vices	5.2198	2.92149	678
Social Virtues	1.4130	1.23487	678
Church Service Attendance	1.5133	1.28586	678
Religious Service Attendance	1.5147	1.08389	678
State Location	.30	.459	678
Religiosity Index	8.5059	4.61061	678

TABLE 99. Correlations

		Count: How many non-traditional items don't you own, but would buy?	Gender	Age	Social Vices	Social Virtues
Pearson Correlation	Count: How many non-traditional items don't you own, but would buy?	1.000	-.003	-.146	.107	.096
	Gender	-.003	1.000	-.089	-.103	.178
	Age	-.146	-.089	1.000	-.207	-.103
	Social Vices	.107	-.103	-.207	1.000	.426
	Social Virtues	.096	.178	-.103	.426	1.000
	Church Service Atten.	.124	.030	-.054	-.066	.208
	Religious Service Atten.	.132	.070	-.079	.008	.233
	State Location	.065	-.171	.028	.161	.166
	Religiosity Index	.176	.075	-.081	.030	.368

Sig. (1-tailed)		Count: How many non-traditional items don't you own, but would buy?	Gender	Age	Social Vices	Social Virtues
	Count: How many non-traditional items don't you own, but would buy?		.470	.000	.003	.006
	Gender	.470		.010	.004	.000
	Age	.000	.010		.000	.004
	Social Vices	.003	.004	.000		.000
	Social Virtues	.006	.000	.004	.000	
	Church Service Atten.	.001	.217	.079	.042	.000
	Religious Service Atten.	.000	.035	.020	.417	.000
	State Location	.046	.000	.234	.000	.000
	Religiosity Index	.000	.026	.017	.219	.000

		Count: How many non-traditional items don't you own, but would buy?	Gender	Age	Social Vices	Social Virtues
N	Count: How many non-traditional items don't you own, but would buy?	678	678	678	678	678
	Gender	678	678	678	678	678
	Age	678	678	678	678	678
	Social Vices	678	678	678	678	678
	Social Virtues	678	678	678	678	678
	Church Service Atten.	678	678	678	678	678
	Religious Service Atten.	678	678	678	678	678
	State Location	678	678	678	678	678
	Religiosity Index	678	678	678	678	678

170

TABLE 100. Correlations

		Church Service Atten.	Religious Service Atten.	State Location	Religiosity Scale
Pearson Correlation	Count: How many non-traditional items don't you own, but would buy?	.124	.132	.065	.176
	Gender	.030	.070	-.171	.075
	Age	-.054	-.079	.028	-.081
	Social Vices	-.066	.008	.161	.030
	Social Virtues	.208	.233	.166	.368
	Church Service Atten.	1.000	.698	.173	.819
	Religious Service Atten.	.698	1.000	.229	.816
	State Location	.173	.229	1.000	.280
	Religiosity Index	.819	.816	.280	1.000

TABLE 100. Continued

		Church Service Atten.	Religious Service Atten.	State Location	Religiosity Scale
Sig. (1-tailed)	Count: How many non-traditional items don't you own, but would buy?	.001	.000	.046	.000
	Gender	.217	.035	.000	.026
	Age	.079	.020	.234	.017
	Social Vices	.042	.417	.000	.219
	Social Virtues	.000	.000	.000	.000
	Church Service Atten.		.000	.000	.000
	Relig. Service Atten.	.000		.000	.000
	State Location	.000	.000		.000
	Religiosity Index	.000	.000	.000	

TABLE 100. Continued

N					
	Count: How many non-traditional items don't you own, but would buy?	678	678	678	678
	Gender	678	678	678	678
	Age	678	678	678	678
	Social Vices	678	678	678	678
	Social Virtues	678	678	678	678
	Church Service Atten.	678	678	678	678
	Religious Service Atten.	678	678	678	678
	State Location	678	678	678	678
	Religiosity Index	678	678	678	678

TABLE 101. Variables Entered/Removed[b]

Model	Variables Entered	Variables Removed	Method
1	Age, Gender		Enter
2	Religiosity Index		Stepwise (Criteria: Probability-of-F-to-enter < = .050, Probability-of-F-to-remove > = .100).
3	Social Vices		Stepwise (Criteria: Probability-of-F-to-enter < = .050, Probability-of-F-to-remove > = .100).

a. All requested variables entered.

b. Dependent Variable: Count: How many non-traditional items don't you own, but would buy?

TABLE 102. Model Summary

Model	R	R Square	Adjusted R Square	Std. Error of the Estimate
1	.146[a]	.021	.019	1.17858
2	.234[c]	.049	.045	1.16262
3		.055	.049	1.16015

TABLE 103. Model Summary

| | Change Statistics | | | | |
Model	R Square Change	F Change	df1	df2	Sig. F Change
1	.021	7.402	2	675	.001
2	.028	19.656	1	674	.000
3	.005	3.870	1	673	.050

a. Predictors: (Constant), Age, Gender

b. Predictors: (Constant), Age, Gender, Religiosity Index

c. Predictors: (Constant), Age, Gender, Religiosity Index, Social Vices

TABLE 104. ANOVA[d]

Model		Sum of Squares	df	Mean Square	F	Sig.
1	Regression	20.563	2	10.281	7.402	.001[a]
	Residual	937.604	675	1.389		
	Total	958.167	677			.000[b]
2	Regression	47.132	3	15.711	11.623	
	Residual	911.035	674	1.352		
	Total	958.167	677			.000[c]
3	Regression	52.341	4	13.085	9.722	
	Residual	905.825	673	1.346		
	Total	958.167	677			

a. Predictors: (Constant), Age, Gender

b. Predictors: (Constant), Age, Gender, Religiosity Index

c. Predictors: (Constant), Age, Gender, Religiosity Index, Social Vices

d. Dependent Variable: Count: How many non-traditional items don't you own, but would buy?

174

TABLE 105. Coefficients[a]

Model		Unstandardized Coefficients		Standardized Coefficients		
		B	Standard Error	Beta	t	Sig.
1	(Constant)	1.491	.105		14.243	.000
	Gender	-.038	.091	-.016	-.417	.676
	Age	-.200	.052	-.147	-3.847	.000
2	(Constant)	1.110	.134		8.270	.000
	Gender	-.065	.090	-.027	-.723	.470
	Age	-.183	.051	-.134	-3.556	.000
	Religiosity Index	.043	.010	.167	4.434	.000

Model		Unstandardized Coefficients		Standardized Coefficients		
		B	Standard Error	Beta	t	Sig.
3	(Constant)	.907	.169		5.366	.000
	Gender	-.043	.090	-.018	-.472	.637
	Age	-.161	.053	-.118	-3.054	.002
	Religiosity Index	.043	.010	.166	4.399	.000
	Social Vices	.031	.016	.076	1.967	.050

a. Dependent Variable: Count: How many non-traditional items don't you own, but would buy?

TABLE 106. Excluded Variables[d]

Model		Beta In	t	Sig.	Partial Correlation	Collinearity Statistics Tolerance
1	Social Vices	.080[a]	2.037	.042	.078	.942
	Social Virtues	.117[a]	2.244	.025	.086	.961
	Church Service Atten.	.122[a]	3.074	.002	.118	.996
	Religious Service Atten.	.068[a]	3.217	.001	.123	.990
	State Location	.167[a]	1.770	.077	.068	.971
	Religiosity Index	.076[b]	4.434	.000	.168	.989
2	Social Vices	.030[b]	1.967	.050	.076	.942
	Social Virtues	-.061[b]	.732	.465	.028	.838
	Church Service Atten.	-.041[b]	-.932	.352	-.036	.328
	Religious Service Atten.	.019[b]	-.634	.526	-.024	.335
	State Location	-.010[c]	.482	.630	.019	.883
3	Social Virtues	-.041[c]	-.216	.829	-.008	.653
	Church Service Atten.	-.037[c]	-.618	.537	-.024	.319
	Religious Service Atten.	.007[c]	-.573	.567	-.022	.334
	State Location		.184	.854	.007	.862

a. Predictors in the Model: (Constant), Age, Gender
b. Predictors in the Model: (Constant), Age, Gender, Religiosity Index
c. Predictors in the Model: (Constant), Age, Gender, Religiosity Index, Social Vices
d. Dependent Variable: Count: How many non-traditional items don't you own, but would buy?

NOTE: DEPENDENT VARIABLE NonTradC.

176

COVARIANTS RQ14_Item52 (gender) abd RQ24 (age).
INDEPENDENT VARIABLE Q23_Bad_Behavior Q23_Good_Behavior State
RQ27_item103b RQ34_item127 RELIGIOSITY2.

REGRESSION
/DESCRIPTIVES MEAN STDDEV CORR SIG N
/MISSING LISTWISE
/STATISTICS COEFF OUTS R ANOVA CHANGE
/CRITERIA = PIN(.05) POUT(.10)
/NOORIGIN
/DEPENDENT NonTradC
/METHOD = ENTER RQ14_Item52 RQ24
/METHOD = STEPWISE Q23_Bad_Behavior Q23_Good_Behavior
RQ27_item103b RQ34_item127 State RELIGIOSITY2 .

Regression

TABLE 107. Descriptive Statistics

	Mean	Standard Deviation	N
Count: How many non-traditional items don't you own, but won't buy?	2.0501	1.69119	678
Gender	.4882	.50023	678
Age	1.5265	.87390	678
Social Vices	5.2198	2.92149	678
Social Virtues	1.4130	1.23487	678
Church Service Attendance	1.5133	1.28586	678
Religious Service Attendance	1.5147	1.08389	678
State Location	.30	.459	678
Religiosity Index	8.5059	4.61061	678

TABLE 108. Correlations

		Count: How many non-traditional items don't you own, but won't buy?	Gender	Age	Social Vices	Social Virtues
Pearson Correlation	Count: How many non-traditional items don't you own, but would buy?	1.000	-.102	.049	-.040	-.268
	Gender	-.102	1.000	-.089	-.103	.178
	Age	.049	-.089	1.000	-.207	-.103
	Social Vices	-.040	-.103	-.207	1.000	.426
	Social Virtues	-.268	.178	-.103	.426	1.000
	Church Service Atten.	-.426	.030	-.054	-.066	.208
	Religious Service Atten.	-.466	.070	-.079	.008	.233
	State Location	-.139	-.171	.028	.161	.166
	Religiosity Index	-.566	.075	-.081	.030	.368
Sig. (1-tailed)	Count: How many non-traditional items don't you own, but would buy?		.004	.101	.152	.000
	Gender	.004		.010	.004	.000
	Age	.101	.010		.000	.004
	Social Vices	.152	.004	.000		.000
	Social Virtues	.000	.000	.004	.000	
	Church Service Atten.	.000	.217	.079	.042	.000
	Religious Service Atten.	.000	.035	.020	.417	.000
	State Location	.000	.000	.234	.000	.000
	Religiosity Index	.000	.026	.017	.219	.000

TABLE 108. Continued

		Count: How many non-traditional items don't you own, but won't buy?	Gender	Age	Social Vices	Social Virtues
N	Count: How many non-traditional items don't you own, but would buy?	678	678	678	678	678
	Gender	678	678	678	678	678
	Age	678	678	678	678	678
	Social Vices	678	678	678	678	678
	Social Virtues	678	678	678	678	678
	Church Service Atten.	678	678	678	678	678
	Religious Service Atten.	678	678	678	678	678
	State Location	678	678	678	678	678
	Religiosity Index	678	678	678	678	678

TABLE 109. Correlations

		Church Service Atten.	Religious Service Atten.	State Location	Religiosity Scale
Pearson Correlation	Count: How many non-traditional items don't you own, but would buy?	-.426	-.466	-.139	-.566
	Gender	.030	.070	-.171	.075
	Age	-.054	-.079	.028	-.081
	Social Vices	-.066	.008	.161	.030
	Social Virtues	.208	.233	.166	.368
	Church Service Atten.	1.000	.698	.173	.819
	Religious Service Atten.	.698	1.000	.229	.816
	State Location	.173	.229	1.000	.280
	Religiosity Index	.819	.816	.280	1.000

TABLE 109. Correlations (continued)

		Church Service Atten.	Religious Service Atten.	State Location	Religiosity Scale
Sig. (1-tailed)	Count: How many non-traditional items don't you own, but would buy?	.000	.000	.000	.000
	Gender	.217	.035	.000	.026
	Age	.079	.020	.234	.017
	Social Vices	.042	.417	.000	.219
	Social Virtues	.000	.000	.000	.000
	Church Service Atten.		.000	.000	.000
	Religious Service Atten.	.000		.000	.000
	State Location	.000	.000		.000
	Religiosity Index	.000	.000	.000	
N	Count: How many non-traditional items don't you own, but would buy?	678	678	678	678
	Gender	678	678	678	678
	Age	678	678	678	678
	Social Vices	678	678	678	678
	Social Virtues	678	678	678	678
	Church Service Atten.	678	678	678	678
	Religious Service Atten.	678	678	678	678
	State Location	678	678	678	678
	Religiosity Index	678	678	678	678

TABLE 110. Variables Entered/Removed[b]

Model	Variables Entered	Variables Removed	Method
1	Age, Gender		Enter
2	Religiosity Index		Stepwise (Criteria: Probability-of-F-to-enter < = .050, Probability-of-F-to-remove > = .100).

a. All requested variables entered.

b. Dependent Variable: Count: How many non-traditional items don't you own, but won't buy?

TABLE 111. Model Summary

Model	R	R Square	Adjusted R Square	Std. Error of the Estimate
1	.110[a]	.012	.009	1.68343
2		.324	.321	1.39394

TABLE 112. Model Summary

Model		Change Statistics			
	R Square Change	F Change	df1	df2	Sig. F Change
1	.012	4.127	2	675	.017
2	.312	310.477	1	674	.000

a. Predictors: (Constant), Age, Gender

b. Predictors: (Constant), Age, Gender, Religiosity Index

TABLE 113. ANOVA[c]

Model		Sum of Squares	df	Mean Square	F	Sig.
1	Regression	23.390	2	11.695	4.127	.017[a]
	Residual	1912.905	675	2.834		
	Total	1936.295	677			.000[b]
2	Regression	626.668	3	208.889	107.505	
	Residual	1309.627	674	1.943		
	Total	1936.295	677			

a. Predictors: (Constant), Age, Gender
b. Predictors: (Constant), Age, Gender, Religiosity Index
c. Dependent Variable: Count: How many non-traditional items don't you own, but won't buy?

TABLE 114. Coefficients[a]

Model		Unstandardized Coefficients		Standardized Coefficients	t	Sig.
		B	Std. Error	Beta		
1	(Constant)	2.094	.150		14.007	.000
	Gender	-.334	.130	-.099	-2.571	.010
	Age	.078	.074	.040	1.049	.294
2	(Constant)	3.907	.161		24.272	.000
	Gender	-.205	.108	-.061	-1.901	.058
	Age	-.004	.062	-.002	-.060	.952
	Religiosity Index	-.206	.012	-.561	-17.620	.000

a. Dependent Variable: Count: How many non-traditional items don't you own, but won't buy?

182

TABLE 115. Excluded Variables[c]

Model		Beta In	t	Sig.	Partial Correlation	Collinearity Statistics Tolerance
1	Social Vices	-.044[a]	-1.116	.265	-.043	.942
	Social Virtues	-.423[a]	-6.786	.000	-.253	.961
	Church Service Atten.	-.461[a]	-12.167	.000	-.424	.996
	Religious Service Atten.	-.162[a]	-13.495	.000	-.461	.990
	State Location	-.561[a]	-4.227	.000	-.161	.971
	Religiosity Index	-.031[b]	-17.620	.000	-.562	.989
2	Social Vices	-.061[b]	-.960	.338	-.037	.942
	Social Virtues	.108[b]	-1.755	.080	-.068	.838
	Church Service Atten.	-.013[b]	1.953	.051	.075	.328
	Religious Service Atten.	.009[b]	-.232	.816	-.009	.335
	State Location		.261	.794	.010	.883

a. Predictors in the Model: (Constant), Age, Gender

b. Predictors in the Model: (Constant), Age, Gender, Religiosity Index

c. Dependent Variable: Count: How many non-traditional items don't you own, but won't buy?

NOTE: DEPENDENT VARIABLE NonTradD.
COVARIANTS RQ14_Item52 (gender) abd RQ24 (age).
INDEPENDENT VARIABLE Q23_Bad_Behavior Q23_Good_Behavior State RQ27_item103b RQ34_item127 RELIGIOSITY2.

REGRESSION
/DESCRIPTIVES MEAN STDDEV CORR SIG N
/MISSING LISTWISE
/STATISTICS COEFF OUTS R ANOVA CHANGE
/CRITERIA = PIN(.05) POUT(.10)
/NOORIGIN
/DEPENDENT NonTradD
/METHOD = ENTER RQ14_Item52 RQ24
/METHOD = STEPWISE Q23_Bad_Behavior Q23_Good_Behavior
RQ27_item103b RQ34_item127 State RELIGIOSITY2 .

Regression

TABLE 116. Descriptive Statistics

	Mean	Standard Deviation	N
Count: How many non-traditional items are you unsure about buying?	.2788	.74556	678
Gender	.4882	.50023	678
Age	1.5265	.87390	678
Social Vices	5.2198	2.92149	678
Social Virtues	1.4130	1.23487	678
Church Service Attendance	1.5133	1.28586	678
Religious Service Attendance	1.5147	1.08389	678
State Location	.30	.459	678
Religiosity Index	8.5059	4.61061	678

TABLE 117. Correlations

		Count: How many non-tra-ditional items don't you own, but would buy?	Gender	Age	Social Vices	Social Virtues
Pearson Correlation	Count: How many non-traditional items are you unsure about buying?	1.000	-.064	.008	.003	-.087
	Gender	-.064	1.000	-.089	-.103	.178
	Age	.008	-.089	1.000	-.207	-.103
	Social Vices	.003	-.103	-.207	1.000	.426
	Social Virtues	-.087	.178	-.103	.426	1.000
	Church Service Atten.	-.119	.030	-.054	-.066	.208
	Religious Service Atten.	-.081	.070	-.079	.008	.233
	State Location	-.012	-.171	.028	.161	.166
	Religiosity Index	-.106	.075	-.081	.030	.368
Sig. (1-tailed)	Count: How many non-traditional items are you unsure about buying?		.047	.419	.469	.012
	Gender	.047		.010	.004	.000
	Age	.419	.010		.000	.004
	Social Vices	.469	.004	.000		.000
	Social Virtues	.012	.000	.004	.000	
	Church Service Atten.	.001	.217	.079	.042	.000
	Religious Service Atten.	.018	.035	.020	.417	.000
	State Location	.374	.000	.234	.000	.000
	Religiosity Index	.003	.026	.017	.219	.000

TABLE 117. Continued

		Count: How many non-tra-ditional items don't you own, but would buy?	Gender	Age	Social Vices	Social Virtues
N	Count: How many non-traditional items are you unsure about buying?	678	678	678	678	678
	Gender	678	678	678	678	678
	Age	678	678	678	678	678
	Social Vices	678	678	678	678	678
	Social Virtues	678	678	678	678	678
	Church Service Atten.	678	678	678	678	678
	Religious Service Atten.	678	678	678	678	678
	State Location	678	678	678	678	678
	Religiosity Index	678	678	678	678	678

TABLE 118. Correlations

		Church Service Atten.	Religious Service Atten.	State Location	Religiosity Scale
Pearson Correlation	Count: How many non-traditional items are you unsure about buying?	-.119	-.081	-.012	-.106
	Gender	.030	.070	-.171	.075
	Age	-.054	-.079	.028	-.081
	Social Vices	-.066	.008	.161	.030
	Social Virtues	.208	.233	.166	.368
	Church Service Atten.	1.000	.698	.173	.819
	Religious Service Atten.	.698	1.000	.229	.816
	State Location	.173	.229	1.000	.280
	Religiosity Index	.819	.816	.280	1.000

186

TABLE 118. Continued

		Church Service Atten.	Religious Service Atten.	State Location	Religiosity Scale
Sig. (1-tailed)	Count: How many non-traditional items are you unsure about buying?	.001	.018	.374	.003
	Gender	.217	.035	.000	.026
	Age	.079	.020	.234	.017
	Social Vices	.042	.417	.000	.219
	Social Virtues	.000	.000	.000	.000
	Church Service Atten.		.000	.000	.000
	Religious Service Atten.	.000		.000	.000
	State Location	.000	.000		.000
	Religiosity Index	.000	.000	.000	
N	Count: How many non-traditional items are you unsure about buying?	678	678	678	678
	Gender	678	678	678	678
	Age	678	678	678	678
	Social Vices	678	678	678	678
	Social Virtues	678	678	678	678
	Church Service Atten.	678	678	678	678
	Religious Service Atten.	678	678	678	678
	State Location	678	678	678	678
	Religiosity Index	678	678	678	678

TABLE 119. Variables Entered/Removed[b]

Model	Variables Entered	Variables Removed	Method
1	Age, Gender		Enter
2	Church Service Attendance		Stepwise (Criteria: Probability-of-F-to-enter <= .050, Probability-of-F-to-remove >= .100).

a. All requested variables entered.

b. Dependent Variable: Count: How many non-traditional items are you unsure about buying?

TABLE 120. Model Summary

Model	R	R Square	Adjusted R Square	Standard Error of the Estimate
1	.064[a]	.004	.001	.74511
2		.018	.013	.74053

TABLE 121. Model Summary

	Change Statistics				
Model	R Square Change	F Change	df1	df2	Sig. F Change
1	.004	1.409	2	675	.245
2	.014	9.363	1	674	.002

a. Predictors: (Constant), Age, Gender
b. Predictors: (Constant), Age, Gender, Church Service Attendance

188

TABLE 122. ANOVA[c]

Model		Sum of Squares	df	Mean Square	F	Sig.
1	Regression	1.564	2	.782	1.409	.245[a]
	Residual	374.750	675	.555		
	Total	376.314	677			.007[b]
2	Regression	6.699	3	2.233	4.072	
	Residual	369.615	674	.548		
	Total	376.314	677			

a. Predictors: (Constant), Age, Gender
b. Predictors: (Constant), Age, Gender, Church Service Attendance
c. Dependent Variable: Count: How many non-traditional items are you unsure about buying?

TABLE 123. Coefficients[a]

Model		Unstandardized Coefficients	
		B	Standard Error
1	(Constant)	.323	.066
	Gender	-.096	.057
	Age	.002	.033
2	(Constant)	.431	.075
	Gender	-.091	.057
	Age	-.003	.033
	Church Service Attendance	-.068	.022

TABLE 124. Coefficients[a]

| Model | | Standardized Coefficients | | |
		Beta	t	Sig.
1	(Constant)		4.876	.000
	Gender	-.064	-1.666	.096
	Age	.002	.057	.955
2	(Constant)		5.770	.000
	Gender	-.061	-1.598	.111
	Age	-.004	-.101	.919
	Church Service Atten.	-.117	-3.060	.002

a. Dependent Variable: Count: How many non-traditional items are you unsure about buying?

TABLE 125. Excluded Variables[c]

Model		Beta In	t	Sig.	Partial Correlation	Collinearity Statistics Tolerance
1	Social Vices	-.003[a]	-.084	.933	-.003	.942
	Social Virtues	-.117[a]	-1.999	.046	-.077	.961
	Church Service Atten.	-.077[a]	-3.060	.002	-.117	.996
	Relig. Service Atten.	-.024[a]	-2.001	.046	-.077	.990
	State Location	-.102[a]	-.619	.536	-.024	.971
	Religiosity Index	-.013[b]	-2.656	.008	-.102	.989
2	Social Vices	-.056[b]	-.320	.749	-.012	.937
	Social Virtues	.009[b]	-1.418	.157	-.055	.921
	Relig. Service Atten.	-.003[b]	.174	.862	.007	.509
	State Location	-.018[b]	-.066	.947	-.003	.938
	Religiosity Index		-.269	.788	-.010	.325

190

TABLE 125. Excluded Variables[c]

Model		Beta In	t	Sig.	Partial Correlation	Collinearity Statistics Tolerance
1	Social Vices	-.003[a]	-.084	.933	-.003	.942
	Social Virtues	-.117[a]	-1.999	.046	-.077	.961
	Church Service Atten.	-.077[a]	-3.060	.002	-.117	.996
	Relig. Service Atten.	-.024[a]	-2.001	.046	-.077	.990
	State Location	-.102[a]	-.619	.536	-.024	.971
	Religiosity Index	-.013[b]	-2.656	.008	-.102	.989
2	Social Vices	-.056[b]	-.320	.749	-.012	.937
	Social Virtues	.009[b]	-1.418	.157	-.055	.921
	Relig. Service Atten.	-.003[b]	.174	.862	.007	.509
	State Location	-.018[b]	-.066	.947	-.003	.938
	Religiosity Index		-.269	.788	-.010	.325

a. Predictors in the Model: (Constant), Age, Gender

b. Predictors in the Model: (Constant), Age, Gender, Church Service Attendance

c. Dependent Variable: Count: How many non-traditional items are you unsure about buying?

Practical Implications

The theoretical and practical implications of this study include, but are not limited to, a better understanding of the role that religious iconography plays in the life of the consumer, the development of more precisely targeted markets by business planners, more effective promotions, fundraisers, and recruitment campaigns conducted by churches, and a foundation for further study of the best practices for marketing religious iconography.

The commercialization of religious icons has reduced them to the objects of fundamental commercial marketing strategies and goals by capitalizing on resource efficiency rather than the needs and desires of the target market. At the most basic level, religious iconography has become a fictionalized symbol secondary to a fundamental business relationship, a marketed contract outlining

191

the commercial interests toward the marketing end goal to optimize sales through the use of "common consumer solution sets," helping to increase sales of other items and, thus, increasing profit. When mass-produced objects fail to align with the interests of the consumer, marketing efforts lose effectiveness as the target market looks for meaningful objects to purchase in order to fulfill its needs and desires.

The evolution of religious iconography that once exclusively inhabited the religious domain has permutated into a multibillion-dollar commercialized industry. The omnipresence of religious iconography has saturated our familiar world with passionate symbolism. This ubiquitous commercialization of iconographic images and symbolism has established a unique system of marketing conventions and principles that organize the visible characteristics of the marketing principles while requiring critical and independent analysis, organization, and documentation.

The emergence of innovative ideas such as those advocated in this research study lead to the formulation of an essential ingredient in the process of strategic change. The inventive process provides impetus to transform the old methods of marketing to a new creative level. The purpose of this research is to examine varieties of the innovative marketing process that discover new effective paths to strategy and emergent strategic marketing techniques and methodologies.

There are four Social behavior perceived to be good cultural Events, Self-improvement, Donating to Charity, and Worship/Bible enjoyment.

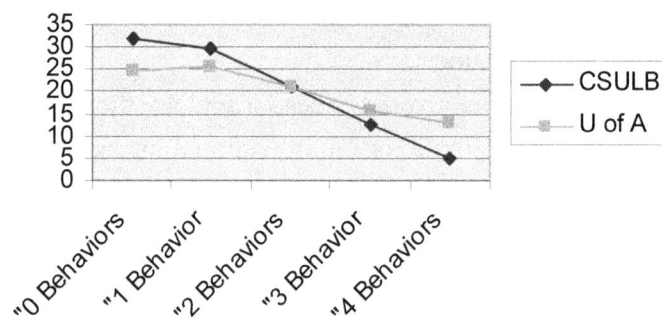

FIGURE 11. Social behavior perceived to be good, by state, variables independent, control, and dependent.

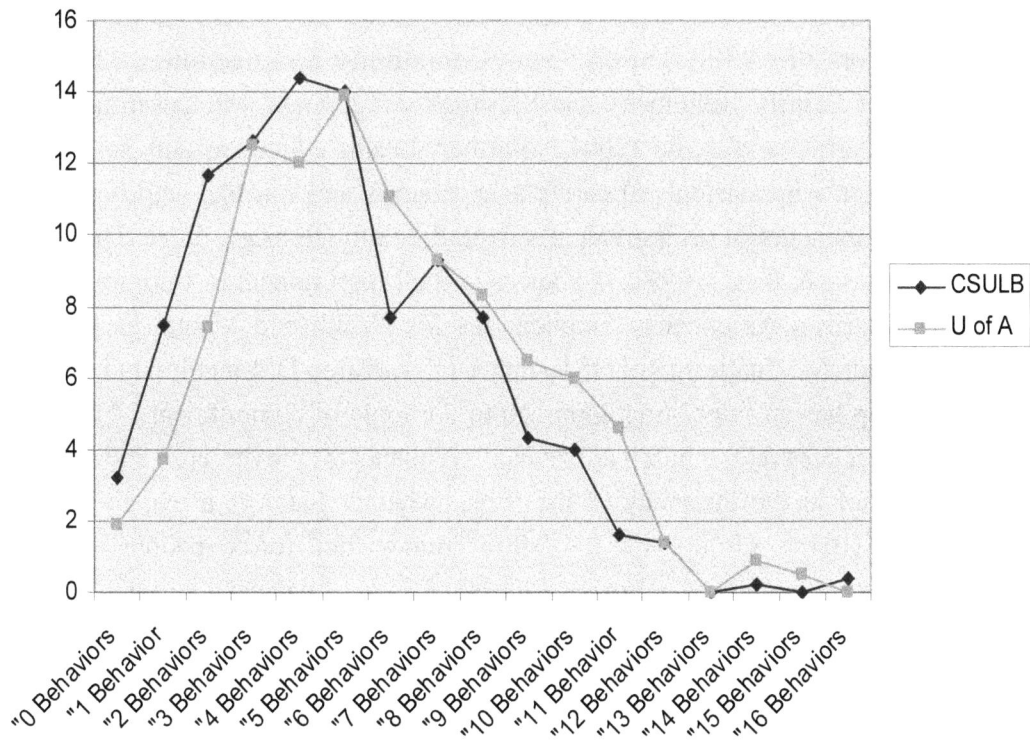

FIGURE 12. Social behavior perceived to be bad, by state, variables independent, control, and dependent

CHAPTER 14

DISCUSSION

The religiosity Index utilizes a permutation of comparable multi-dimensional indicators used in four academic studies: (1) the (May 2007) study of The Influence of Religiosity on Contraceptive Use among Roman Catholic Women in the United States (Ohlendorf and Fehring, May 2007). (2) the (2005) study of Indicators of Child, Family, and Community Connections: The Measurement of Family Religiosity and Spirituality (Lippman, Michelsen, and Roehlekepartain, 2005). (3) the (2001) "Further, health education and health promotion efforts are increasingly attentive to spirituality and spiritual well-being as important components of an individual's overall health (Bensley, 1991; Diax, 1993; Waite, Hawks & Gast, 1999). Advances in the Measurement of Religiosity Among Older African Americans: Implications for Health and Mental Health Researchers, Linda M. Chatters, Robert Joseph Taylor, Karen D. Lincoln; and (4) "the Barna Group has an interesting approach to the topic of commitment. They evaluate eight practices (e.g., church attendance, frequency of prayer, etc.) and ten beliefs (e.g., belief in the inerrancy of the Bible, whether Satan is a real living entity, etc.)." (Barna Group, n.d.): More money but fewer people" at: http://www.barna.org/cgi-bin/PagePress Release.asp? "Annual survey of America's faith shows no significant changes in past year," 1999-MAR-8, at: http://www.barna.org/cgi-bin/PagePress Release.asp?, "An inside look at today's churches reveals current statistics on Protestant churches," 1997-Oct.-30, at: http://www.barna.org/cgi-bin/PagePressRelease.asp?

The CAGS survey question 16a that reads: "Which if any of the following persons' recommendations influenced your decision to purchase the items from the product list" measures those respondents who are influenced by Clergy Survey question 23a reads: "Which of the following forms of Printed Media influenced your decision to purchase" measures those respondents who are influenced by "religious printed media." The concept of the influence of "Clergy" and religious "Printed Media" in the context of questions 16a and 23a is not dissimilar to the employment of the conceptual use of Influence as utilized in the study of The (2007) Influence of Religiosity on Contraceptive Use among Roman Catholic Women in the United States (Ohlendorf and Fehring, May 2007).

195

There also, Dr. Fehring is Professor and Director, Marquette University College of Nursing Institute for Natural Family Planning.

The Influence of Religiosity on Contraceptive Use among Roman Catholic Women in the United States found that "there seems to be some influence of religion on the family planning choices of RC women." The two conceptual utilizations of influence closely resemble each other, but the influence in the study of Religiosity on Contraceptive Use among Roman Catholics conceptually rates stronger than questions 16a and 23a in the CAGS study. However, degree of intensity is of negligible significance in the context of degree as this study further validates the role of "religious influences" as an important component of the religiosity Index.

The greatest number of religiosity indicator questions 5): (20a, Influence of religious printed media. 46a 6). Purchased item for special enlightenment purposes. 47a, Respondent classified themselves as seriously religious. 51a, Respondent classified themselves as very religious. 51b Respondent enjoys worship/Bible. 86a, Respondent believes in life after death. 129a.) parallel similar indicators worthy of comparison appear in the 2005 study: Indicators of Child, Family, and Community Connections: The Measurement of Family Religiosity and Spirituality (Lippman, Michelsen, and Roehlekepartain, 2005). The CAGS survey question 20a (Did your Sunday School/Church Education influence your decision to purchase?) measures the influence of church education. The influence of church education is paralleled in the 2005 study, which uses religious education indicators in "1 Learning more about religion, and attitudes about one's house of worship/interest in learning more about religion . . ."

In the CAGS survey, question 46a measures religiosity in terms of a person's belief in the use of religious iconography for worship purposes. The 2005 study (Indicators of Child, Family and Community Connections . . .) is equal in most respects, since it uses, for example, ". . . belief in the inerrancy of the Bible, whether Satan is a real living entity, etc.), and specific religious practices across religions and spiritual practices (e.g., the presence of religious altars in the home)" as indicators which can compare with the purpose of CAGS question. Beyond the 2005 study, the Barna Group uses "Believer commitment" as an additional indicator that parallels the use of CAGS survey question 46a (Select all the purposes for which you purchased the items listed in the product list: Purchased item for worship purposes). Likewise, CAGS question 47a (Select all the purposes for which you purchased the items listed in the product list: Purchased item for special enlightenment purposes) is comparable to the similar findings of the (2001) research Advances in the Measurement of Religiosity Among Older African Americans: Implications for Health and Mental Health by Researchers, Linda M. Chatters, Robert Joseph Taylor, Karen D. Lincoln.

Questions 51a and 51b of the CAGS survey are nearly identical in meaning to the 2005 study of Indicators of Child, Family, and Community Connections . . . which measures "religious identity" (i.e., "Do you think of yourself as a religious person?") as an indicator. The CAGS survey question 51a asks respondents whether they classify themselves as "seriously religious," and CAGS survey question 51b allows the respondents to choose a lesser degree of "very religious" which is comparable to the 2005 study in regard to their "religious identity." CAGS survey question 129a asks respondents about belief in life after death, similarly to the 2005 study, which delves into "the nature and influence of religious beliefs / religious beliefs (e.g., life after death, existence of angels, miracles, beliefs about God, moving spiritual experiences, personal commitment to live one's life for God)."

Two indicators used in this research study utilized CAGS question num--ber 29a as an indicator of religiosity. CAGS question 29a is centered on the perceived value of spirituality (question 29a: Which of the following influenced your decision to purchase items from the product list? Spiritual value), and for this purpose, the CAGS question uses "spiritual value" similarly to an indicator in a study researched by Linda M. Chatters, Robert Joseph Taylor, and Karen D. Lincoln on Advances in the Measurement of Religiosity Among Older African Americans: Implications for Health and Mental Health (2001) did, which specifically cited that "Further, health education and health promotion efforts are increasingly attentive to spirituality and spiritual well-being as important components of an individual's overall health (Bensley, 1991; Diax, 1993; Waite, Hawks & Gast, 1999). CAGS question 86a is centered on the respondents' perceived enjoyment of worship, question 86a: (I enjoy [Select all that apply.]: worship / Bible); for this study the CAGS question is used as an indicator of religiosity. This indicator of "worship enjoyment" is supported by comparable usage in the Barna Group, which "evaluate eight practices (e.g., church attendance, frequency of prayer, etc.), and ten beliefs (e.g., belief in the inerrancy of the Bible, whether Satan is a real living entity, etc.)." Questions 103a and 103b (I attend church services: a More than weekly and b Weekly) [sic] are centered on respondents' perceived practices; for this study the CAGS question 103 (all answers were used) is used as an indicator of religiosity.

CHAPTER 15

CONCLUSIONS

The CAGS survey found a correlation between the respondents' Consumer Social Behaviors viewed as vices by religious organizations and their propensity to purchase religious iconography. This correlation may be used by business enterprises to identify target markets for religious iconography, as well as to design their product lines. The multidimensional method utilized in this survey offers improvement in the identification and classification of the target market for religious iconography and compares past studies that utilized unidimensional methods.

Limitations, Sources of Bias

This survey was applied to a small sample of the population, consisting of students at two universities. The demographic characteristics, including race, gender, and age groups, varied. The total number of respondents was less than 1,000 (494 California State University, Long Beach, students and 216 University of Arkansas, but that sample does provide a meaningful starting point for further research.) A survey of a larger group might provide stronger evidence in support of these findings. "The role of religiousness as a variable in models of consumer marketing behavior is not well-established. Research findings in this area tend to be sparse and conflicting, and measurement issues have yet to be addressed." (Wilkes et al., 1986). This study has laid the foundation for future research in this area.

It should be noted that the Consumer Social Behaviors viewed as vices may, in fact, be virtues to others. These behaviors will need to be further explored in respect to study participants.

The use of students in the CAGS survey does limit the general demographic findings, since there are specialized characteristics unique to students from the general population. It is widely accepted that collegiate students have limited to lower incomes, are younger, and more educated than the general population. This reflects a limitation to the research study.

A source of bias is shown in the social consumer behaviors vice "playing sports" (survey questionnaire items 71 through 90) because it is understood that playing sports also has a positive influence in encouraging participants to remain healthy and physically engaged. However, this research study has found that playing sports can be both a vice and a virtue. For the purposes of this research, playing sports is defined as a vice. This is not to say that it does not acknowledge that this may be seen as a bias.

APPENDIX A

SUMMARY STEPWISE MULTIPLE REGRESSION TABLES
FOR TRADITIONAL ICONOGRAPHY

TABLE A1. Summary Stepwise Multiple Regression Table for Traditional Iconography Status[1]

Step	Own Item	Don't Own Would Buy	Don't Own Won't Buy	Unsure
1	Gender, Age[2]	Gender, Age	Gender, Age	Gender, Age
2	Relig. Index (14.8%)[3]	Social Vices (6.4%)	Relig. Index (16.2%)	Church Atten. (1.1%)
3	State Location	State Location	Social Vices	—
4	Social Vices	—	Social Virtues	—
5	Church Attendance	—	—	—
6	Religious Attendance	—	—	—
Mean[4]	2.78	1.38	2.18	0.48
S.D.	2.26	1.72	2.34	1.19
Range	0 to 7	0 to 7	0 to 7	0 to 7
Adj R^2	21.0%	7.1%	20.5%	1.2%

     1. Status consists of four categories: Respondent owns the item, Don't Own – Will Buy, Don't Own – Won't Buy, and Unsure. Traditional items include: Painting or Print, Statuette, Pendant or Medal, Holy Book, Cross, Crucifix, Rosary.

     2. Control variables: Gender, Age.

     3. Step 2 accounts for the greatest amount of variance for each analysis (Adjusted R Square scores are in parentheses). The Religiosity Index appears as the best predictor in two of four outcome variables.

     4. The mean, standard deviation, range, and adjusted R squared are for each of the status categories. See Tables 15–18 for standardized coefficients.

TABLE A2. Summary Stepwise Multiple Regression Table for Non-Traditional Iconography[1]

Step	Own Item	Don't Own Would Buy	Don't Own Won't Buy	Unsure
1	Gender, Age[2]	Gender, Age	Gender, Age	Gender, Age
2	Relig. Index (33.1%)[3]	Relig. Index (2.8%)	Relig. Index (31.2%)	Church Atten. (1.4%)
3	Social Virtues	Social Vices	—	—
4	—	—	—	—
5	—	—	—	—
6	—	—	—	—
Mean[4]	1.39	1.17	2.03	0.29
S.D.	1.36	1.19	1.69	0.78
Range	0 to 5	0 to 5	0 to 5	0 to 5
Adj R^2	35.8%	4.9%	32.1%	1.4%

1. Status consists of four categories: Respondent owns the item, Don't Own—Will Buy, Don't Own—Won't Buy, and Unsure. Non-traditional items include: DVD or VCR Movie, Music CD, Jewelry Other, Religious Books, Bumper Sticker.

2. Control variables: Gender, Age.

3. Step 2 accounts for the greatest amount of variance for each analysis (Adjusted R Square scores are in parentheses). The Religiosity Index appears as the best predictor in two of four outcome variables.

4. The mean, standard deviation, range, and adjusted R squared are for each of the status categories. See Tables 19–22 for standardized coefficients.

APPENDIX B

DISTRIBUTION PERCENTAGE TABLES

TABLE B1. Percent Distribution of Gender, Age, Marital Status, and Ethnicity by State

		State Location			
		California		Arkansas	
		Count	Col. N %	Count	Col. N %
Gender	Males	224	45.8%	134	64.1%
	Females	265	54.2%	75	35.9%
	Total	489	100.0%	209	100.0%
Age	< 24 years	326	68.2%	136	65.4%
	25–29 years	89	18.6%	38	18.3%
	30–34 years	36	7.5%	22	10.6%
	35 years or older	27	5.6%	12	5.8%
	Total	478	100.0%	208	100.0%
Marital Status	Single	419	84.8%	151	69.9%
	Married	58	11.7%	52	24.1%
	Other	17	3.4%	13	6.0%
	Total	494	100.0%	216	100.0%
Ethnicity	African-American	13	2.7%	5	2.3%
	Asian/Pacific Islander	154	31.5%	15	7.0%
	Hispanic	107	21.9%	10	4.7%
	European Descent	64	13.1%	31	14.6%
	American	58	11.9%	127	59.6%
	Other	93	19.0%	25	11.7%
	Total	489	100.0%	213	100.0%

TABLE B2. Pearson Chi-Square Tests

		State Location
Gender	Chi-square	19.642
	df	1
	Sig.	.000[*]
Age	Chi-square	1.774
	df	3
	Sig.	.621
Marital Status	Chi-square	21.279
	df	2
	Sig.	.000[*]
Ethnicity	Chi-square	196.554
	df	5
	Sig.	.000[*]

Results are based on non-empty rows and columns in each innermost subtable.
*The Chi-square statistic is significant at the 0.05 level.

TABLE B3. Percent Distribution of Annual Income, Employment Status, College Graduation Status, and Class Status by State

| | | State Location | | | |
| | | California | | Arkansas | |
		Count	Col. N %	Count	Col. N %
Annual Income	$9,999 or below	191	41.4%	80	41.5%
	$10,000 to $19,999	126	27.3%	29	15.0%
	$20,000 to $29,999	64	13.9%	20	10.4%
	$30,000 or higher	80	17.4%	64	33.2%
	Total	461	100.0%	193	100.0%
Employment Status	Sales/Marketing	73	14.8%	43	19.9%
	Clerical/Retail/Service	76	15.4%	24	11.1%
	Middle-Upper Management	25	5.1%	37	17.1%
	No Response	320	64.8%	112	51.9%
	Total	494	100.0%	216	100.0%
College Grad Status	Business	319	64.6%	190	88.0%
	Arts, Education & Engineering	72	14.6%	15	6.9%
	No Response	103	20.9%	11	5.1%
	Total	494	100.0%	216	100.0%
Class Status	Freshman	7	1.4%	0	.0%
	Sophomore	25	5.1%	2	1.0%
	Junior	146	30.0%	95	45.5%
	Senior	284	58.4%	37	17.7%
	Graduate	24	4.9%	75	35.9%
	Total	486	100.0%	209	100.0%

TABLE B4. Pearson Chi-Square Tests

		State Location
Annual Income	Chi-square	25.444
	df	3
	Sig.	.000[*]
Employment Status	Chi-square	33.564
	df	3
	Sig.	.000[*]
College Graduation Status	Chi-square	41.849
	df	2
	Sig.	.000[*]
Class Status	Chi-square	170.381
	df	4
	Sig.	.000[*,a]

Results are based on non-empty rows and columns in each innermost subtable.
*The Chi-square statistic is significant at the 0.05 level.
a. More than 20% of cells in this subtable have expected cell counts less than 5. Chi-square results may be invalid.

TABLE B5. Percent Distribution of "Owned Iconography" by State

		State Location			
		California		Arkansas	
		Count	Col. N %	Count	Col. N %
Iconography Owned	DVD or VHS	118	28.5%	55	27.2%
	Music CD	137	33.1%	91	45.0%
	Painting or print	159	38.4%	52	25.7%
	Statuette	153	37.0%	50	24.8%
	Pendant or medal	201	48.6%	78	38.6%
	Jewelry Other	202	48.8%	84	41.6%
	Holy Book	357	86.2%	189	93.6%
	Book Other	162	39.1%	103	51.0%
	Bumper sticker	22	5.3%	16	7.9%
	Cross	229	55.3%	109	54.0%
	Crucifix	159	38.4%	40	19.8%
	Rosary	151	36.5%	44	21.8%
	Other	123	29.7%	45	22.3%
	Total	414	100.0%	202	100.0%

TABLE B6. Pearson Chi-Square Tests

		State Location
Iconography Owned	Chi-square	91.041
	df	13
	Sig.	.000[*]

Results are based on non-empty rows and columns in each innermost subtable.
*The Chi-square statistic is significant at the 0.05 level.

TABLE B7. Percent Distribution of "Do Not Own, Would Buy" Iconography by State

		State Location			
		California		Arkansas	
		Count	Col. N %	Count	Col. N %
Don't Own, Would Buy	DVD or VHS	165	47.4%	98	56.3%
	Music CD	93	26.7%	52	29.9%
	Painting or print	141	40.5%	102	58.6%
	Statuette	108	31.0%	65	37.4%
	Pendant or medal	96	27.6%	52	29.9%
	Jewelry Other	100	28.7%	54	31.0%
	Holy Book	40	11.5%	9	5.2%
	Book Other	88	25.3%	38	21.8%
	Bumper sticker	100	28.7%	40	23.0%
	Cross	71	20.4%	54	31.0%
	Crucifix	80	23.0%	58	33.3%
	Rosary	66	19.0%	34	19.5%
	Other	106	30.5%	61	35.1%
	Total	348	100.0%	174	100.0%

TABLE B8. Pearson Chi-Square Tests

		State Location
Don't Own, Would Buy	Chi-square	45.119
	df	13
	Sig.	.000[*]

Results are based on non-empty rows and columns in each innermost subtable.
*The Chi-square statistic is significant at the 0.05 level.

TABLE B9. Percent Distribution of "Do Not Own, Would Not Buy" Iconography by State

		State Location			
		California		Arkansas	
		Count	Col. N %	Count	Col. N %
Don't Own, Won't Buy	DVD or VHS	168	39.7%	46	26.1%
	Music CD	229	54.1%	62	35.2%
	Painting or print	145	34.3%	39	22.2%
	Statuette	180	42.6%	69	39.2%
	Pendant or medal	151	35.7%	64	36.4%
	Jewelry Other	140	33.1%	61	34.7%
	Holy Book	72	17.0%	11	6.3%
	Book Other	204	48.2%	62	35.2%
	Bumper sticker	333	78.7%	136	77.3%
	Cross	158	37.4%	34	19.3%
	Crucifix	200	47.3%	88	50.0%
	Rosary	229	54.1%	105	59.7%
	Other	181	42.8%	63	35.8%
	Total	423	100.0%	176	100.0%

TABLE B10. Pearson Chi-Square Tests

		State Location
Don't Own, Won't Buy	Chi-square	80.810
	df	13
	Sig.	.000*

Results are based on non-empty rows and columns in each innermost subtable.
*The Chi-square statistic is significant at the 0.05 level.

210

TABLE B11. Percent Distribution of "Unsure" Iconography by State

| | | State Location | | | |
| | | California | | Arkansas | |
		Count	Col. N %	Count	Col. N %
Unsure	DVD or VHS	34	23.4%	14	20.9%
	Music CD	22	15.2%	6	9.0%
	Painting or print	37	25.5%	18	26.9%
	Statuette	37	25.5%	25	37.3%
	Pendant or medal	31	21.4%	18	26.9%
	Jewelry Other	36	24.8%	13	19.4%
	Holy Book	13	9.0%	4	6.0%
	Book Other	27	18.6%	8	11.9%
	Bumper sticker	26	17.9%	19	28.4%
	Cross	20	13.8%	11	16.4%
	Crucifix	38	26.2%	24	35.8%
	Rosary	35	24.1%	27	40.3%
	Other	72	49.7%	40	59.7%
	Total	145	100.0%	67	100.0%

TABLE B12. Pearson Chi-Square Tests

		State Location
Unsure	Chi-square	21.336
	df	13
	Sig.	.067

Results are based on non-empty rows and columns in each innermost subtable.

TABLE B13. Percent Distribution of Roof and McKinney Divisions by State

| | | State Location | | | |
| | | California | | Arkansas | |
		Count	Col. N %	Count	Col. N %
Roof and McKinney	Liberal Protestants	19	4.1%	17	8.2%
	Moderate Protestants	65	13.9%	32	15.5%
	Black Protestants	1	.2%	5	2.4%
	Conservative Protestants	21	4.5%	57	27.5%
	Catholics	155	33.3%	40	19.3%
	Others	7	1.5%	3	1.4%
	No Religious Preference	66	14.2%	16	7.7%
	Other Christian	42	9.0%	20	9.7%
	Secular / Agnostic / Atheist	29	6.2%	9	4.3%
	Other Non-Christians	61	13.1%	8	3.9%
	Total	466	100.0%	207	100.0%

TABLE B14. Pearson Chi-Square Tests

		State Location
Roof and McKinney Divisions	Chi-square	105.525
	df	9
	Sig.	.000[*]

Results are based on non-empty rows and columns in each innermost subtable.
*The Chi-square statistic is significant at the 0.05 level.

TABLE B15. Percent Distribution of World Christian Encyclopedia Divisions by State

		California		Arkansas	
		Count	Col. N %	Count	Col. N %
World Christian Encyclopedia	Angelicans	8	1.7%	8	3.9%
	Protestants	98	21.0%	103	49.8%
	Catholics	155	33.3%	40	19.3%
	Marginal Protestants	7	1.5%	3	1.4%
	Independent Christians	66	14.2%	16	7.7%
	Orthodox	42	9.0%	20	9.7%
	No Preference	0	.0%	0	.0%
	Secular / Agnostic / Atheist	29	6.2%	9	4.3%
	Other Non-Christian	61	13.1%	8	3.9%
	Total	466	100.0%	207	100.0%

TABLE B16. Pearson Chi-Square Tests

		State Location
World Christian Encyclopedia Divisions	Chi-square	69.728
	df	7
	Sig.	.000[*,a]

Results are based on non-empty rows and columns in each innermost subtable.

*The Chi-square statistic is significant at the 0.05 level.

a. More than 20% of cells in this subtable have expected cell counts less than 5. Chi-square results may be invalid.

TABLE B17. Percent Distribution of the Religiosity Index, Social Virtues and Social Vices by State

		State Location					
		California		Arkansas		Total	
		Count	Col. N %	Count	Col. N %	Count	Col. N %
Religiosity Index	Low	292	59.1%	69	31.9%	361	50.8%
	High	202	40.9%	147	68.1%	349	49.2%
	Total	494	100.0%	216	100.0%	710	100.0%
Social Virtues	Low	303	61.3%	108	50.0%	411	57.9%
	High	191	38.7%	108	50.0%	299	42.1%
	Total	494	100.0%	216	100.0%	710	100.0%
Social Vices	Low	244	49.4%	81	37.5%	325	45.8%
	High	250	50.6%	135	62.5%	385	54.2%
	Total	494	100.0%	216	100.0%	710	100.0%

TABLE B18. Pearson Chi-Square Tests

		State Location
Religiosity Index	Chi-square	44.373
	df	1
	Sig.	.000[*]
Social Virtues	Chi-square	7.922
	df	1
	Sig.	.005[*]
Social Vices	Chi-square	8.564
	df	1
	Sig.	.003[*]

Results are based on non-empty rows and columns in each innermost subtable.

*The Chi-square statistic is significant at the 0.05 level.

TABLE B19. Percent Distribution of Religiosity Measures (1–5) by State

		State Location			
		California		Arkansas	
		Count	Col. N %	Count	Col. N %
Level of Religiousness	Unsure/Not	167	33.8%	34	15.7%
	Somewhat	232	47.0%	108	50.0%
	Very	69	14.0%	55	25.5%
	Seriously	26	5.3%	19	8.8%
	Total	494	100.0%	216	100.0%
Church Attendance	Less than Weekly	373	75.5%	145	67.1%
	Weekly or More	121	24.5%	71	32.9%
	Total	494	100.0%	216	100.0%
Religious Attendance	Never	141	28.5%	36	16.7%
	1–2 Visits/Year	126	25.5%	27	12.5%
	Occasionally	141	28.5%	88	40.7%
	Nearly every week or more	86	17.4%	65	30.1%
	Total	494	100.0%	216	100.0%
Enjoy Worship/Bible	No	372	75.3%	105	48.6%
	Yes	122	24.7%	111	51.4%
	Total	494	100.0%	216	100.0%
Do you believe there is life after death?	Not Applicable	47	9.5%	15	6.9%
	No	50	10.1%	14	6.5%
	Unsure	93	18.8%	24	11.1%
	Yes	304	61.5%	163	75.5%
	Total	494	100.0%	216	100.0%

TABLE B20. Pearson Chi-Square Tests

		State Location
Religiousness Level	Chi-square	31.945
	df	3
	Sig.	.000[*]
Church Attendance	Chi-square	5.345
	df	1
	Sig.	.021[*]
Religious Attendance	Chi-square	38.601
	df	3
	Sig.	.000[*]
Enjoy Worship/Bible	Chi-square	48.567
	df	1
	Sig.	.000[*]
Do you believe there is life after death?	Chi-square	13.204
	df	3
	Sig.	.004[*]

Results are based on non-empty rows and columns in each innermost subtable.
*The Chi-square statistic is significant at the 0.05 level.

TABLE B21. Percent Distribution of Religiosity Measures (6–11) by State

| | | State Location | | | |
| | | California | | Arkansas | |
		Count	Col. N %	Count	Col. N %
Clergy	No	462	93.5%	182	84.3%
	Yes	32	6.5%	34	15.7%
	Total	494	100.0%	216	100.0%
Church Education	No	334	67.6%	108	50.0%
	Yes	160	32.4%	108	50.0%
	Total	494	100.0%	216	100.0%
Church Newsletters	No	460	93.1%	192	88.9%
	Yes	34	6.9%	24	11.1%
	Total	494	100.0%	216	100.0%
Spiritual Value	No	286	57.9%	81	37.5%
	Yes	208	42.1%	135	62.5%
	Total	494	100.0%	216	100.0%
Worship	No	346	70.0%	111	51.4%
	Yes	148	30.0%	105	48.6%
	Total	494	100.0%	216	100.0%
Special Enlightenment	No	361	73.1%	134	62.0%
	Yes	133	26.9%	82	38.0%
	Total	494	100.0%	216	100.0%

TABLE B22. Pearson Chi-Square Tests

		State Location
Clergy	Chi-square	15.294
	df	1
	Sig.	.000[*]
Church Education	Chi-square	19.837
	df	1
	Sig.	.000[*]
Church Newsletters	Chi-square	3.582
	df	1
	Sig.	.058
Spiritual Value	Chi-square	25.033
	df	1
	Sig.	.000[*]
Worship	Chi-square	22.795
	df	1
	Sig.	.000[*]
Special Enlightenment	Chi-square	8.676
	df	1
	Sig.	.003[*]

Results are based on non-empty rows and columns in each innermost subtable.
*The Chi-square statistic is significant at the 0.05 level.

218

TABLE B23. Percent Distribution of Influential Factors of Iconography Purchases by State

| | | State Location | | | |
| | | California | | Arkansas | |
		Count	Col. N %	Count	Col. N %
Influence Decision	Clergy	32	11.8%	34	21.3%
	Church Education	160	58.8%	108	67.5%
	Church Newsletters	34	12.5%	24	15.0%
	Spiritual Value	208	76.5%	135	84.4%
	Total	272	100.0%	160	100.0%

TABLE B24. Pearson Chi-Square Tests

		State Location
Influence Decision	Chi-square	14.612
	df	4
	Sig.	.006[*]

Results are based on non-empty rows and columns in each innermost subtable.
*The Chi-square statistic is significant at the 0.05 level.

TABLE B25. Percent Distribution of Purposes for Purchased Iconography by State

		State Location			
		California		Arkansas	
		Count	Col. N %	Count	Col. N %
Purpose of Purchase	Worship	148	65.2%	105	77.2%
	Special Enlightenment	133	58.6%	82	60.3%
	Total	227	100.0%	136	100.0%

TABLE B26. Pearson Chi-Square Tests

		State Location
Purpose of Purchase	Chi-square	5.908
	df	2
	Sig.	.052

Results are based on non-empty rows and columns in each innermost subtable.

TABLE B27. Percent Distribution of Expected Users of Purchased Iconography by State

| | | State Location | | | |
| | | California | | Arkansas | |
		Count	Col. N %	Count	Col. N %
Household Member	Self	233	58.4%	142	75.5%
	Spouse	42	10.5%	45	23.9%
	Household	52	13.0%	44	23.4%
	Parent	190	47.6%	78	41.5%
	Grandparent	67	16.8%	45	23.9%
	Sibling	82	20.6%	48	25.5%
	Child 2–17	27	6.8%	24	12.8%
	Infant < 2	6	1.5%	10	5.3%
	Roommate	31	7.8%	31	16.5%
	Other Adult	50	12.5%	24	12.8%
	Total	399	100.0%	188	100.0%

TABLE B28. Pearson Chi-Square Tests

		State Location
Household Member	Chi-square	75.618
	df	10
	Sig.	.000[*]

Results are based on non-empty rows and columns in each innermost subtable.
*The Chi-square statistic is significant at the 0.05 level.

TABLE B29. Percent Distribution of Consumer Social Behaviors by State

| | | State Location | | | |
| | | California | | Arkansas | |
		Count	Col. N %	Count	Col. N %
Social Behaviors	Cigarette/Cigars	85	17.6%	49	23.0%
	Dancing	242	50.1%	100	46.9%
	Beer, wine, etc.	246	50.9%	149	70.0%
	Concerts	275	56.9%	149	70.0%
	Night clubbing	198	41.0%	102	47.9%
	Video Games	199	41.2%	93	43.7%
	TV Shopping	34	7.0%	11	5.2%
	Computer/Internet	326	67.5%	160	75.1%
	Self-improvement	227	47.0%	106	49.8%
	Cultural Events	178	36.9%	76	35.7%
	Casino Gambling	152	31.5%	67	31.5%
	Lottery/Sweepstakes	61	12.6%	27	12.7%
	Astrology/Horoscope	94	19.5%	33	15.5%
	Tarot Cards	31	6.4%	8	3.8%
	Psychic Readings	34	7.0%	9	4.2%
	Enjoy Worship/Bible	122	25.3%	111	52.1%
	Politics	102	21.1%	69	32.4%
	Donating to charity	112	23.2%	68	31.9%
	Hunting/Shooting	49	10.1%	62	29.1%
	Watch/play Sports	301	62.3%	160	75.1%
	Total	483	100.0%	213	100.0%

TABLE B30. Pearson Chi-Square Tests

		State Location
Social Behaviors	Chi-square	164.318
	df	20
	Sig.	.000[*]

Results are based on non-empty rows and columns in each innermost subtable.

*The Chi-square statistic is significant at the 0.05 level.

222

APPENDIX C

CASE PROCESSING AND CROSS-TAB TABLES

APPENDIX C

TABLE C1.

Case Processing Summary

	Cases					
	Valid		Missing		Total	
	N	Percent	N	Percent	N	Percent
Clergy * State Location	710	100.0%	0	.0%	710	100.0%
Church Education * State Location	710	100.0%	0	.0%	710	100.0%
Church Newsletters * State Location	710	100.0%	0	.0%	710	100.0%
Spiritual Value * State Location	710	100.0%	0	.0%	710	100.0%

TABLE C2. Clergy * State Location

Crosstab

| | | | State Location | | Total |
			California	Arkansas	
Clergy	No	Count	462	182	644
		% within Clergy	71.7%	28.3%	100.0%
		% within State Location	93.5%	84.3%	90.7%
		% of Total	65.1%	25.6%	90.7%
	Yes	Count	32	34	66
		% within Clergy	48.5%	51.5%	100.0%
		% within State Location	6.5%	15.7%	9.3%
		% of Total	4.5%	4.8%	9.3%
Total		Count	494	216	710
		% within Clergy	69.6%	30.4%	100.0%
		% within State Location	100.0%	100.0%	100.0%
		% of Total	69.6%	30.4%	100.0%

TABLE C3

Chi-Square Tests

	Value	df	Asymp. Sig. (2-sided)	Exact Sig. (2-sided)	Exact Sig. (1-sided)
Pearson Chi-Square	15.294[a]	1	.000		
Continuity Correction[b]	14.215	1	.000		
Likelihood Ratio	14.141	1	.000		
Fisher's Exact Test				.000	.000
Linear-by-Linear Association	15.272	1	.000		
N of Valid Cases	710				

a. 0 cells (.0%) have expected count less than 5. The minimum expected count is 20.08.

b. Computed only for a 2x2 table

TABLE C4. Church Education * State Location

Crosstab

| | | | State Location | | Total |
			California	Arkansas	
Church Education	No	Count	334	108	442
		% within Church Education	75.6%	24.4%	100.0%
		% within State Location	67.6%	50.0%	62.3%
		% of Total	47.0%	15.2%	62.3%
	Yes	Count	160	108	268
		% within Church Education	59.7%	40.3%	100.0%
		% within State Location	32.4%	50.0%	37.7%
		% of Total	22.5%	15.2%	37.7%
Total		Count	494	216	710
		% within Church Education	69.6%	30.4%	100.0%
		% within State Location	100.0%	100.0%	100.0%
		% of Total	69.6%	30.4%	100.0%

TABLE C5

Chi-Square Tests

	Value	df	Asymp. Sig. (2-sided)	Exact Sig. (2-sided)	Exact Sig. (1-sided)
Pearson Chi-Square	19.837[a]	1	.000		
Continuity Correction[b]	19.094	1	.000		
Likelihood Ratio	19.542	1	.000		
Fisher's Exact Test				.000	.000
Linear-by-Linear Association	19.809	1	.000		
N of Valid Cases	710				

a. 0 cells (.0%) have expected count less than 5. The minimum expected count is 81.53.

b. Computed only for a 2x2 table

TABLE C6. Church Newsletters * State Location

Crosstab

			State Location		Total
			California	Arkansas	
Church Newsletters	No	Count	460	192	652
		% within Church Newsletters	70.6%	29.4%	100.0%
		% within State Location	93.1%	88.9%	91.8%
		% of Total	64.8%	27.0%	91.8%
	Yes	Count	34	24	58
		% within Church Newsletters	58.6%	41.4%	100.0%
		% within State Location	6.9%	11.1%	8.2%
		% of Total	4.8%	3.4%	8.2%
Total		Count	494	216	710
		% within Church Newsletters	69.6%	30.4%	100.0%
		% within State Location	100.0%	100.0%	100.0%
		% of Total	69.6%	30.4%	100.0%

TABLE C7. Chi-Square Tests

Chi-Square Tests

	Value	df	Asymp. Sig. (2-sided)	Exact Sig. (2-sided)	Exact Sig. (1-sided)
Pearson Chi-Square	3.582 [a]	1	.058		
Continuity Correction[b]	3.041	1	.081		
Likelihood Ratio	3.407	1	.065		
Fisher's Exact Test				.073	.043
Linear-by-Linear Association	3.577	1	.059		
N of Valid Cases	710				

a. 0 cells (.0%) have expected count less than 5. The minimum expected count is 17.65.

b. Computed only for a 2x2 table

TABLE C8. Spiritual Value * State Location

Crosstab

			State Location		Total
			California	Arkansas	
Spiritual Value	No	Count	286	81	367
		% within Spiritual Value	77.9%	22.1%	100.0%
		% within State Location	57.9%	37.5%	51.7%
		% of Total	40.3%	11.4%	51.7%
	Yes	Count	208	135	343
		% within Spiritual Value	60.6%	39.4%	100.0%
		% within State Location	42.1%	62.5%	48.3%
		% of Total	29.3%	19.0%	48.3%
Total		Count	494	216	710
		% within Spiritual Value	69.6%	30.4%	100.0%
		% within State Location	100.0%	100.0%	100.0%
		% of Total	69.6%	30.4%	100.0%

TABLE C9

Chi-Square Tests

	Value	df	Asymp. Sig. (2-sided)	Exact Sig. (2-sided)	Exact Sig. (1-sided)
Pearson Chi-Square	25.033[a]	1	.000		
Continuity Correction[b]	24.223	1	.000		
Likelihood Ratio	25.200	1	.000		
Fisher's Exact Test				.000	.000
Linear-by-Linear Association	24.998	1	.000		
N of Valid Cases	710				

a. 0 cells (.0%) have expected count less than 5. The minimum expected count is 104.35.

b. Computed only for a 2x2 table

TABLE C10

Case Processing Summary

	Cases					
	Valid		Missing		Total	
	N	Percent	N	Percent	N	Percent
Worship * State Location	710	100.0%	0	.0%	710	100.0%
Special Enlightenment *State Location	710	100.0%	0	.0%	710	100.0%

TABLE C11. Worship * State Location

Crosstab

| | | | State Location | | Total |
			California	Arkansas	
Worship	No	Count	346	111	457
		% within Worship	75.7%	24.3%	100.0%
		% within State Location	70.0%	51.4%	64.4%
		% of Total	48.7%	15.6%	64.4%
	Yes	Count	148	105	253
		% within Worship	58.5%	41.5%	100.0%
		% within State Location	30.0%	48.6%	35.6%
		% of Total	20.8%	14.8%	35.6%
Total		Count	494	216	710
		% within Worship	69.6%	30.4%	100.0%
		% within State Location	100.0%	100.0%	100.0%
		% of Total	69.6%	30.4%	100.0%

TABLE C12

Chi-Square Tests

	Value	df	Asymp. Sig. (2-sided)	Exact Sig. (2-sided)	Exact Sig. (1-sided)
Pearson Chi-Square	22.795[a]	1	.000		
Continuity Correction[b]	21.989	1	.000		
Likelihood Ratio	22.353	1	.000		
Fisher's Exact Test				.000	.000
Linear-by-Linear Association	22.763	1	.000		
N of Valid Cases	710				

a. 0 cells (.0%) have expected count less than 5. The minimum expected count is 76.97.

b. Computed only for a 2x2 table

TABLE C13. Special Enlightenment * State Location

Crosstab

| | | | State Location | | |
			California	Arkansas	Total
Special Enlightenment	No	Count	361	134	495
		% within Special Enlightenment	72.9%	27.1%	100.0%
		% within State Location	73.1%	62.0%	69.7%
		% of Total	50.8%	18.9%	69.7%
	Yes	Count	133	82	215
		% within Special Enlightenment	61.9%	38.1%	100.0%
		% within State Location	26.9%	38.0%	30.3%
		% of Total	18.7%	11.5%	30.3%
Total		Count	494	216	710
		% within Special Enlightenment	69.6%	30.4%	100.0%
		% within State Location	100.0%	100.0%	100.0%
		% of Total	69.6%	30.4%	100.0%

TABLE C14

Chi-Square Tests

	Value	df	Asymp. Sig. (2-sided)	Exact Sig. (2-sided)	Exact Sig. (1-sided)
Pearson Chi-Square	8.676[a]	1	.003		
Continuity Correction[b]	8.161	1	.004		
Likelihood Ratio	8.490	1	.004		
Fisher's Exact Test				.004	.002
Linear-by-Linear Association	8.664	1	.003		
N of Valid Cases	710				

a. 0 cells (.0%) have expected count less than 5. The minimum expected count is 65.41.

b. Computed only for a 2x2 table

Case Processing Summary

	Cases					
	Valid		Missing		Total	
	N	Percent	N	Percent	N	Percent
Self * State Location	710	100.0%	0	.0%	710	100.0%
Spouse * State Location	710	100.0%	0	.0%	710	100.0%
Household * State Location	710	100.0%	0	.0%	710	100.0%
Parent * State Location	710	100.0%	0	.0%	710	100.0%
Grandparent * State Location	710	100.0%	0	.0%	710	100.0%
Sibling * State Location	710	100.0%	0	.0%	710	100.0%
Child 2–17 * State Location	710	100.0%	0	.0%	710	100.0%
Infant < 2 * State Location	710	100.0%	0	.0%	710	100.0%
Roommate * State Location	710	100.0%	0	.0%	710	100.0%
Other Adult * State Location	710	100.0%	0	.0%	710	100.0%

TABLE C16. Self * State Location

Crosstab

			State Location		Total
			California	Arkansas	
Self	No	Count	261	74	335
		% within Self	77.9%	22.1%	100.0%
		% within State Location	52.8%	34.3%	47.2%
		% of Total	36.8%	10.4%	47.2%
	Yes	Count	233	142	375
		% within Self	62.1%	37.9%	100.0%
		% within State Location	47.2%	65.7%	52.8%
		% of Total	32.8%	20.0%	52.8%
Total		Count	494	216	710
		% within Self	69.6%	30.4%	100.0%
		% within State Location	100.0%	100.0%	100.0%
		% of Total	69.6%	30.4%	100.0%

TABLE C17. Chi-Square Tests

Chi-Square Tests

	Value	df	Asymp. Sig. (2-sided)	Exact Sig. (2-sided)	Exact Sig. (1-sided)
Pearson Chi-Square	20.807[a]	1	.000		
Continuity Correction[b]	20.068	1	.000		
Likelihood Ratio	21.109	1	.000		
Fisher's Exact Test				.000	.000
Linear-by-Linear Association	20.778	1	.000		
N of Valid Cases	710				

a. 0 cells (.0%) have expected count less than 5. The minimum expected count is 101.92.

b. Computed only for a 2x2 table

TABLE C18. Spouse * State Location

Crosstab

			State Location California	State Location Arkansas	Total
Spouse No		Count	452	171	623
		% within Spouse	72.6%	27.4%	100.0%
		% within State Location	91.5%	79.2%	87.7%
		% of Total	63.7%	24.1%	87.7%
	Yes	Count	42	45	87
		% within Spouse	48.3%	51.7%	100.0%
		% within State Location	8.5%	20.8%	12.3%
		% of Total	5.9%	6.3%	12.3%
Total		Count	494	216	710
		% within Spouse	69.6%	30.4%	100.0%
		% within State Location	100.0%	100.0%	100.0%
		% of Total	69.6%	30.4%	100.0%

234

TABLE C19

Chi-Square Tests

	Value	df	Asymp. Sig. (2-sided)	Exact Sig. (2-sided)	Exact Sig. (1-sided)
Pearson Chi-Square	21.254[a]	1	.000		
Continuity Correction[b]	20.123	1	.000		
Likelihood Ratio	19.719	1	.000		
Fisher's Exact Test				.000	.000
Linear-by-Linear Association	21.225	1	.000		
N of Valid Cases	710				

a. 0 cells (.0%) have expected count less than 5. The minimum expected count is 26.47.

b. Computed only for a 2x2 table

TABLE C20. Household * State Location

Crosstab

			State Location		Total
			California	Arkansas	
Household	No	Count	442	172	614
		% within Household	72.0%	28.0%	100.0%
		% within State Location	89.5%	79.6%	86.5%
		% of Total	62.3%	24.2%	86.5%
	Yes	Count	52	44	96
		% within Household	54.2%	45.8%	100.0%
		% within State Location	10.5%	20.4%	13.5%
		% of Total	7.3%	6.2%	13.5%
Total		Count	494	216	710
		% within Household	69.6%	30.4%	100.0%
		% within State Location	100.0%	100.0%	100.0%
		% of Total	69.6%	30.4%	100.0%

TABLE C21. Chi-Square Tests

Chi-Square Tests

	Value	df	Asymp. Sig. (2-sided)	Exact Sig. (2-sided)	Exact Sig. (1-sided)
Pearson Chi-Square	12.455[a]	1	.000		
Continuity Correction[b]	11.627	1	.001		
Likelihood Ratio	11.736	1	.001		
Fisher's Exact Test				.001	.000
Linear-by-Linear Association	12.438	1	.000		
N of Valid Cases	710				

a. 0 cells (.0%) have expected count less than 5. The minimum expected count is 29.21.

b. Computed only for a 2x2 table

TABLE C22. Parent * State Location

Crosstab

			State Location		Total
			California	Arkansas	
Parent	No	Count	304	138	442
		% within Parent	68.8%	31.2%	100.0%
		% within State Location	61.5%	63.9%	62.3%
		% of Total	42.8%	19.4%	62.3%
	Yes	Count	190	78	268
		% within Parent	70.9%	29.1%	100.0%
		% within State Location	38.5%	36.1%	37.7%
		% of Total	26.8%	11.0%	37.7%
Total		Count	494	216	710
		% within Parent	69.6%	30.4%	100.0%
		% within State Location	100.0%	100.0%	100.0%
		% of Total	69.6%	30.4%	100.0%

236

TABLE C23. Chi-Square Tests

Chi-Square Tests

	Value	df	Asymp. Sig. (2-sided)	Exact Sig. (2-sided)	Exact Sig. (1-sided)
Pearson Chi-Square	.353[a]	1	.552		
Continuity Correction[b]	.260	1	.610		
Likelihood Ratio	.355	1	.552		
Fisher's Exact Test				.614	.306
Linear-by-Linear Association	.353	1	.553		
N of Valid Cases	710				

a. 0 cells (.0%) have expected count less than 5. The minimum expected count is 81.53.

b. Computed only for a 2x2 table

TABLE C24. Grandparent * State Location

Crosstab

| | | | State Location | | Total |
			California	Arkansas	
Grandparent No		Count	427	171	598
		% within Grandparent	71.4%	28.6%	100.0%
		% within State Location	86.4%	79.2%	84.2%
		% of Total	60.1%	24.1%	84.2%
	Yes	Count	67	45	112
		% within Grandparent	59.8%	40.2%	100.0%
		% within State Location	13.6%	20.8%	15.8%
		% of Total	9.4%	6.3%	15.8%
Total		Count	494	216	710
		% within Grandparent	69.6%	30.4%	100.0%
		% within State Location	100.0%	100.0%	100.0%
		% of Total	69.6%	30.4%	100.0%

TABLE C25

Chi-Square Tests

	Value	df	Asymp. Sig. (2-sided)	Exact Sig. (2-sided)	Exact Sig. (1-sided)
Pearson Chi-Square	5.979[a]	1	.014		
Continuity Correction[b]	5.445	1	.020		
Likelihood Ratio	5.744	1	.017		
Fisher's Exact Test				.018	.011
Linear-by-Linear Association	5.971	1	.015		
N of Valid Cases	710				

a. 0 cells (.0%) have expected count less than 5. The minimum expected count is 34.07.

b. Computed only for a 2x2 table

238

TABLE C26. Sibling * State Location

Crosstab

| | | | State Location | | Total |
			California	Arkansas	
Sibling No	Count		412	168	580
	% within Sibling		71.0%	29.0%	100.0%
	% within State Location		83.4%	77.8%	81.7%
	% of Total		58.0%	23.7%	81.7%
Yes	Count		82	48	130
	% within Sibling		63.1%	36.9%	100.0%
	% within State Location		16.6%	22.2%	18.3%
	% of Total		11.5%	6.8%	18.3%
Total	Count		494	216	710
	% within Sibling		69.6%	30.4%	100.0%
	% within State Location		100.0%	100.0%	100.0%
	% of Total		69.6%	30.4%	100.0%

TABLE C27

Chi-Square Tests

	Value	df	Asymp. Sig. (2-sided)	Exact Sig. (2-sided)	Exact Sig. (1-sided)
Pearson Chi-Square	3.177[a]	1	.075		
Continuity Correction[b]	2.812	1	.094		
Likelihood Ratio	3.092	1	.079		
Fisher's Exact Test				.091	.048
Linear-by-Linear Association	3.172	1	.075		
N of Valid Cases	710				

a. 0 cells (.0%) have expected count less than 5. The minimum expected count is 39.55.

b. Computed only for a 2x2 table

TABLE C28. Child 2–17 * State Location

Crosstab

| | | | State Location | | Total |
			California	Arkansas	
Child 2–17	No	Count	467	192	659
		% within Child 2–17	70.9%	29.1%	100.0%
		% within State Location	94.5%	88.9%	92.8%
		% of Total	65.8%	27.0%	92.8%
	Yes	Count	27	24	51
		% within Child 2–17	52.9%	47.1%	100.0%
		% within State Location	5.5%	11.1%	7.2%
		% of Total	3.8%	3.4%	7.2%
Total		Count	494	216	710
		% within Child 2–17	69.6%	30.4%	100.0%
		% within State Location	100.0%	100.0%	100.0%
		% of Total	69.6%	30.4%	100.0%

TABLE C29

Chi-Square Tests

	Value	df	Asymp. Sig. (2-sided)	Exact Sig. (2-sided)	Exact Sig. (1-sided)
Pearson Chi-Square	7.184[a]	1	.007		
Continuity Correction[b]	6.363	1	.012		
Likelihood Ratio	6.703	1	.010		
Fisher's Exact Test				.011	.007
Linear-by-Linear Association	7.174	1	.007		
N of Valid Cases	710				

a. 0 cells (.0%) have expected count less than 5. The minimum expected count is 15.52.

b. Computed only for a 2x2 table

240

TABLE C30. Infant < 2 * State Location

Crosstab

| | | | State Location | | Total |
			California	Arkansas	
Infant < 2	No	Count	488	206	694
		% within Infant < 2	70.3%	29.7%	100.0%
		% within State Location	98.8%	95.4%	97.7%
		% of Total	68.7%	29.0%	97.7%
	Yes	Count	6	10	16
		% within Infant < 2	37.5%	62.5%	100.0%
		% within State Location	1.2%	4.6%	2.3%
		% of Total	.8%	1.4%	2.3%
Total		Count	494	216	710
		% within Infant < 2	69.6%	30.4%	100.0%
		% within State Location	100.0%	100.0%	100.0%
		% of Total	69.6%	30.4%	100.0%

TABLE C31

Chi-Square Tests

	Value	df	Asymp. Sig. (2-sided)	Exact Sig. (2-sided)	Exact Sig. (1-sided)
Pearson Chi-Square	7.957[a]	1	.005		
Continuity Correction[b]	6.482	1	.011		
Likelihood Ratio	7.163	1	.007		
Fisher's Exact Test				.010	.007
Linear-by-Linear Association	7.946	1	.005		
N of Valid Cases	710				

a. 1 cells (25.0%) have expected count less than 5. The minimum expected count is 4.87.
b. Computed only for a 2x2 table

241

TABLE C32. Roommate * State Location

Crosstab

			State Location		Total
			California	Arkansas	
Roommate No		Count	463	185	648
		% within Roommate	71.5%	28.5%	100.0%
		% within State Location	93.7%	85.6%	91.3%
		% of Total	65.2%	26.1%	91.3%
	Yes	Count	31	31	62
		% within Roommate	50.0%	50.0%	100.0%
		% within State Location	6.3%	14.4%	8.7%
		% of Total	4.4%	4.4%	8.7%
Total		Count	494	216	710
		% within Roommate	69.6%	30.4%	100.0%
		% within State Location	100.0%	100.0%	100.0%
		% of Total	69.6%	30.4%	100.0%

TABLE C33

Chi-Square Tests

	Value	df	Asymp. Sig. (2-sided)	Exact Sig. (2-sided)	Exact Sig. (1-sided)
Pearson Chi-Square	12.301[a]	1	.000		
Continuity Correction[b]	11.308	1	.001		
Likelihood Ratio	11.405	1	.001		
Fisher's Exact Test				.001	.001
Linear-by-Linear Association	12.283	1	.000		
N of Valid Cases	710				

a. 0 cells (.0%) have expected count less than 5. The minimum expected count is 18.86.

b. Computed only for a 2x2 table

242

TABLE C34. Other Adult * State Location

Crosstab

| | | | State Location | | Total |
			California	Arkansas	
Other Adult	No	Count	444	192	636
		% within Other Adult	69.8%	30.2%	100.0%
		% within State Location	89.9%	88.9%	89.6%
		% of Total	62.5%	27.0%	89.6%
	Yes	Count	50	24	74
		% within Other Adult	67.6%	32.4%	100.0%
		% within State Location	10.1%	11.1%	10.4%
		% of Total	7.0%	3.4%	10.4%
Total		Count	494	216	710
		% within Other Adult	69.6%	30.4%	100.0%
		% within State Location	100.0%	100.0%	100.0%
		% of Total	69.6%	30.4%	100.0%

TABLE C35

Chi-Square Tests

	Value	df	Asymp. Sig. (2-sided)	Exact Sig. (2-sided)	Exact Sig. (1-sided)
Pearson Chi-Square	.158[a]	1	.691		
Continuity Correction[b]	.069	1	.792		
Likelihood Ratio	.156	1	.693		
Fisher's Exact Test				.690	.391
Linear-by-Linear Association	.157	1	.692		
N of Valid Cases	710				

a. 0 cells (.0%) have expected count less than 5. The minimum expected count is 22.51.

b. Computed only for a 2x2 table

TABLE C36. Relationship between Social Vices and Traditional Iconography among Respondents Who Own the Item.

Correlations

		Painting or print	Statuette	Pendant or medal	Holy Book	Cross	Crucifix	Rosary
Cigarette / Cigars	Pearson Correlation	-.022	-.018	-.027	.059	-.035	-.029	-.006
	Sig. (2-tailed)	.554	.624	.473	.114	.358	.448	.863
	N	710	710	710	710	710	710	710
Dancing	Pearson Correlation	.175	.176	.154	.094	.176	.133	.146
	Sig. (2-tailed)	.000	.000	.000	.013	.000	.000	.000
	N	710	710	710	710	710	710	710
Beer, wine, etc.	Pearson Correlation	-.102	-.069	-.030	.022	.074	.008	.035
	Sig. (2-tailed)	.007	.068	.420	.562	.050	.829	.351
	N	710	710	710	710	710	710	710
Concerts	Pearson Correlation	.025	-.021	.032	.115	.139	.020	.010
	Sig. (2-tailed)	.504	.585	.399	.002	.000	.591	.791
	N	710	710	710	710	710	710	710
Night clubbing	Pearson Correlation	.043	.065	.106	.043	.172	.107	.132
	Sig. (2-tailed)	.256	.086	.005	.257	.000	.004	.000
	N	710	710	710	710	710	710	710
Video Games	Pearson Correlation	-.086	-.054	-.045	-.031	-.052	.014	-.053
	Sig. (2-tailed)	.021	.152	.227	.411	.169	.715	.162
	N	710	710	710	710	710	710	710
TV Shopping	Pearson Correlation	.021	.015	-.020	-.022	.018	.005	.034
	Sig. (2-tailed)	.584	.700	.596	.558	.627	.895	.363
	N	710	710	710	710	710	710	710
Computer / Internet	Pearson Correlation	-.029	-.013	-.012	.023	-.002	-.015	-.051
	Sig. (2-tailed)	.434	.727	.744	.533	.953	.691	.176
	N	710	710	710	710	710	710	710
Casino Gambling	Pearson Correlation	-.061	-.011	-.038	-.003	.005	.072	.067
	Sig. (2-tailed)	.107	.772	.314	.936	.904	.055	.073
	N	710	710	710	710	710	710	710
Lottery / Sweepstakes	Pearson Correlation	.045	.036	.074	.003	.061	.089	.094
	Sig. (2-tailed)	.228	.334	.050	.930	.105	.018	.012
	N	710	710	710	710	710	710	710
Astrology / Horoscope	Pearson Correlation	.034	.022	.106	.012	.085	.134	.116
	Sig. (2-tailed)	.362	.561	.005	.757	.024	.000	.002
	N	710	710	710	710	710	710	710
Tarot Cards	Pearson Correlation	.060	.066	.059	-.044	.018	.084	.059
	Sig. (2-tailed)	.112	.077	.115	.243	.637	.026	.114
	N	710	710	710	710	710	710	710
Psychic Readings	Pearson Correlation	.016	.061	.013	-.057	-.017	.039	.055
	Sig. (2-tailed)	.675	.102	.723	.129	.644	.302	.140
	N	710	710	710	710	710	710	710
Politics	Pearson Correlation	.037	.001	.012	.082	.043	.030	-.007
	Sig. (2-tailed)	.320	.983	.746	.029	.247	.427	.850
	N	710	710	710	710	710	710	710
Hunting / Shooting	Pearson Correlation	-.051	.019	.019	.043	-.007	.025	.022
	Sig. (2-tailed)	.176	.605	.615	.256	.862	.507	.561
	N	710	710	710	710	710	710	710
Watch / play Sports	Pearson Correlation	.013	-.005	-.013	.094	.045	.025	-.024
	Sig. (2-tailed)	.731	.888	.729	.012	.236	.508	.525
	N	710	710	710	710	710	710	710

TABLE C37. Relationship between Social Vices and Non-Traditional Iconography among Respondents Who Own the Item.

Correlations

		DVD or VHS	Music CD	Jewelry Other	Book Other	Bumper sticker
Cigarette / Cigars	Pearson Correlation	.011	-.016	-.044	.030	-.035
	Sig. (2-tailed)	.763	.677	.243	.430	.355
	N	710	710	710	710	710
Dancing	Pearson Correlation	.037	.080	.197	.089	.009
	Sig. (2-tailed)	.322	.034	.000	.017	.817
	N	710	710	710	710	710
Beer, wine, etc.	Pearson Correlation	-.140	-.090	-.070	-.038	-.065
	Sig. (2-tailed)	.000	.016	.062	.316	.085
	N	710	710	710	710	710
Concerts	Pearson Correlation	.038	.104	.136	.099	-.009
	Sig. (2-tailed)	.311	.006	.000	.008	.814
	N	710	710	710	710	710
Night clubbing	Pearson Correlation	-.074	-.051	.088	-.029	-.077
	Sig. (2-tailed)	.050	.175	.019	.436	.041
	N	710	710	710	710	710
Video Games	Pearson Correlation	-.028	-.115	-.080	-.024	-.046
	Sig. (2-tailed)	.462	.002	.034	.530	.219
	N	710	710	710	710	710
TV Shopping	Pearson Correlation	-.040	-.030	.034	.014	-.036
	Sig. (2-tailed)	.288	.420	.368	.702	.336
	N	710	710	710	710	710
Computer / Internet	Pearson Correlation	.025	.013	-.017	.023	-.027
	Sig. (2-tailed)	.501	.739	.649	.548	.471
	N	710	710	710	710	710
Casino Gambling	Pearson Correlation	-.088	-.100	-.070	-.068	-.037
	Sig. (2-tailed)	.019	.008	.063	.071	.327
	N	710	710	710	710	710
Lottery / Sweepstakes	Pearson Correlation	.016	-.066	.075	-.052	-.013
	Sig. (2-tailed)	.680	.077	.047	.169	.720
	N	710	710	710	710	710
Astrology / Horoscope	Pearson Correlation	-.017	-.077	.096	-.049	-.029
	Sig. (2-tailed)	.658	.040	.010	.195	.435
	N	710	710	710	710	710
Tarot Cards	Pearson Correlation	-.022	-.086	.079	.031	-.002
	Sig. (2-tailed)	.565	.021	.035	.406	.949
	N	710	710	710	710	710
Psychic Readings	Pearson Correlation	-.048	-.086	.032	-.001	-.034
	Sig. (2-tailed)	.203	.022	.391	.987	.364
	N	710	710	710	710	710
Politics	Pearson Correlation	.026	.015	.014	.083	-.002
	Sig. (2-tailed)	.496	.695	.705	.027	.953
	N	710	710	710	710	710
Hunting / Shooting	Pearson Correlation	.036	-.039	-.037	.013	-.016
	Sig. (2-tailed)	.342	.305	.321	.738	.666
	N	710	710	710	710	710
Watch / play Sports	Pearson Correlation	.053	.057	-.010	.061	.017
	Sig. (2-tailed)	.160	.132	.786	.106	.643
	N	710	710	710	710	710

TABLE C38. Relationship between Social Virtues and Traditional Iconography among Respondents Who Own the Item.

Correlations

		Painting or print	Statuette	Pendant or medal	Holy Book	Cross	Crucifix	Rosary
Self Improvement	Pearson Correlation	.043	.024	.059	.046	.082	.036	.029
	Sig. (2-tailed)	.247	.529	.119	.218	.029	.343	.445
	N	710	710	710	710	710	710	710
Cultural Events	Pearson Correlation	.119	.067	.121	.005	.077	.097	.067
	Sig. (2-tailed)	.001	.072	.001	.901	.040	.010	.073
	N	710	710	710	710	710	710	710
Enjoy Worship/Bible	Pearson Correlation	.182	.069	.040	.283	.145	-.009	-.094
	Sig. (2-tailed)	.000	.066	.293	.000	.000	.817	.012
	N	710	710	710	710	710	710	710
Donating to charity	Pearson Correlation	.124	.018	.068	.112	.145	.076	.004
	Sig. (2-tailed)	.001	.629	.070	.003	.000	.043	.913
	N	710	710	710	710	710	710	710

TABLE C39. Relationship between Social Virtues and Non-Traditional Iconography among Respondents Who Own the Item.

Correlations

		DVD or VHS	Music CD	Jewelry Other	Book Other	Bumper sticker
Self Improvement	Pearson Correlation	.025	.025	.028	.092	-.023
	Sig. (2-tailed)	.500	.513	.457	.015	.543
	N	710	710	710	710	710
Cultural Events	Pearson Correlation	.062	.053	.106	.080	-.021
	Sig. (2-tailed)	.097	.158	.005	.033	.580
	N	710	710	710	710	710
Enjoy Worship/Bible	Pearson Correlation	.267	.419	.178	.428	.167
	Sig. (2-tailed)	.000	.000	.000	.000	.000
	N	710	710	710	710	710
Donating to charity	Pearson Correlation	.054	.105	.109	.153	.020
	Sig. (2-tailed)	.152	.005	.004	.000	.601
	N	710	710	710	710	710

TABLE C40. Relationship between Social Vices and Traditional Iconography among Respondents Who Don't Own, But Will Buy.

Correlations

		Painting or print	Statuette	Pendant or medal	Holy Book	Cross	Crucifix	Rosary
Cigarette / Cigars	Pearson Correlation	.084	.036	.045	.011	.098	.145	.084
	Sig. (2-tailed)	.024	.332	.232	.776	.009	.000	.025
	N	710	710	710	710	710	710	710
Dancing	Pearson Correlation	.018	.037	.054	.082	-.031	-.010	.015
	Sig. (2-tailed)	.641	.322	.154	.028	.407	.780	.693
	N	710	710	710	710	710	710	710
Beer, wine, etc.	Pearson Correlation	.154	.091	.060	.075	.041	.080	.052
	Sig. (2-tailed)	.000	.015	.108	.045	.280	.032	.167
	N	710	710	710	710	710	710	710
Concerts	Pearson Correlation	.132	.158	.061	.031	-.005	.062	.060
	Sig. (2-tailed)	.000	.000	.105	.409	.897	.097	.110
	N	710	710	710	710	710	710	710
Night clubbing	Pearson Correlation	.116	.159	.116	.105	.031	.077	.031
	Sig. (2-tailed)	.002	.000	.002	.005	.405	.040	.414
	N	710	710	710	710	710	710	710
Video Games	Pearson Correlation	.091	.059	.100	.089	.102	.023	.048
	Sig. (2-tailed)	.015	.116	.008	.018	.006	.532	.198
	N	710	710	710	710	710	710	710
TV Shopping	Pearson Correlation	.007	.041	.052	.112	.016	.033	.061
	Sig. (2-tailed)	.846	.277	.170	.003	.664	.381	.105
	N	710	710	710	710	710	710	710
Computer / Internet	Pearson Correlation	.087	.124	.095	.017	.051	.019	.074
	Sig. (2-tailed)	.020	.001	.012	.643	.173	.605	.047
	N	710	710	710	710	710	710	710
Casino Gambling	Pearson Correlation	.045	.033	.048	.023	.068	.019	-.034
	Sig. (2-tailed)	.228	.381	.205	.546	.072	.618	.370
	N	710	710	710	710	710	710	710
Lottery / Sweepstakes	Pearson Correlation	.008	.035	.028	.083	.051	.010	-.029
	Sig. (2-tailed)	.833	.346	.457	.027	.178	.797	.434
	N	710	710	710	710	710	710	710
Astrology / Horoscope	Pearson Correlation	.074	.026	-.004	.032	-.013	.049	.043
	Sig. (2-tailed)	.049	.487	.909	.389	.727	.189	.248
	N	710	710	710	710	710	710	710
Tarot Cards	Pearson Correlation	.035	-.007	.028	.129	.002	.007	.116
	Sig. (2-tailed)	.358	.847	.449	.001	.954	.862	.002
	N	710	710	710	710	710	710	710
Psychic Readings	Pearson Correlation	.041	-.048	.030	.047	-.040	-.020	.067
	Sig. (2-tailed)	.277	.203	.431	.208	.289	.590	.075
	N	710	710	710	710	710	710	710
Politics	Pearson Correlation	.017	.049	.043	.042	-.001	.015	.065
	Sig. (2-tailed)	.648	.196	.248	.269	.981	.696	.081
	N	710	710	710	710	710	710	710
Hunting / Shooting	Pearson Correlation	.123	.036	.008	-.041	.106	.043	.026
	Sig. (2-tailed)	.001	.342	.827	.279	.005	.248	.483
	N	710	710	710	710	710	710	710
Watch / play Sports	Pearson Correlation	.101	.135	.108	-.021	.068	.040	.068
	Sig. (2-tailed)	.007	.000	.004	.574	.068	.284	.068
	N	710	710	710	710	710	710	710

TABLE C41. Relationship between Social Vices and Non-Traditional Iconography among Respondents Who Don't Own, But Will Buy.

Correlations

		DVD or VHS	Music CD	Jewelry Other	Book Other	Bumper sticker
Cigarette / Cigars	Pearson Correlation	-.012	.006	.061	-.017	-.031
	Sig. (2-tailed)	.746	.880	.107	.655	.410
	N	710	710	710	710	710
Dancing	Pearson Correlation	.078	.036	-.035	.039	-.003
	Sig. (2-tailed)	.038	.338	.346	.297	.934
	N	710	710	710	710	710
Beer, wine, etc.	Pearson Correlation	.145	.087	.071	.051	-.028
	Sig. (2-tailed)	.000	.021	.059	.173	.461
	N	710	710	710	710	710
Concerts	Pearson Correlation	.065	-.004	.000	-.002	-.004
	Sig. (2-tailed)	.083	.911	.995	.961	.907
	N	710	710	710	710	710
Night clubbing	Pearson Correlation	.106	.111	.076	.073	.020
	Sig. (2-tailed)	.005	.003	.044	.052	.588
	N	710	710	710	710	710
Video Games	Pearson Correlation	.041	.017	.074	-.044	-.076
	Sig. (2-tailed)	.281	.655	.049	.246	.043
	N	710	710	710	710	710
TV Shopping	Pearson Correlation	.016	-.003	-.025	.030	.031
	Sig. (2-tailed)	.672	.942	.511	.418	.411
	N	710	710	710	710	710
Computer / Internet	Pearson Correlation	.000	-.032	.034	-.034	.009
	Sig. (2-tailed)	.997	.395	.370	.370	.813
	N	710	710	710	710	710
Casino Gambling	Pearson Correlation	.075	-.005	.085	.001	-.047
	Sig. (2-tailed)	.046	.884	.023	.977	.207
	N	710	710	710	710	710
Lottery / Sweepstakes	Pearson Correlation	.048	.011	-.011	.027	-.004
	Sig. (2-tailed)	.203	.772	.764	.478	.920
	N	710	710	710	710	710
Astrology / Horoscope	Pearson Correlation	.076	.019	-.014	.014	.046
	Sig. (2-tailed)	.044	.617	.714	.708	.223
	N	710	710	710	710	710
Tarot Cards	Pearson Correlation	.020	-.045	.008	-.015	.020
	Sig. (2-tailed)	.597	.226	.829	.692	.588
	N	710	710	710	710	710
Psychic Readings	Pearson Correlation	.025	-.011	-.005	-.025	.008
	Sig. (2-tailed)	.500	.761	.901	.502	.837
	N	710	710	710	710	710
Politics	Pearson Correlation	.086	.033	.055	-.029	.011
	Sig. (2-tailed)	.021	.375	.142	.443	.778
	N	710	710	710	710	710
Hunting / Shooting	Pearson Correlation	.007	.051	.018	.054	.001
	Sig. (2-tailed)	.850	.172	.630	.152	.977
	N	710	710	710	710	710
Watch / play Sports	Pearson Correlation	.026	.050	.086	.025	.038
	Sig. (2-tailed)	.491	.182	.022	.512	.314
	N	710	710	710	710	710

TABLE C42. Relationship between Social Virtues and Traditional Iconography among Respondents Who Don't Own, But Will Buy.

Correlations

		Painting or print	Statuette	Pendant or medal	Holy Book	Cross	Crucifix	Rosary
Self Improvement	Pearson Correlation	.083	.111	.018	.056	-.012	-.027	.025
	Sig. (2-tailed)	.026	.003	.633	.137	.748	.480	.504
	N	710	710	710	710	710	710	710
Cultural Events	Pearson Correlation	-.006	.008	-.065	.017	-.090	-.047	-.015
	Sig. (2-tailed)	.878	.840	.085	.650	.016	.208	.690
	N	710	710	710	710	710	710	710
Enjoy Worship/Bible	Pearson Correlation	.090	.064	.070	-.119	.126	.112	.088
	Sig. (2-tailed)	.016	.086	.064	.001	.001	.003	.019
	N	710	710	710	710	710	710	710
Donating to charity	Pearson Correlation	-.011	.039	-.028	-.005	-.057	.000	.034
	Sig. (2-tailed)	.771	.302	.455	.886	.130	.998	.366
	N	710	710	710	710	710	710	710

TABLE C43. Relationship between Social Virtues and Non-Traditional Iconography among Respondents Who Don't Own, But Will Buy.

Correlations

		DVD or VHS	Music CD	Jewelry Other	Book Other	Bumper sticker
Self Improvement	Pearson Correlation	.033	.028	.040	.036	.038
	Sig. (2-tailed)	.380	.457	.293	.335	.314
	N	710	710	710	710	710
Cultural Events	Pearson Correlation	.024	.037	-.043	.022	.044
	Sig. (2-tailed)	.527	.320	.248	.550	.245
	N	710	710	710	710	710
Enjoy Worship/Bible	Pearson Correlation	.135	-.042	.047	-.011	.219
	Sig. (2-tailed)	.000	.269	.211	.778	.000
	N	710	710	710	710	710
Donating to charity	Pearson Correlation	.069	-.030	.015	.000	.020
	Sig. (2-tailed)	.065	.422	.682	.990	.587
	N	710	710	710	710	710

TABLE C44. Relationship between Social Vices and Traditional Iconography among Respondents Who Don't Own, Won't Buy.

Correlations

		Painting or print	Statuette	Pendant or medal	Holy Book	Cross	Crucifix	Rosary
Cigarette / Cigars	Pearson Correlation	-.031	-.030	.003	-.063	-.051	-.076	-.036
	Sig. (2-tailed)	.415	.423	.930	.091	.179	.043	.334
	N	710	710	710	710	710	710	710
Dancing	Pearson Correlation	-.120	-.136	-.151	-.131	-.124	-.079	-.078
	Sig. (2-tailed)	.001	.000	.000	.000	.001	.036	.037
	N	710	710	710	710	710	710	710
Beer, wine, etc.	Pearson Correlation	-.054	-.015	-.010	-.046	-.107	-.042	-.073
	Sig. (2-tailed)	.150	.690	.791	.224	.004	.267	.053
	N	710	710	710	710	710	710	710
Concerts	Pearson Correlation	-.143	-.100	-.046	-.112	-.121	-.029	-.031
	Sig. (2-tailed)	.000	.007	.219	.003	.001	.438	.403
	N	710	710	710	710	710	710	710
Night clubbing	Pearson Correlation	-.089	-.169	-.160	-.098	-.181	-.143	-.132
	Sig. (2-tailed)	.017	.000	.000	.009	.000	.000	.000
	N	710	710	710	710	710	710	710
Video Games	Pearson Correlation	-.024	-.020	-.040	-.028	-.032	-.020	.009
	Sig. (2-tailed)	.523	.587	.287	.457	.395	.593	.803
	N	710	710	710	710	710	710	710
TV Shopping	Pearson Correlation	-.035	-.046	-.033	-.023	-.054	-.062	-.083
	Sig. (2-tailed)	.350	.223	.379	.546	.149	.100	.027
	N	710	710	710	710	710	710	710
Computer / Internet	Pearson Correlation	-.069	-.098	-.080	-.064	-.037	-.026	-.052
	Sig. (2-tailed)	.067	.009	.032	.087	.325	.497	.163
	N	710	710	710	710	710	710	710
Casino Gambling	Pearson Correlation	.002	-.050	.005	-.015	-.063	-.080	-.067
	Sig. (2-tailed)	.964	.184	.904	.686	.092	.034	.073
	N	710	710	710	710	710	710	710
Lottery / Sweepstakes	Pearson Correlation	-.027	-.070	-.062	-.057	-.085	-.058	-.055
	Sig. (2-tailed)	.467	.061	.100	.129	.024	.121	.145
	N	710	710	710	710	710	710	710
Astrology / Horoscope	Pearson Correlation	-.058	-.035	-.044	-.021	-.044	-.101	-.101
	Sig. (2-tailed)	.123	.352	.245	.574	.239	.007	.007
	N	710	710	710	710	710	710	710
Tarot Cards	Pearson Correlation	-.058	-.048	-.038	-.030	-.008	-.035	-.103
	Sig. (2-tailed)	.123	.205	.314	.425	.840	.345	.006
	N	710	710	710	710	710	710	710
Psychic Readings	Pearson Correlation	-.015	.011	.000	.036	.045	.007	-.074
	Sig. (2 tailed)	.682	.762	.994	.335	.233	.858	.050
	N	710	710	710	710	710	710	710
Politics	Pearson Correlation	-.040	-.055	-.027	-.113	-.054	-.009	-.016
	Sig. (2-tailed)	.288	.143	.471	.003	.153	.808	.668
	N	710	710	710	710	710	710	710
Hunting / Shooting	Pearson Correlation	-.051	-.040	-.022	.000	-.087	-.024	-.025
	Sig. (2-tailed)	.174	.287	.557	.994	.020	.525	.506
	N	710	710	710	710	710	710	710
Watch / play Sports	Pearson Correlation	-.104	-.122	-.081	-.118	-.091	-.048	-.041
	Sig. (2-tailed)	.005	.001	.031	.002	.016	.201	.280
	N	710	710	710	710	710	710	710

250

TABLE C45. Relationship between Social Vices and Non-Traditional
Iconography among Respondents Who Don't Own, Won't Buy.

		DVD or VHS	Music CD	Jewelry Other	Book Other	Bumper sticker
		Correlations				
Cigarette / Cigars	Pearson Correlation	.005	.023	-.007	-.016	.004
	Sig. (2-tailed)	.899	.549	.842	.663	.922
	N	710	710	710	710	710
Dancing	Pearson Correlation	-.074	-.064	-.155	-.088	.060
	Sig. (2-tailed)	.048	.088	.000	.019	.110
	N	710	710	710	710	710
Beer, wine, etc.	Pearson Correlation	.000	.024	.014	.012	.048
	Sig. (2-tailed)	.993	.529	.716	.754	.198
	N	710	710	710	710	710
Concerts	Pearson Correlation	-.118	-.075	-.109	-.058	.018
	Sig. (2-tailed)	.002	.047	.004	.120	.637
	N	710	710	710	710	710
Night clubbing	Pearson Correlation	-.003	-.011	-.126	-.014	.029
	Sig. (2-tailed)	.944	.763	.001	.708	.439
	N	710	710	710	710	710
Video Games	Pearson Correlation	-.056	.083	.015	.033	.055
	Sig. (2-tailed)	.135	.026	.693	.378	.142
	N	710	710	710	710	710
TV Shopping	Pearson Correlation	-.007	.018	-.022	-.010	-.009
	Sig. (2-tailed)	.850	.627	.553	.785	.814
	N	710	710	710	710	710
Computer / Internet	Pearson Correlation	-.036	-.001	-.024	-.019	-.026
	Sig. (2-tailed)	.335	.975	.521	.608	.492
	N	710	710	710	710	710
Casino Gambling	Pearson Correlation	.020	.113	-.020	.069	.028
	Sig. (2-tailed)	.597	.003	.589	.066	.457
	N	710	710	710	710	710
Lottery / Sweepstakes	Pearson Correlation	-.042	.078	-.056	.044	.008
	Sig. (2-tailed)	.262	.039	.135	.237	.834
	N	710	710	710	710	710
Astrology / Horoscope	Pearson Correlation	-.026	.082	-.081	.049	-.007
	Sig. (2-tailed)	.485	.029	.031	.195	.854
	N	710	710	710	710	710
Tarot Cards	Pearson Correlation	.017	.138	-.069	.005	-.010
	Sig. (2-tailed)	.655	.000	.065	.895	.791
	N	710	710	710	710	710
Psychic Readings	Pearson Correlation	.039	.113	-.015	.047	.007
	Sig. (2-tailed)	.298	.003	.683	.207	.843
	N	710	710	710	710	710
Politics	Pearson Correlation	-.119	-.034	-.025	-.041	-.007
	Sig. (2-tailed)	.002	.365	.507	.272	.860
	N	710	710	710	710	710
Hunting / Shooting	Pearson Correlation	-.029	-.012	.039	-.029	-.019
	Sig. (2-tailed)	.437	.754	.295	.445	.613
	N	710	710	710	710	710
Watch / play Sports	Pearson Correlation	-.038	-.078	-.075	-.071	-.053
	Sig. (2-tailed)	.309	.038	.045	.057	.157
	N	710	710	710	710	710

TABLE C46. Relationship between Social Virtues and Traditional Iconography among Respondents Who Don't Own, Won't Buy.

Correlations

		Painting or print	Statuette	Pendant or medal	Holy Book	Cross	Crucifix	Rosary
Self Improvement	Pearson Correlation	-.099	-.105	-.067	-.078	-.077	-.041	-.043
	Sig. (2-tailed)	.009	.005	.076	.037	.041	.279	.250
	N	710	710	710	710	710	710	710
Cultural Events	Pearson Correlation	-.066	-.068	-.038	-.015	-.011	-.018	-.021
	Sig. (2-tailed)	.079	.069	.314	.680	.767	.629	.585
	N	710	710	710	710	710	710	710
Enjoy Worship/Bible	Pearson Correlation	-.256	-.130	-.082	-.236	-.250	-.101	.008
	Sig. (2-tailed)	.000	.001	.029	.000	.000	.007	.824
	N	710	710	710	710	710	710	710
Donating to charity	Pearson Correlation	-.079	-.062	-.053	-.101	-.107	-.092	-.024
	Sig. (2-tailed)	.036	.099	.159	.007	.004	.014	.526
	N	710	710	710	710	710	710	710

TABLE C47. Relationship between Social Virtues and Non-Traditional Iconography among Respondents Who Don't Own, Won't Buy.

Correlations

		DVD or VHS	Music CD	Jewelry Other	Book Other	Bumper sticker
Self Improvement	Pearson Correlation	-.033	-.054	-.083	-.098	-.018
	Sig. (2-tailed)	.380	.147	.027	.009	.638
	N	710	710	710	710	710
Cultural Events	Pearson Correlation	-.042	-.072	-.065	-.080	-.011
	Sig. (2-tailed)	.264	.054	.085	.033	.769
	N	710	710	710	710	710
Enjoy Worship/Bible	Pearson Correlation	-.354	-.351	-.226	-.367	-.304
	Sig. (2-tailed)	.000	.000	.000	.000	.000
	N	710	710	710	710	710
Donating to charity	Pearson Correlation	-.115	-.071	-.107	-.097	-.013
	Sig. (2-tailed)	.002	.059	.004	.010	.729
	N	710	710	710	710	710

TABLE C48. Relationship between Social Vices and Traditional Iconography among Unsure Respondents.

Correlations

		Painting or print	Statuette	Pendant or medal	Holy Book	Cross	Crucifix	Rosary
Cigarette / Cigars	Pearson Correlation	-.059	.029	-.032	-.052	-.033	-.047	-.034
	Sig. (2-tailed)	.116	.436	.396	.166	.386	.209	.359
	N	710	710	710	710	710	710	710
Dancing	Pearson Correlation	-.090	-.059	-.073	-.022	-.068	-.029	-.079
	Sig. (2-tailed)	.017	.119	.051	.560	.070	.447	.036
	N	710	710	710	710	710	710	710
Beer, wine, etc.	Pearson Correlation	.036	.025	.008	-.027	-.003	-.025	.045
	Sig. (2-tailed)	.337	.503	.826	.472	.928	.505	.228
	N	710	710	710	710	710	710	710
Concerts	Pearson Correlation	.002	.020	-.037	-.078	-.035	-.041	.010
	Sig. (2-tailed)	.965	.593	.325	.038	.347	.276	.792
	N	710	710	710	710	710	710	710
Night clubbing	Pearson Correlation	-.099	-.032	-.075	-.041	-.071	-.022	.008
	Sig. (2-tailed)	.009	.390	.045	.279	.058	.555	.829
	N	710	710	710	710	710	710	710
Video Games	Pearson Correlation	.036	.056	.010	.000	-.010	-.005	.036
	Sig. (2-tailed)	.336	.138	.799	.997	.780	.893	.345
	N	710	710	710	710	710	710	710
TV Shopping	Pearson Correlation	.011	-.019	.020	-.041	.001	.042	.022
	Sig. (2-tailed)	.767	.613	.587	.278	.979	.259	.560
	N	710	710	710	710	710	710	710
Computer / Internet	Pearson Correlation	.015	-.005	.017	.047	.012	.049	.092
	Sig. (2-tailed)	.683	.900	.643	.212	.758	.193	.014
	N	710	710	710	710	710	710	710
Casino Gambling	Pearson Correlation	.023	.042	-.013	-.025	-.023	-.023	.063
	Sig. (2-tailed)	.537	.265	.721	.509	.535	.542	.091
	N	710	710	710	710	710	710	710
Lottery / Sweepstakes	Pearson Correlation	-.013	-.010	-.052	-.003	-.018	-.026	.005
	Sig. (2-tailed)	.728	.783	.168	.937	.639	.497	.899
	N	710	710	710	710	710	710	710
Astrology / Horoscope	Pearson Correlation	-.080	-.014	-.113	-.049	-.064	-.092	-.053
	Sig. (2-tailed)	.032	.706	.003	.192	.090	.014	.156
	N	710	710	710	710	710	710	710
Tarot Cards	Pearson Correlation	-.047	-.009	-.066	.003	-.021	-.053	-.031
	Sig. (2-tailed)	.214	.813	.080	.943	.572	.161	.413
	N	710	710	710	710	710	710	710
Psychic Readings	Pearson Correlation	-.051	-.037	-.069	.037	.004	-.037	-.016
	Sig. (2-tailed)	.171	.329	.066	.319	.925	.329	.674
	N	710	710	710	710	710	710	710
Politics	Pearson Correlation	-.003	.047	-.023	-.024	.009	-.034	-.011
	Sig. (2-tailed)	.936	.207	.533	.530	.819	.363	.772
	N	710	710	710	710	710	710	710
Hunting / Shooting	Pearson Correlation	-.038	-.037	-.025	-.042	-.016	-.037	-.010
	Sig. (2-tailed)	.316	.325	.499	.263	.669	.325	.800
	N	710	710	710	710	710	710	710
Watch / play Sports	Pearson Correlation	-.030	-.003	.002	-.001	-.016	-.013	.029
	Sig. (2-tailed)	.426	.943	.954	.984	.665	.727	.445
	N	710	710	710	710	710	710	710

253

TABLE C49. Relationship between Social Vices and Non-Traditional Iconography among Unsure Respondents.

Correlations

		DVD or VHS	Music CD	Jewelry Other	Book Other	Bumper sticker
Cigarette / Cigars	Pearson Correlation	-.015	-.024	-.032	-.027	.067
	Sig. (2-tailed)	.686	.527	.396	.478	.076
	N	710	710	710	710	710
Dancing	Pearson Correlation	-.057	-.051	-.040	-.037	-.089
	Sig. (2-tailed)	.126	.179	.286	.322	.018
	N	710	710	710	710	710
Beer, wine, etc.	Pearson Correlation	-.008	.035	.019	.007	.046
	Sig. (2-tailed)	.832	.348	.605	.854	.220
	N	710	710	710	710	710
Concerts	Pearson Correlation	.038	-.011	-.026	-.038	.025
	Sig. (2-tailed)	.310	.777	.495	.306	.505
	N	710	710	710	710	710
Night clubbing	Pearson Correlation	-.060	-.041	-.064	-.010	.000
	Sig. (2-tailed)	.110	.270	.088	.782	.997
	N	710	710	710	710	710
Video Games	Pearson Correlation	.071	.037	.043	.074	.088
	Sig. (2-tailed)	.057	.331	.248	.048	.019
	N	710	710	710	710	710
TV Shopping	Pearson Correlation	.045	.036	.020	-.059	.004
	Sig. (2-tailed)	.230	.333	.587	.115	.926
	N	710	710	710	710	710
Computer / Internet	Pearson Correlation	.038	.044	.029	.057	.065
	Sig. (2-tailed)	.313	.240	.434	.132	.085
	N	710	710	710	710	710
Casino Gambling	Pearson Correlation	-.010	-.010	.035	-.011	.064
	Sig. (2-tailed)	.795	.791	.356	.766	.088
	N	710	710	710	710	710
Lottery / Sweepstakes	Pearson Correlation	-.016	-.010	-.018	-.007	.025
	Sig. (2-tailed)	.667	.783	.630	.859	.507
	N	710	710	710	710	710
Astrology / Horoscope	Pearson Correlation	-.038	-.038	-.026	-.021	-.031
	Sig. (2-tailed)	.314	.313	.496	.569	.411
	N	710	710	710	710	710
Tarot Cards	Pearson Correlation	-.016	-.017	-.017	-.026	.013
	Sig. (2-tailed)	.677	.649	.654	.483	.722
	N	710	710	710	710	710
Psychic Readings	Pearson Correlation	-.021	-.021	.001	-.031	.031
	Sig (2-tailed)	.570	.574	.984	.416	.411
	N	710	710	710	710	710
Politics	Pearson Correlation	.019	.021	-.049	-.022	.029
	Sig. (2-tailed)	.615	.572	.189	.563	.437
	N	710	710	710	710	710
Hunting / Shooting	Pearson Correlation	-.008	.012	-.025	-.044	.063
	Sig. (2-tailed)	.836	.741	.499	.239	.093
	N	710	710	710	710	710
Watch / play Sports	Pearson Correlation	-.061	-.048	.002	-.024	.022
	Sig. (2-tailed)	.106	.199	.954	.531	.566
	N	710	710	710	710	710

TABLE C50. Relationship between Social Virtues and Traditional Iconography among Unsure Respondents.

Correlations

		Painting or print	Statuette	Pendant or medal	Holy Book	Cross	Crucifix	Rosary
Self Improvement	Pearson Correlation	-.061	-.031	-.033	-.055	-.021	.029	-.011
	Sig. (2-tailed)	.103	.413	.377	.144	.572	.437	.774
	N	710	710	710	710	710	710	710
Cultural Events	Pearson Correlation	-.073	.009	-.053	-.002	-.001	-.054	-.044
	Sig. (2-tailed)	.051	.820	.162	.967	.972	.151	.247
	N	710	710	710	710	710	710	710
Enjoy Worship/Bible	Pearson Correlation	-.068	-.025	-.072	-.109	-.076	.018	.007
	Sig. (2-tailed)	.071	.507	.055	.003	.043	.640	.853
	N	710	710	710	710	710	710	710
Donating to charity	Pearson Correlation	-.048	.026	.007	-.070	-.014	.049	.015
	Sig. (2-tailed)	.204	.486	.844	.062	.717	.191	.696
	N	710	710	710	710	710	710	710

TABLE C51. Relationship between Social Virtues and Non-Traditional Iconography among Unsure Respondents.

Correlations

		DVD or VHS	Music CD	Jewelry Other	Book Other	Bumper sticker
Self Improvement	Pearson Correlation	-.051	-.002	.011	-.071	-.024
	Sig. (2-tailed)	.177	.959	.763	.060	.516
	N	710	710	710	710	710
Cultural Events	Pearson Correlation	-.084	-.015	-.018	-.021	-.025
	Sig. (2-tailed)	.025	.683	.637	.583	.501
	N	710	710	710	710	710
Enjoy Worship/Bible	Pearson Correlation	-.081	-.065	-.048	-.131	.052
	Sig. (2-tailed)	.032	.086	.199	.000	.165
	N	710	710	710	710	710
Donating to charity	Pearson Correlation	-.002	-.018	-.044	-.103	-.005
	Sig. (2-tailed)	.954	.627	.245	.006	.885
	N	710	710	710	710	710

APPENDIX D

INTER-CORRELATION MATRIXES TABLES

TABLE D1. Inter-correlation Matrix of the Religiosity Index and its Components

Correlations

		Religiosity Scale	Church Service Attendance	Religious Service Attendance	Level of Religiousness	Enjoy Worship/Bible	Spiritual Value	Worship	Church Education	Do you believe there is life after death?	Special Enlightenment	Clergy	Church Newsletters
Religiosity Scale	Pearson Correlation	1	.809	.807	.751	.669	.657	.596	.542	.529	.360	.300	.284
	Sig. (2-tailed)		.000	.000	.000	.000	.000	.000	.000	.000	.000	.000	.000
	N	710	710	710	710	710	710	710	710	710	710	710	710
Church Service Attendance	Pearson Correlation	.809	1	.674	.564	.486	.392	.396	.396	.241	.162	.192	.168
	Sig. (2-tailed)	.000		.000	.000	.000	.000	.000	.000	.000	.000	.000	.000
	N	710	710	710	710	710	710	710	710	710	710	710	710
Religious Service Attendance	Pearson Correlation	.807	.674	1	.551	.467	.440	.401	.328	.312	.214	.188	.129
	Sig. (2-tailed)	.000	.000		.000	.000	.000	.000	.000	.000	.000	.000	.001
	N	710	710	710	710	710	710	710	710	710	710	710	710
Level of Religiousness	Pearson Correlation	.751	.564	.551	1	.511	.494	.368	.290	.292	.200	.166	.176
	Sig. (2-tailed)	.000	.000	.000		.000	.000	.000	.000	.000	.000	.000	.000
	N	710	710	710	710	710	710	710	710	710	710	710	710
Enjoy Worship/Bible	Pearson Correlation	.669	.486	.467	.511	1	.429	.413	.353	.279	.192	.169	.153
	Sig. (2-tailed)	.000	.000	.000	.000		.000	.000	.000	.000	.000	.000	.000
	N	710	710	710	710	710	710	710	710	710	710	710	710
Spiritual Value	Pearson Correlation	.657	.392	.440	.494	.429	1	.428	.364	.285	.332	.205	.164
	Sig. (2-tailed)	.000	.000	.000	.000	.000		.000	.000	.000	.000	.000	.000
	N	710	710	710	710	710	710	710	710	710	710	710	710
Worship	Pearson Correlation	.596	.396	.401	.368	.413	.428	1	.343	.244	.182	.157	.218
	Sig. (2-tailed)	.000	.000	.000	.000	.000	.000		.000	.000	.000	.000	.000
	N	710	710	710	710	710	710	710	710	710	710	710	710
Church Education	Pearson Correlation	.542	.396	.328	.290	.353	.364	.343	1	.188	.176	.171	.245
	Sig. (2-tailed)	.000	.000	.000	.000	.000	.000	.000		.000	.000	.000	.000
	N	710	710	710	710	710	710	710	710	710	710	710	710
Do you believe there is life after death?	Pearson Correlation	.529	.241	.312	.292	.279	.285	.244	.188	1	.099	.065	.059
	Sig. (2-tailed)	.000	.000	.000	.000	.000	.000	.000	.000		.008	.082	.114
	N	710	710	710	710	710	710	710	710	710	710	710	710
Special Enlightenment	Pearson Correlation	.360	.162	.214	.200	.192	.332	.182	.176	.099	1	.106	.094
	Sig. (2-tailed)	.000	.000	.000	.000	.000	.000	.000	.000	.008		.005	.012
	N	710	710	710	710	710	710	710	710	710	710	710	710
Clergy	Pearson Correlation	.300	.192	.188	.166	.169	.205	.157	.171	.065	.106	1	.152
	Sig. (2-tailed)	.000	.000	.000	.000	.000	.000	.000	.000	.082	.005		.000
	N	710	710	710	710	710	710	710	710	710	710	710	710
Church Newsletters	Pearson Correlation	.284	.168	.129	.176	.153	.164	.218	.245	.059	.094	.152	1
	Sig. (2-tailed)	.000	.000	.001	.000	.000	.000	.000	.000	.114	.012	.000	
	N	710	710	710	710	710	710	710	710	710	710	710	710

There is no significant relationship between social vices and iconography status. When examining traditional items, we reject the null hypotheses for vices—ownership, will buy and won't buy as well as for hypotheses for virtues—ownership and won't buy. As vices and virtues increase, the decision to not buy goes down. Likewise, there is a positive relationship between virtues and ownership of traditional items.

TABLE D2. Social Behaviors Indices by Traditional Iconography Ownership Status

Correlations

		Own	Don't Own, Will Buy	Don't Own, Won't Buy	Unsure
Social Vices	Pearson Correlation	.095	.188	-.181	-.047
	Sig. (2-tailed)	.011	.000	.000	.208
	N	710	710	710	710
Social Virtues	Pearson Correlation	.156	.046	-.162	-.054
	Sig. (2-tailed)	.000	.225	.000	.152
	N	710	710	710	710

When reviewing non-traditional items, we reject the null for vices – will buy and for virtues to ownership, will buy, won't buy and for those who are unsure. Non-traditional iconography has positive relationship with social virtues. In contrast, social virtues has a negative relationship with the decision not to buy.

258

TABLE D3. Social Behaviors Indices by Non-Traditional Iconography Ownership Status

Correlations

		Own	Don't Own, Will Buy	Don't Own, Won't Buy	Unsure
Social Vices	Pearson Correlation	-.008	.098	-.037	-.002
	Sig. (2-tailed)	.838	.009	.321	.952
	N	710	710	710	710
Social Virtues	Pearson Correlation	.291	.094	-.269	-.083
	Sig. (2-tailed)	.000	.013	.000	.027
	N	710	710	710	710

TABLE D4. Social Vices by Traditional Iconography Ownership Status

Correlations

		Own	Don't Own, Will Buy	Don't Own, Won't Buy	Unsure
Cigarette / Cigars	Pearson Correlation	-.013	.002	.002	-.008
	Sig. (2-tailed)	.733	.953	.953	.834
	N	710	710	710	710
Dancing	Pearson Correlation	.143	.043	-.089	-.083
	Sig. (2-tailed)	.000	.253	.018	.027
	N	710	710	710	710
Beer, wine, etc.	Pearson Correlation	-.124	.120	.027	.029
	Sig. (2-tailed)	.001	.001	.466	.439
	N	710	710	710	710
Concerts	Pearson Correlation	.130	.023	-.094	-.002
	Sig. (2-tailed)	.001	.542	.012	.967
	N	710	710	710	710
Night clubbing	Pearson Correlation	-.032	.137	-.034	-.054
	Sig. (2-tailed)	.394	.000	.372	.152
	N	710	710	710	710
Video Games	Pearson Correlation	-.093	.008	.038	.095
	Sig. (2-tailed)	.013	.825	.313	.011
	N	710	710	710	710
TV Shopping	Pearson Correlation	-.012	.017	-.008	.015
	Sig. (2-tailed)	.757	.650	.832	.690
	N	710	710	710	710
Computer / Internet	Pearson Correlation	.010	-.007	-.029	.069
	Sig. (2-tailed)	.797	.851	.434	.065
	N	710	710	710	710
Casino Gambling	Pearson Correlation	-.117	.042	.061	.023
	Sig. (2-tailed)	.002	.259	.107	.546
	N	710	710	710	710
Lottery / Sweepstakes	Pearson Correlation	-.012	.026	.011	-.008
	Sig. (2-tailed)	.757	.482	.767	.836
	N	710	710	710	710
Astrology / Horoscope	Pearson Correlation	-.019	.052	.007	-.046
	Sig. (2-tailed)	.611	.166	.851	.222
	N	710	710	710	710
Tarot Cards	Pearson Correlation	.003	-.002	.025	-.018
	Sig. (2-tailed)	.940	.947	.505	.631
	N	710	710	710	710
Psychic Readings	Pearson Correlation	-.039	-.001	.055	-.011
	Sig. (2-tailed)	.302	.985	.143	.774
	N	710	710	710	710
Politics	Pearson Correlation	.047	.060	-.063	-.002
	Sig. (2-tailed)	.208	.113	.096	.966
	N	710	710	710	710
Hunting / Shooting	Pearson Correlation	-.014	.044	-.014	.000
	Sig. (2-tailed)	.718	.241	.701	.995
	N	710	710	710	710
Watch / play Sports	Pearson Correlation	.057	.078	-.089	-.031
	Sig. (2-tailed)	.131	.039	.018	.411
	N	710	710	710	710

TABLE D4. Continued

Correlations

		Own	Don't Own, Will Buy	Don't Own, Won't Buy	Unsure
Cigarette / Cigars	Pearson Correlation	-.013	.002	.002	-.008
	Sig. (2-tailed)	.733	.953	.953	.834
	N	710	710	710	710
Dancing	Pearson Correlation	.143	.043	-.089	-.083
	Sig. (2-tailed)	.000	.253	.018	.027
	N	710	710	710	710
Beer, wine, etc.	Pearson Correlation	-.124	.120	.027	.029
	Sig. (2-tailed)	.001	.001	.466	.439
	N	710	710	710	710
Concerts	Pearson Correlation	.130	.023	-.094	-.002
	Sig. (2-tailed)	.001	.542	.012	.967
	N	710	710	710	710
Night clubbing	Pearson Correlation	-.032	.137	-.034	-.054
	Sig. (2-tailed)	.394	.000	.372	.152
	N	710	710	710	710
Video Games	Pearson Correlation	-.093	.008	.038	.095
	Sig. (2-tailed)	.013	.825	.313	.011
	N	710	710	710	710
TV Shopping	Pearson Correlation	-.012	.017	-.008	.015
	Sig. (2-tailed)	.757	.650	.832	.690
	N	710	710	710	710
Computer / Internet	Pearson Correlation	.010	-.007	-.029	.069
	Sig. (2-tailed)	.797	.851	.434	.065
	N	710	710	710	710
Casino Gambling	Pearson Correlation	-.117	.042	.061	.023
	Sig. (2-tailed)	.002	.259	.107	.546
	N	710	710	710	710
Lottery / Sweepstakes	Pearson Correlation	-.012	.026	.011	-.008
	Sig. (2-tailed)	.757	.482	.767	.836
	N	710	710	710	710
Astrology / Horoscope	Pearson Correlation	-.019	.052	.007	-.046
	Sig. (2-tailed)	.611	.166	.851	.222
	N	710	710	710	710
Tarot Cards	Pearson Correlation	.003	-.002	.025	-.018
	Sig. (2-tailed)	.940	.947	.505	.631
	N	710	710	710	710
Psychic Readings	Pearson Correlation	-.039	-.001	.055	-.011
	Sig. (2-tailed)	.302	.985	.143	.774
	N	710	710	710	710
Politics	Pearson Correlation	.047	.060	-.063	-.002
	Sig. (2-tailed)	.208	.113	.096	.966
	N	710	710	710	710
Hunting / Shooting	Pearson Correlation	-.014	.044	-.014	.000
	Sig. (2-tailed)	.718	.241	.701	.995
	N	710	710	710	710
Watch / play Sports	Pearson Correlation	.057	.078	-.089	-.031
	Sig. (2-tailed)	.131	.039	.018	.411
	N	710	710	710	710

261

TABLE D5. Social Vices by Non-Traditional Iconography Ownership Status

Correlations

		Own	Don't Own, Will Buy	Don't Own, Won't Buy	Unsure
Cigarette / Cigars	Pearson Correlation	-.018	.117	-.053	-.044
	Sig. (2-tailed)	.641	.002	.156	.237
	N	710	710	710	710
Dancing	Pearson Correlation	.215	.033	-.155	-.089
	Sig. (2-tailed)	.000	.386	.000	.018
	N	710	710	710	710
Beer, wine, etc.	Pearson Correlation	-.012	.129	-.066	.016
	Sig. (2-tailed)	.750	.001	.078	.661
	N	710	710	710	710
Concerts	Pearson Correlation	.066	.121	-.108	-.026
	Sig. (2-tailed)	.078	.001	.004	.489
	N	710	710	710	710
Night clubbing	Pearson Correlation	.138	.145	-.189	-.066
	Sig. (2-tailed)	.000	.000	.000	.078
	N	710	710	710	710
Video Games	Pearson Correlation	-.063	.114	-.029	.029
	Sig. (2-tailed)	.094	.002	.445	.446
	N	710	710	710	710
TV Shopping	Pearson Correlation	.010	.064	-.067	.012
	Sig. (2-tailed)	.781	.086	.076	.741
	N	710	710	710	710
Computer / Internet	Pearson Correlation	-.020	.111	-.081	.047
	Sig. (2-tailed)	.588	.003	.030	.210
	N	710	710	710	710
Casino Gambling	Pearson Correlation	.005	.048	-.054	.015
	Sig. (2-tailed)	.884	.203	.149	.697
	N	710	710	710	710
Lottery / Sweepstakes	Pearson Correlation	.083	.037	-.080	-.025
	Sig. (2-tailed)	.027	.320	.034	.513
	N	710	710	710	710
Astrology / Horoscope	Pearson Correlation	.105	.048	-.081	-.097
	Sig. (2-tailed)	.005	.202	.031	.010
	N	710	710	710	710
Tarot Cards	Pearson Correlation	.062	.059	-.063	-.049
	Sig. (2-tailed)	.097	.117	.093	.189
	N	710	710	710	710
Psychic Readings	Pearson Correlation	.023	.013	-.001	-.042
	Sig. (2-tailod)	.548	.722	.969	.267
	N	710	710	710	710
Politics	Pearson Correlation	.040	.050	-.055	-.007
	Sig. (2-tailed)	.289	.186	.142	.860
	N	710	710	710	710
Hunting / Shooting	Pearson Correlation	.013	.078	-.049	-.042
	Sig. (2-tailed)	.720	.039	.192	.269
	N	710	710	710	710
Watch / play Sports	Pearson Correlation	.026	.122	-.113	-.006
	Sig. (2-tailed)	.482	.001	.003	.872
	N	710	710	710	710

TABLE D6. Social Vices by Traditional Iconography Ownership Status

		Own	Don't Own, Will Buy	Don't Own, Won't Buy	Unsure
Cigarette / Cigars	Pearson Correlation	-.018	.117	-.053	-.044
	Sig. (2-tailed)	.641	.002	.156	.237
	N	710	710	710	710
Dancing	Pearson Correlation	.215	.033	-.155	-.089
	Sig. (2-tailed)	.000	.386	.000	.018
	N	710	710	710	710
Beer, wine, etc.	Pearson Correlation	-.012	.129	-.066	.016
	Sig. (2-tailed)	.750	.001	.078	.661
	N	710	710	710	710
Concerts	Pearson Correlation	.066	.121	-.108	-.026
	Sig. (2-tailed)	.078	.001	.004	.489
	N	710	710	710	710
Night clubbing	Pearson Correlation	.138	.145	-.189	-.066
	Sig. (2-tailed)	.000	.000	.000	.078
	N	710	710	710	710
Video Games	Pearson Correlation	-.063	.114	-.029	.029
	Sig. (2-tailed)	.094	.002	.445	.446
	N	710	710	710	710
TV Shopping	Pearson Correlation	.010	.064	-.067	.012
	Sig. (2-tailed)	.781	.086	.076	.741
	N	710	710	710	710
Computer / Internet	Pearson Correlation	-.020	.111	-.081	.047
	Sig. (2-tailed)	.588	.003	.030	.210
	N	710	710	710	710
Casino Gambling	Pearson Correlation	.005	.048	-.054	.015
	Sig. (2-tailed)	.884	.203	.149	.697
	N	710	710	710	710
Lottery / Sweepstakes	Pearson Correlation	.083	.037	-.080	-.025
	Sig. (2-tailed)	.027	.320	.034	.513
	N	710	710	710	710
Astrology / Horoscope	Pearson Correlation	.105	.048	-.081	-.097
	Sig. (2-tailed)	.005	.202	.031	.010
	N	710	710	710	710
Tarot Cards	Pearson Correlation	.062	.059	-.063	-.049
	Sig. (2-tailed)	.097	.117	.093	.189
	N	710	710	710	710
Psychic Readings	Pearson Correlation	.023	.013	-.001	-.042
	Sig. (2-tailed)	.548	.722	.969	.267
	N	710	710	710	710
Politics	Pearson Correlation	.040	.050	-.055	-.007
	Sig. (2-tailed)	.289	.186	.142	.860
	N	710	710	710	710
Hunting / Shooting	Pearson Correlation	.013	.078	-.049	-.042
	Sig. (2-tailed)	.720	.039	.192	.269
	N	710	710	710	710
Watch / play Sports	Pearson Correlation	.026	.122	-.113	-.006
	Sig. (2-tailed)	.482	.001	.003	.872
	N	710	710	710	710

TABLE D7

Correlations

		Own	Don't Own, Will Buy	Don't Own, Won't Buy	Unsure
Self Improvement	Pearson Correlation	.066	.060	-.096	-.034
	Sig. (2-tailed)	.080	.113	.010	.363
	N	710	710	710	710
Cultural Events	Pearson Correlation	.114	-.046	-.046	-.049
	Sig. (2-tailed)	.002	.216	.219	.194
	N	710	710	710	710
Enjoy Worship/Bible	Pearson Correlation	.124	.111	-.190	-.057
	Sig. (2-tailed)	.001	.003	.000	.127
	N	710	710	710	710
Donating to charity	Pearson Correlation	.112	-.006	-.097	.001
	Sig. (2-tailed)	.003	.863	.010	.982
	N	710	710	710	710

TABLE D8. Social Virtues by Non-Traditional Iconography Ownership Status

Correlations

		Own	Don't Own, Will Buy	Don't Own, Won't Buy	Unsure
Self Improvement	Pearson Correlation	.055	.061	-.080	-.041
	Sig. (2-tailed)	.141	.106	.033	.280
	N	710	710	710	710
Cultural Events	Pearson Correlation	.101	.029	-.076	-.051
	Sig. (2-tailed)	.007	.440	.044	.178
	N	710	710	710	710
Enjoy Worship/Bible	Pearson Correlation	.471	.126	-.449	-.079
	Sig. (2-tailed)	.000	.001	.000	.036
	N	710	710	710	710
Donating to charity	Pearson Correlation	.150	.030	-.112	-.050
	Sig. (2-tailed)	.000	.423	.003	.183
	N	710	710	710	710

APPENDIX E

DISTRIBUTION PERCENTAGE TABLES
WITH PEARSON CHI-SQUARE TESTS

APPENDIX E

TABLE E1. Percent Distribution of Roof and McKinney Divisions by State

Roof and McKinney Divisions	State Location	
	California	
	Count	Column N %
Liberal Protestants	19	4.1%
Moderate Protestants	65	13.9%
Black Protestants	1	.2%
Conservative Protestants	21	4.5%
Catholics	155	33.3%
Others	7	1.5%
No Religious Preference	66	14.2%
Other Christian	42	9.0%
Secular / Agnostic / Atheist	29	6.2%
Other Nonchristians	61	13.1%
Total	466	100.0%

TABLE E2. Percent Distribution of Roof and McKinney Divisions by State

		State Location	
		Arkansas	
		Count	Column N %
Roof and McKinney Divisions	Liberal Protestants	17	8.2%
	Moderate Protestants	32	15.5%
	Black Protestants	5	2.4%
	Conservative Protesta	57	27.5%
	Catholics	40	19.3%
	Others	3	1.4%
	No Religious Prefere1	16	7.7%
	Other Christian	20	9.7%
	Secular / Agnostic / Atl	9	4.3%
	Other Nonchristians	8	3.9%
	Total	207	100.0%

TABLE E3
Pearson Chi-Square Tests

		State Location
Roof and McKinney Divisions	Chi-square	105.525
	df	9
	Sig.	

Results are based on non-empty rows and columns in each innermost subtable.
*The Chi-square statistic is significant at the 0.05 level.

TABLE E4. Percent Distribution of World Christian Encyclopedia Divisions by State

		California	
		Count	Col. N %
World Christian	Angelicans	8	1.7%
Encyclopedia Divisions	Protestants	98	21.0%
	Catholics	155	33.3%
	Marginal Protestants	7	1.5%
	Independent Christians	66	14.2%
	Orthodox	42	9.0%
	No Preference	0	.0%
	Secular / Agnostic / Atheist	29	6.2%
	Other Nonchristian	61	13.1%
	Total	466	100.0%

TABLE E5. Percent Distribution of World Christian Encyclopedia Divisions by State

		State Location Arkansas	
		Count	Col. N %
World Christian	Angelicans	8	3.9%
Encyclopedia Divisions	Protestants	103	49.8%
	Catholics	40	19.3%
	Marginal Protestants	3	1.4%
	Independent Christians	16	7.7%
	Orthodox	20	9.7%
	No Preference	0	.0%
	Secular / Agnostic / Atheist	9	4.3%
	Other Nonchristian	8	3.9%
	Total	207	100.0%

TABLE E6. Pearson Chi-Square Tests

		State Location
World Christian Encyclopedia Divisions	Chi-square	69.728
	df	7
	Sig.	

Results are based on non-empty rows and columns in each innermost subtable.
*The Chi-square statistic is significant at the 0.05 level.
a. More than 20% of cells in this subtable have expected cell counts less than 5. Chi-square results may be invalid.

TABLE E7. Percent Distribution of Religiosity Measures by State

		State Location California	
		Count	Col. N %
Religiosity Index	Low	292	59.1%
	High	202	40.9%
	Total	494	100.0%
Level of Religiousness	Unsure/Not	167	33.8%
	Somewhat	232	47.0%
	Very	69	14.0%
	Seriously	26	5.3%
	Total	494	100.0%
Church Service Attendance	Less than Weekly	373	75.5%
	Weekly or More	121	24.5%
	Total	494	100.0%
Religious Service Attendance	Never	141	28.5%
	1–2 Visits per Year	126	25.5%
	Occasionally attend	141	28.5%
	Nearly every week or more	86	17.4%
	Total	494	100.0%
Enjoy Worship/Bible	No	372	75.3%
	Yes	122	24.7%
	Total	494	100.0%
Do you believe there is life after death?	Not Applicable	47	9.5%
	No	50	10.1%
	Unsure	93	18.8%
	Yes	304	61.5%
	Total	494	100.0%

TABLE E7. Continued

		State Location California	
		Count	Column N %
Social Virtues	Low	303	61.3%
	High	191	38.7%
	Total	494	100.0%
Social Vices	Low	244	49.4%
	High	250	50.6%
	Total	494	100.0%

TABLE E8. Percent Distribution of Religiosity Measures by State

		State Location Arkansas	
		Count	Col. N %
Religiosity Index	Low	69	31.9%
	High	147	68.1%
	Total	216	100.0%
Level of Religiousness	Unsure/Not	34	15.7%
	Somewhat	108	50.0%
	Very	55	25.5%
	Seriously	19	8.8%
	Total	216	100.0%
Church Service Attendance	Less than Weekly	145	67.1%
	Weekly or More	71	32.9%
	Total	216	100.0%
Religious Service Attendance	Never	36	16.7%
	1–2 Visits per Year	27	12.5%
	Occasionally attend	88	40.7%
	Nearly every week or more	65	30.1%
	Total	216	100.0%
Enjoy Worship/Bible	No	105	48.6%
	Yes	111	51.4%
	Total	216	100.0%
Do you believe there is life after death?	Not Applicable	15	6.9%
	No	14	6.5%
	Unsure	24	11.1%
	Yes	163	75.5%
	Total	216	100.0%

TABLE E8. Continued

		State Location Arkansas	
		Count	Col. N %
Social Virtues	Low	108	50.0%
	High	108	50.0%
	Total	216	100.0%
Social Vices	Low	81	37.5%
	High	135	62.5%
	Total	216	100.0%

TABLE E9

Pearson Chi-Square Tests

		State Location
Religiosity Index	Chi-square	44.373
	df	1
	Sig.	
Level of Religiousness	Chi-square	31.945
	df	3
	Sig.	
Church Service Attendance	Chi-square	5.345
	df	1
	Sig.	
Religious Service Attendance	Chi-square	38.601
	df	3
	Sig.	
Enjoy Worship/Bible	Chi-square	48.567
	df	1
	Sig.	
Do you believe there is life after death?	Chi-square	13.204
	df	3
	Sig.	
Social Virtues	Chi-square	7.922
	df	1
	Sig.	
Social Vices	Chi-square	8.564
	df	1
	Sig.	

Results are based on non-empty rows and columns in each innermost subtable.
*The Chi-square statistic is significant at the 0.05 level.

270

TABLE E10. Percent Distribution of Religiosity Measures by State

		State Location California	
		Count	Col. N %
Religiosity Index	Low	292	59.1%
	High	202	40.9%
	Total	494	100.0%
Level of Religiousness	Unsure/Not	167	33.8%
	Somewhat	232	47.0%
	Very	69	14.0%
	Seriously	26	5.3%
	Total	494	100.0%
Church Service Attendance	Less than Weekly	373	75.5%
	Weekly or More	121	24.5%
	Total	494	100.0%
Religious Service Atten.	Never	141	28.5%
	1–2 Visits per Year	126	25.5%
	Occasionally attend	141	28.5%
	Nearly every week or more	86	17.4%
	Total	494	100.0%

TABLE E11. Percent Distribution of Religiosity Measures by State

		State Location Arkansas	
		Count	Col. N %
Religiosity Index	Low	69	31.9%
	High	147	68.1%
	Total	216	100.0%
Level of Religiousness	Unsure/Not	34	15.7%
	Somewhat	108	50.0%
	Very	55	25.5%
	Seriously	19	8.8%
	Total	216	100.0%
Church Service Attendance	Less than Weekly	145	67.1%
	Weekly or More	71	32.9%
	Total	216	100.0%
Religious Service Attendance	Never	36	16.7%
	1–2 Visits per Year	27	12.5%
	Occasionally attend	88	40.7%
	Nearly every week or more	65	30.1%
	Total	216	100.0%

272

TABLE E12. Pearson Chi-Square Tests

		State Location
Religiosity Index	Chi-square	44.373
	df	1
	Sig.	
Level of Religiousness	Chi-square	31.945
	df	3
	Sig.	
Church Service Attendance	Chi-square	5.345
	df	1
	Sig.	
Religious Service Attendance	Chi-square	38.601
	df	3
	Sig.	

Results are based on non-empty rows and columns in each innermost subtable.
*The Chi-square statistic is significant at the 0.05 level.

TABLE E13. Percent Distribution of Religiosity Measures by State

| | | State Location | | | |
| | | California | | Arkansas | |
		Count	Col. N %	Count	Col. N %
Enjoy Worship/Bible	No	372	75.3%	105	48.6%
	Yes	122	24.7%	111	51.4%
	Total	494	100.0%	216	100.0%
Do you believe there is life after death?	Not Applicable	47	9.5%	15	6.9%
	No	50	10.1%	14	6.5%
	Unsure	93	18.8%	24	11.1%
	Yes	304	61.5%	163	75.5%
	Total	494	100.0%	216	100.0%
Clergy	No	462	93.5%	182	84.3%
	Yes	32	6.5%	34	15.7%
	Total	494	100.0%	216	100.0%
Church Education	No	334	67.6%	108	50.0%
	Yes	160	32.4%	108	50.0%
	Total	494	100.0%	216	100.0%
Church Newsletters	No	460	93.1%	192	88.9%
	Yes	34	6.9%	24	11.1%
	Total	494	100.0%	216	100.0%
Spiritual Value	No	286	57.9%	81	37.5%
	Yes	208	42.1%	135	62.5%
	Total	494	100.0%	216	100.0%
Worship	No	346	70.0%	111	51.4%
	Yes	148	30.0%	105	48.6%
	Total	494	100.0%	216	100.0%
Special Enlightenment	No	361	73.1%	134	62.0%
	Yes	133	26.9%	82	38.0%
	Total	494	100.0%	216	100.0%

TABLE E14. Pearson Chi-Square Tests

		State Location
Enjoy Worship/Bible	Chi-square	48.567
	df	1
	Sig.	
Do you believe there is life after death?	Chi-square	13.204
	df	3
	Sig.	
Clergy	Chi-square	15.294
	df	1
	Sig.	
Church Education	Chi-square	19.837
	df	1
	Sig.	
Church Newsletters	Chi-square	3.582
	df	1
	Sig.	.058
Spiritual Value	Chi-square	25.033
	df	1
	Sig.	
Worship	Chi-square	22.795
	df	1
	Sig.	
Special Enlightenment	Chi-square	8.676
	df	1
	Sig.	

Results are based on non-empty rows and columns in each innermost subtable.
*The Chi-square statistic is significant at the 0.05 level.

APPENDIX F

DISTRIBUTION PERCENTAGE
OF INFLUENTIAL FACTOR TABLES

TABLE F1. Percent Distribution of Influential Factors of Iconography Purchases by State

| | | State Location | | | |
| | | California | | Arkansas | |
		Count	Col. N %	Count	Col. N %
Influence Decision	Clergy	32	11.8%	34	21.3%
	Church Education	160	58.8%	108	67.5%
	Church Newsletters	34	12.5%	24	15.0%
	Spiritual Value	208	76.5%	135	84.4%
	Total	272	100.0%	160	100.0%

TABLE F2. Pearson Chi-Square Tests

		State Location
Influence Decision	Chi-square	14.612
	df	4
	Sig.	

Results are based on non-empty rows and columns in each innermost subtable.
*The Chi-square statistic is significant at the 0.05 level.

TABLE F3. Percent Distribution of Purposes for Purchased Iconography by State

| | | State Location | | | |
| | | California | | Arkansas | |
		Count	Col. N %	Count	Col. N %
Purpose of Purchase	Worship	148	65.2%	105	77.2%
	Special Enlightenment	133	58.6%	82	60.3%
	Total	227	100.0%	136	100.0%

TABLE F4

Pearson Chi-Square Tests

		State Location
Purpose of Purchase	Chi-square	5.908
	df	2
	Sig.	.052

Results are based on non-empty rows and columns in each innermost subtable.

TABLE F5. Percent Distribution of Expected Users of Purchased Iconography by State

| | | State Location | | | |
| | | California | | Arkansas | |
		Count	Col. N %	Count	Col. N %
Household Member	Self	233	58.4%	142	75.5%
	Spouse	42	10.5%	45	23.9%
	Household	52	13.0%	44	23.4%
	Parent	190	47.6%	78	41.5%
	Grandparent	67	16.8%	45	23.9%
	Sibling	82	20.6%	48	25.5%
	Child 2–17	27	6.8%	24	12.8%
	Infant < 2	6	1.5%	10	5.3%
	Roommate	31	7.8%	31	16.5%
	Other Adult	50	12.5%	24	12.8%
	Total	399	100.0%	188	100.0%

278

TABLE F6

Pearson Chi-Square Tests

		State Location
Household Member	Chi-square	75.618
	df	10
	Sig.	

Results are based on non-empty rows and columns in each innermost subtable.
*The Chi-square statistic is significant at the 0.05 level.

TABLE F7. Percent Distribution of Consumer Social Behaviors by State

		State Location			
		California		Arkansas	
		Count	Col. N %	Count	Col. N %
Social	Cigarette/Cigars	85	17.6%	49	23.0%
Behaviors	Dancing	242	50.1%	100	46.9%
	Beer, wine, etc.	246	50.9%	149	70.0%
	Concerts	275	56.9%	149	70.0%
	Night clubbing	198	41.0%	102	47.9%
	Video Games	199	41.2%	93	43.7%
	TV Shopping	34	7.0%	11	5.2%
	Computer/Internet	326	67.5%	160	75.1%
	Self-improvement	227	47.0%	106	49.8%
	Cultural Events	178	36.9%	76	35.7%
	Casino Gambling	152	31.5%	67	31.5%
	Lottery/Sweepstakes	61	12.6%	27	12.7%
	Astrology/Horoscope	94	19.5%	33	15.5%
	Tarot Cards	31	6.4%	8	3.8%
	Psychic Readings	34	7.0%	9	4.2%
	Enjoy Worship/Bible	122	25.3%	111	52.1%
	Politics	102	21.1%	69	32.4%
	Donating to charity	112	23.2%	68	31.9%
	Hunting/Shooting	49	10.1%	62	29.1%
	Watch/play Sports	301	62.3%	160	75.1%
	Total	483	100.0%	213	100.0%

TABLE F8. Pearson Chi-Square Tests

		State Location
Social Behaviors	Chi-square	164.318
	df	20
	Sig.	

Results are based on non-empty rows and columns in each innermost subtable.
*The Chi-square statistic is significant at the 0.05 level.

APPENDIX G

DISTRIBUTION PERCENTAGE
OF DEMOGRAPHIC TABLES

281

TABLE G1. Percent Distribution of Annual Income, Employment Status, College Graduation Status and Class Status by State

| | | State Location | | | |
| | | California | | Arkansas | |
		Count	Col. N %	Count	Col. N %
Annual Income	$9,999 or below	191	41.4%	80	41.5%
	$10,000 to $19,999	126	27.3%	29	15.0%
	$20,000 to $29,999	64	13.9%	20	10.4%
	$30,000 or higher	80	17.4%	64	33.2%
	Total	461	100.0%	193	100.0%
Employment Status	Sales/Marketing	73	14.8%	43	19.9%
	Clerical/Retail/Service	76	15.4%	24	11.1%
	Middle-Upper Management	25	5.1%	37	17.1%
	No Response	320	64.8%	112	51.9%
	Total	494	100.0%	216	100.0%
College Graduation Status	Business	319	64.6%	190	88.0%
	Arts, Education and Engineering	72	14.6%	15	6.9%
	No Response	103	20.9%	11	5.1%
	Total	494	100.0%	216	100.0%
Class Status	Freshman	7	1.4%	0	.0%
	Sophomore	25	5.1%	2	1.0%
	Junior	146	30.0%	95	45.5%
	Senior	284	58.4%	37	17.7%
	Graduate	24	4.9%	75	35.9%
	Total	486	100.0%	209	100.0%

282

TABLE G2
Pearson Chi-Square Tests

		State Location
Annual Income	Chi-square	25.444
	df	3
	Sig.	
Employment Status	Chi-square	33.564
	df	3
	Sig.	
College Graduation Status	Chi-square	41.849
	df	2
	Sig.	
Class Status	Chi-square	170.381
	df	4
	Sig.	

Results are based on non-empty rows and columns in each innermost subtable.
*The Chi-square statistic is significant at the 0.05 level.
a. More than 20% of cells in this subtable have expected cell counts less than 5.
    Chi-square results may be invalid.

TABLE G3. Percent Distribution of Roof and McKinney Divisions by State

		State Location			
		California		Arkansas	
		Count	Col. N %	Count	Col. N %
Roof and McKinney Divisions	Liberal Protestants	19	4.1%	17	8.2%
	Moderate Protestants	65	13.9%	32	15.5%
	Black Protestants	1	.2%	5	2.4%
	Conservative Protestants	21	4.5%	57	27.5%
	Catholics	155	33.3%	40	19.3%
	Others	7	1.5%	3	1.4%
	No Religious Preference	66	14.2%	16	7.7%
	Other Christian	42	9.0%	20	9.7%
	Secular / Agnostic / Atheist	29	6.2%	9	4.3%
	Other Non-Christians	61	13.1%	8	3.9%
Total		466	100.0%	207	100.0%

TABLE G4
Pearson Chi-Square Tests

		State Location
Roof and McKinney Divisions	Chi-square	105.525
	df	9
	Sig.	

Results are based on non-empty rows and columns in each innermost subtable.
*The Chi-square statistic is significant at the 0.05 level.

TABLE G5. Percent Distribution of World Christian Encyclopedia Divisions by State

		State Location			
		California		Arkansas	
		Count	Col. N %	Count	Col. N %
World Christian Encyclopedia Divisions	Angelicans	8	1.7%	8	3.9%
	Protestants	98	21.0%	103	49.8%
	Catholics	155	33.3%	40	19.3%
	Marginal Protestants	7	1.5%	3	1.4%
	Independent Christians	66	14.2%	16	7.7%
	Orthodox	42	9.0%	20	9.7%
	No Preference	0	.0%	0	.0%
	Secular/Agnostic/Atheist	29	6.2%	9	4.3%
	Other Non-Christian	61	13.1%	8	3.9%
	Total	466	100.0%	207	100.0%

TABLE G6. Pearson Chi-Square Tests

		State Location
World Christian Encyclopedia Divisions	Chi-square	69.728
	df	7
	Sig.	

Results are based on non-empty rows and columns in each innermost subtable.
*The Chi-square statistic is significant at the 0.05 level.
a. More than 20% of cells in this subtable have expected cell counts less than 5. Chi-square results may be invalid.

TABLE G7. Percent Distribution of Religiosity Measures by State

		State Location			
		California		Arkansas	
		Count	Col. N %	Count	Col. N %
Religiosity Index	Low	292	59.1%	69	31.9%
	High	202	40.9%	147	68.1%
	Total	494	100.0%	216	100.0%
Religiousness Level	Unsure/Not	167	33.8%	34	15.7%
	Somewhat	232	47.0%	108	50.0%
	Very	69	14.0%	55	25.5%
	Seriously	26	5.3%	19	8.8%
	Total	494	100.0%	216	100.0%
Church Service Atten.	Less than Weekly	373	75.5%	145	67.1%
	Weekly or More	121	24.5%	71	32.9%
	Total	494	100.0%	216	100.0%
Religious Service Atten.	Never	141	28.5%	36	16.7%
	1–2 Visits per Year	126	25.5%	27	12.5%
	Occasionally attend	141	28.5%	88	40.7%
	Nearly every week or more	86	17.4%	65	30.1%
	Total	494	100.0%	216	100.0%

285

TABLE G7. Continued

| | | State Location | | | |
| | | California | | Arkansas | |
		Count	Col. N %	Count	Col. N %
Enjoy Worship/Bible	No	372	75.3%	105	48.6%
	Yes	122	24.7%	111	51.4%
	Total	494	100.0%	216	100.0%
Do you believe	Not Applicable	47	9.5%	15	6.9%
there is life after	No	50	10.1%	14	6.5%
death?	Unsure	93	18.8%	24	11.1%
	Yes	304	61.5%	163	75.5%
	Total	494	100.0%	216	100.0%
Social Virtues	Low	303	61.3%	108	50.0%
	High	191	38.7%	108	50.0%
	Total	494	100.0%	216	100.0%
Social Vices	Low	244	49.4%	81	37.5%
	High	250	50.6%	135	62.5%
	Total	494	100.0%	216	100.0%

TABLE G8
Pearson Chi-Square Tests

		State Location
Religiosity Index	Chi-square	44.373
	df	1
	Sig.	
Religiousness Level	Chi-square	31.945
	df	3
	Sig.	
Church Service Attendance	Chi-square	5.345
	df	1
	Sig.	
Religious Service Attendance	Chi-square	38.601
	df	3
	Sig.	

286

TABLE G8. Continued

		State Location
Enjoy Worship/Bible	Chi-square	48.567
	df	1
	Sig.	
Do you believe there is life after death?	Chi-square	13.204
	df	3
	Sig.	
Social Virtues	Chi-square	7.922
	df	1
	Sig.	
Social Vices	Chi-square	8.564
	df	1
	Sig.	

Results are based on non-empty rows and columns in each innermost subtable.
*The Chi-square statistic is significant at the 0.05 level.

TABLE G9. Percent Distribution of Religiosity Measures by State

		State Location			
		California		Arkansas	
		Count	Col. N %	Count	Col. N %
Religiosity Index	Low	292	59.1%	69	31.9%
	High	202	40.9%	147	68.1%
	Total	494	100.0%	216	100.0%
Religiousness Level	Unsure/Not	167	33.8%	34	15.7%
	Somewhat	232	47.0%	108	50.0%
	Very	69	14.0%	55	25.5%
	Seriously	26	5.3%	19	8.8%
	Total	494	100.0%	216	100.0%
Church Service Atten.	Less than Weekly	373	75.5%	145	67.1%
	Weekly or More	121	24.5%	71	32.9%
	Total	494	100.0%	216	100.0%
Religious Service Attendance	Never	141	28.5%	36	16.7%
	1–2 Visits per Year	126	25.5%	27	12.5%
	Occasionally attend	141	28.5%	88	40.7%
	Nearly every week or more	86	17.4%	65	30.1%
	Total	494	100.0%	216	100.0%

TABLE G10. Pearson Chi-Square Tests

		State Location
Religiosity Index	Chi-square	44.373
	df	1
	Sig.	
Religiousness Level	Chi-square	31.945
	df	3
	Sig.	
Church Service Attendance	Chi-square	5.345
	df	1
	Sig.	
Religious Service Attendance	Chi-square	38.601
	df	3
	Sig.	

Results are based on non-empty rows and columns in each innermost subtable.
*The Chi-square statistic is significant at the 0.05 level.

288

APPENDIX H

CONSUMER BEHAVIOR
OF VICES AND VIRTUES TABLES

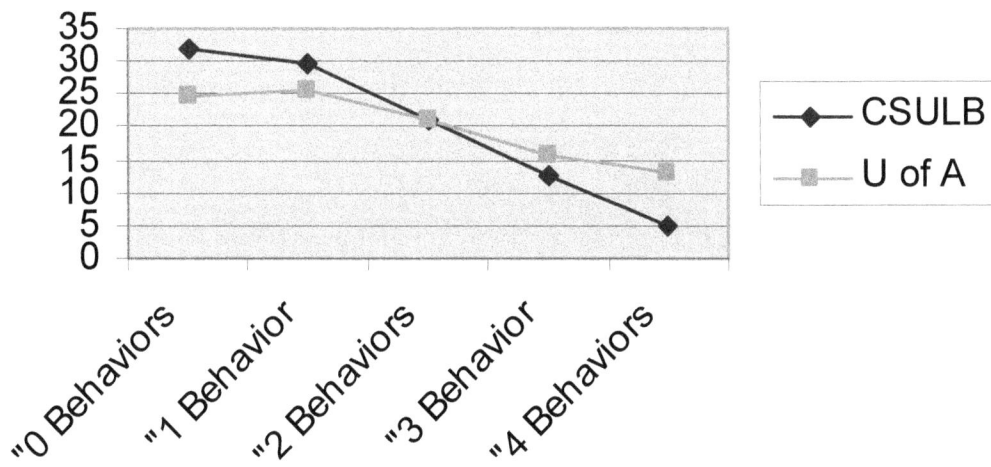

Good Behaviors (Virtues)

TABLE H1. Good Behaviors (Virtues) and Bad behaviors (Vices) Tables

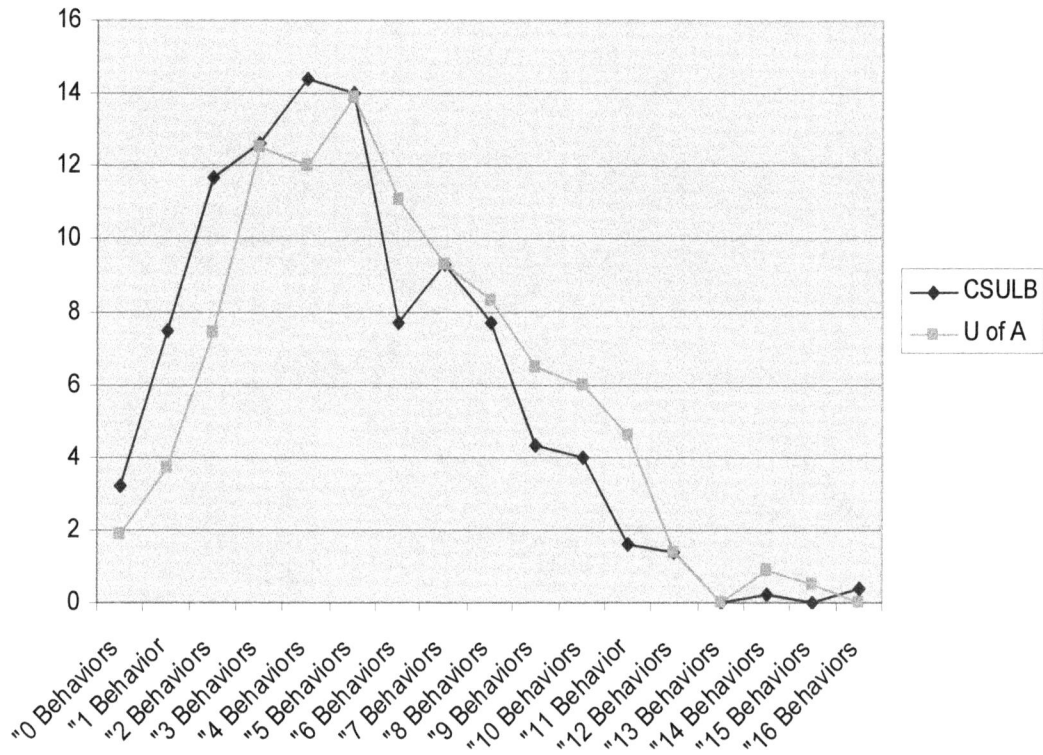

TABLE H2. Bad behaviors (Vices)

APPENDIX I

INTER-CORRELATION MATRIXES

APPENDIX I

Diagram I—Target Market Group Venn diagram

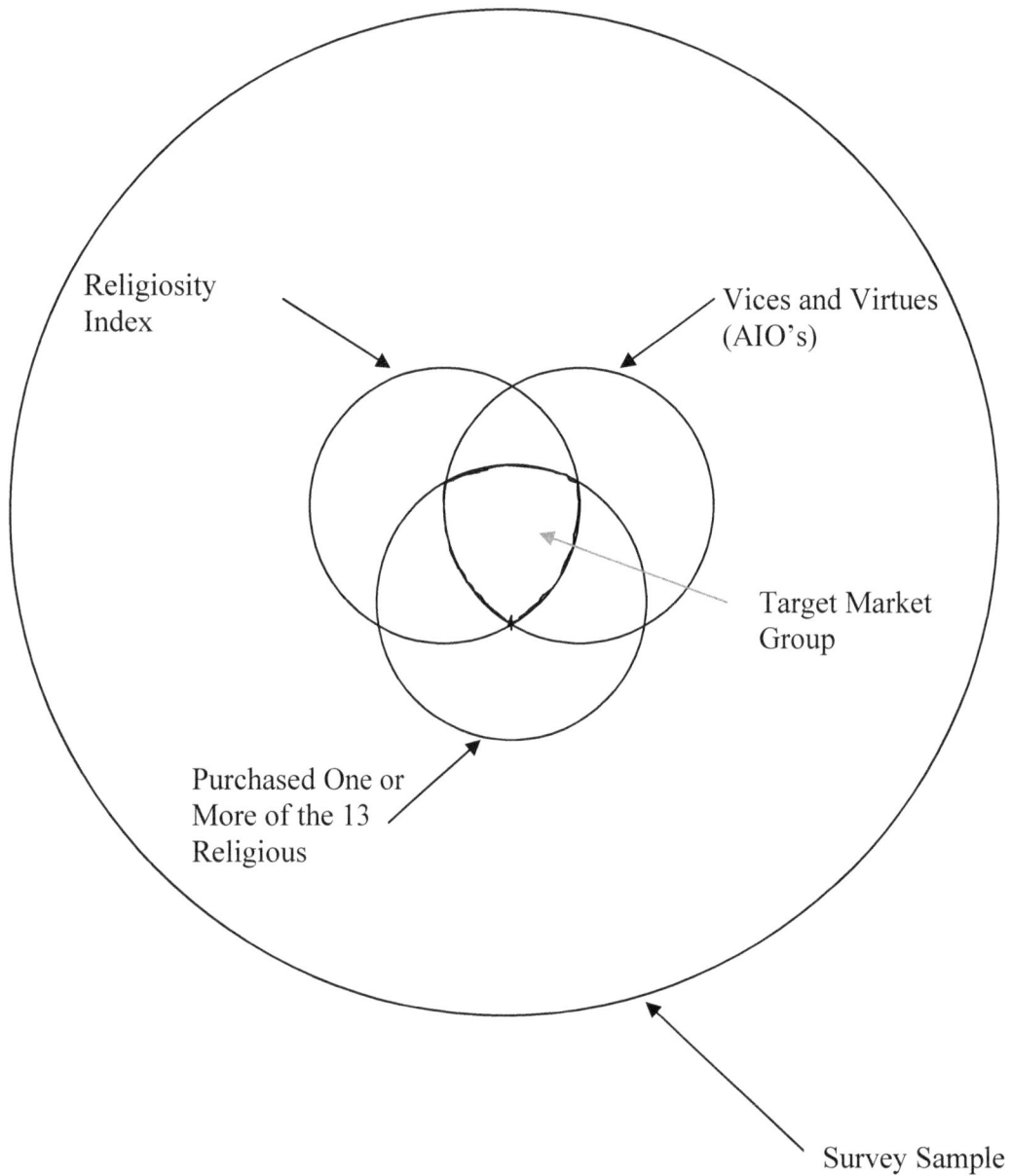

Religiosity Index

Vices and Virtues (AIO's)

Target Market Group

Purchased One or More of the 13 Religious

Survey Sample

APPENDIX J

SURVEY QUESTIONNAIRE PROTOCOL STATEMENT

APPENDIX J
Survey Questionnaire Protocol Statement (script)

I would like to introduce ourselves (STATE NAMES)

We would like to conduct a 20-minute survey. It is completely voluntary. I would like to first of all thank (PROFESSORS NAME) and you in advance for your help.

The survey is anonymous and will be used for the purposes of completing a thesis for a graduate degree. We will pass out the survey questionnaire and Scantron. If you do not want to participate, please remain seated and turn in your blank questionnaire. In the upper top corner, please fill in the starting time and enter the class number. Under the portion that asks for your last 4 digits, you can use any four digits such as your favorite four numbers, your last four digits of your phone number, your pet's birthday, your birthday, any four numbers you feel like using. The number is not to identify you; it is allow the questionnaire data to have a unique file name.

If you have any questions, please raise your hand.

(COMMON ANSWERS TO QUESTIONS THAT MIGHT OCCUR)

Questions 13a, 13b, 13c, and 13d refer to all other religious items not specified in the categories of religious items stated in Questions 1–12 but are specified by Christian denominations as having a relevant religious meaning (e.g., Mormons have holy undergarments). Pay close attention to the Question Numbers, as some answers are numbered, e.g., 12a and 13a. Others are numbered 14a, 14b, and 14c. The answer is the Scantron number, and the questions alphanumeric, which will be what place on the question number in the Scantron. Basically, as students you are all used to using Scantrons.

43a wearables—refers to placement on clothes, such as with a lapel pin. It can also refer to placement on the body itself.

128a refers to what you consider yourself first, as in any DENOMINA-TIONAL NAME (e.g., Catholic) or a Christian.

If you think of yourself as a DENOMINATIONAL NAME (e.g., Catholic), then the answer to 128a is YES.

If you think of yourself as a Christian first before your DENOMINATION (e.g., Catholic), then the answer to 128b is NO.

128c is unsure; this is self-explanatory

128e is N/A (NON-APPLICABLE) this refers to those who have no preference or for those who are Secular, Agnostic, or Atheist.

N/A (NON-APPLICABLE) always refers to those who have no preference or for those who are Secular, Agnostic, or Atheist.

130e refers to students who have a Bachelor's degree and are completing a Master's Degree.

APPENDIX K

SURVEY QUESTIONNAIRE FORM

APPENDIX K

K: Survey Questionnaire (page 1 of 7)

Start Time _____   Finish Time _____   Class Code _____   _____
                                                                          Last 4 Digits SS ###

Item 1: A religious DVD or VCR movie (e.g., Passion of Christ, Ten Commandments)

[a] Yes, I own the item   [b] No, don't own, but would buy   [c] No, don't own, won't buy   [d] Unsure

Item 2: A religious Music CD (e.g., Jessica Simpson)

[a] Yes, I own the item   [b] No, don't own, but would buy   [c] No, don't own, won't buy   [d] Unsure

Item 3: A religious painting or print (e.g., Last Supper, Angels)

[a] Yes, I own the item   [b] No, don't own, but would buy   [c] No, don't own, won't buy   [d] Unsure

Item 4: A religious statuette (e.g., Sacred Heart)

[a] Yes, I own the item   [b] No, don't own, but would buy   [c] No, don't own, won't buy   [d] Unsure

Item 5: A religious pendant or medal (e.g., St. Christopher, Virgin Mary, other)

[a] Yes, I own the item   [b] No, don't own, but would buy   [c] No, don't own, won't buy   [d] Unsure

Item 6: Any other religious jewelry

[a] Yes, I own the item   [b] No, don't own, but would buy   [c] No, don't own, won't buy   [d] Unsure

Item 7: A holy book (e.g., Bible, Book of Mormon, New Testament, other Holy Books)

[a] Yes, I own the item   [b] No, don't own, but would buy   [c] No, don't own, won't buy   [d] Unsure

Item 8: A religious book (e.g., Billy Graham, Chuck Missler, Hal Lindsey)

[a] Yes, I own the item   [b] No, don't own, but would buy   [c] No, don't own, won't buy   [d] Unsure

298

Item 9: A religious bumper sticker (e.g., fish)

        a | Yes, I own the item   b | No, don't own, but would buy   c | No, don't own, won't buy   d | Unsure

Item 10: A cross

        a | Yes, I own the item   b | No, don't own, but would buy   c | No, don't own, won't buy   d | Unsure

Item 11: A crucifix

        a | Yes, I own the item   b | No, don't own, but would buy   c | No, don't own, won't buy   d | Unsure

Item 12: A rosary

        a | Yes, I own the item   b | No, don't own, but would buy   c | No, don't own, won't buy   d | Unsure

Item 13: Other religious iconography

        a | Yes, I own the item   b | No, don't own, but would buy   c | No, don't own, won't buy   d | Unsure

TABLE K. Continued

Which, if any, of the following persons' recommendations influenced your decision to purchase the items from the product list? (Select **ALL** that apply.)
14 [a] Religious leader, non-clergy   15 [a] Friend / acquaintance   16 [a] Clergy   17 [a] Family   18 [a] N/A

Did you have prior knowledge of the products before you purchased them? (Refer to product list. Select only ONE.)
19 [a] Yes   [b] No   [c] N/A

Did your Sunday School / Church Education influence your decision to purchase? (Select only ONE.)
20 [a] Yes   [b] No   [c] Never attended Sunday School / Church Education

Which of the following forms of printed media influenced your decision to purchase? (Select **ALL** that apply.)
21 [a] Books   22 [a] Magazines   23 [a] Church newsletters   24 [a] Other printed media   25 [a] N/A

Which of the following price considerations affected your decision to purchase? (Select **ALL** that apply.)
26 [a] Sales price   27 [a] Sales rebate   28 [a] Value for price

Which of the following influenced your decision to purchase items from the product list? (Select **ALL** that apply.)
29 [a] Spiritual value   30 [a] Tradition   31 [a] Guilt   32 [a] N/A

Which of the following were important to you in purchasing items from the product list? (Select **ALL** that apply.)
33 [a] Quality   34 [a] Durability   35 [a] Style and appearance   36 [a] Brand   37 [a] N/A

Did a sales representative or the reputation of the dealer influence your decision to purchase items from the product list?
(Answer Yes or No, and select one or both options.)
38 [a] Yes   [b] No   39 [a] Sales Representative   [b] Reputation of the dealer   [c] Both   [d] None   [e] N/A

Where did you place the items you purchased? (Refer to product list. Select **ALL** that apply.)
40 [a] Home   41 [a] Auto   42 [a] Office   43 [a] Wearables   44 [a] N/A

Select all the purposes for which you purchased the items listed in the product list. (Select **ALL** that apply.)
45 [a] Display only   46 [a] Worship   47 [a] Special enlightenment   48 [a] Wear / Jewelry   49 [a] N/A

Do you ever purchase any of the items listed in the product list as gifts for family, friends, or others?
50 [a] Yes   [b] No   [c] N/A

TABLE K. Continued

TABLE K. Continued

Do you work full or part time and where: 62 [a] Working part time from home	[b] Full time outside home [c] Working full time from home	[d] Full time outside home [e] N/A

Are you a: (Check **ALL** that apply.)

63 [a] Student   64 [a] Veteran   65 [a] Retired   66 [a] Homemaker

Are you a: (Check **ALL** that apply.)

67 [a] Active Military   68 [a] Self-employed / Business owner   69 [a] Other   70 [a] N/A

I enjoy: (Select **ALL** that apply.)

71 [a] Cigarette / Cigar	72 [a] Dancing	73 [a] Beer, wine, etc.	74 [a] Concerts	75 [a] Night clubbing
76 [a] Video games	77 [a] TV shopping	78 [a] Computer / Internet	79 [a] Self-improvement	80 [a] Cultural events
81 [a] Casino gambling	82 [a] Lottery / Sweepstakes	83 [a] Astrology / Horoscope	84 [a] Tarot cards	85 [a] Psychic readings
86 [a] Worship / Bible	87 [a] Politics	88 [a] Donating to charity	89 [a] Hunting / Shooting	90 [a] Watch / Play sports

Age Part 1 — What is your age group?

91 [a] Under 18	[b] 18-24	[c] 25-29	[d] 30-34	[e] 35-39
92 [a] 40-44	[b] 45-49	[c] 50-54	[d] 55-59	[e] 60-64
93 [a] 65-69	[b] 70-74	[c] 75-79	[d] 80 or older	[e]

Income Part 1 — Annual income

94 [a] Under $4,999	[b] $5,000-9,999	[c] $10,000-14,999	[d] $15,000-19,999	[e] $20,000-24,999
95 [a] $25,000-29,999	[b] $30,000-34,999	[c] $35,000-39,999	[d] $40,000-44,999	[e] $45,000-49,999
96 [a] $50,000-54,999	[b] $55,000-59,999	[c] $60,000-64,999	[d] $65,000-79,999	[e] Over $80,000

302

TABLE K. Continued

303

TABLE K. Continued

LIST OF TABLES

LIST OF TABLES

307

310

312

APPENDIX D TABLES

LIST OF FIGURES

FIGURES   Page

REFERENCES

REFERENCES

ABC News. (2010, Oct 12). *Video games linked to poor relationships.* Retrieved from http://abclocal.go.com/kabc/story?Section=news/ health&id=6621759

Affinity. (2011). In *Oxford English Dictionary.* Retrieved from http://www.oed.com. mcc1.library.csulb.edu/view/Entry/3417?redirected From=affinity#eid

Alexius, Patriarch. (2007). The church, society and politics: A view from Moscow. *European View,* (6)(1), 111–116, doi: 10.1007/s12290-007-0016-4.

American Psychological Association. (2010). *Publication manual of the American Psychological Association* (6th ed.). Washington, DC: Author.

American Psychological Association. (2001). *Publication manual of the American Psychological Association* (5th ed.). Washington, DC: Author.

Americans more likely to accept politics in religion, new poll says. (2005, June 7). *San Jose Mercury News.*

Barna Group. (n.d.). *Approach to the topic of commitment.* Retrieved from http://www.barna.org

Barna Research Group of Glendale, California. (1996). Poll—Fewer go to church each year: Church attendance has suffered a five-year decline and sunk to its lowest level in two decades. *Birmingham News.* Retrieved from http://community.seattletimes.nwsource.com/archive/?date= 19960831 &slug=2346772

Barnet, S., & Stubbs M. (Eds.). (1997). *A short guide to writing about art.* (5th ed.). NY York: Longman.

Brady Center. (2007). Brady *Campaign to Prevent Gun Violence.* Retrieved from www.bradycampaign.org/gunsoncampus

Buzzle.com. (2010). *Types of advertising techniques.* Retrieved from
    http://www.buzzle.com/articles/types-of-advertising-techniques.html

Collett, J. L. & Lizardo, O. (2009). A power-control theory of gender and
    religiosity. *Journal for the Scientific Study of Religion,* (*48*)(2), 212–214.

DemandTec Inc. (2009). *The collaborative optimization network for retailers and
    consumers products companies. Analytical Services.* Retrieved from
    Demandtec.com/c/document_library/ get_file?uuid=ccd25214-449a-4195-
    87bb-cc 59a7353872&groupId=10128

DeRushia, K. D. (2010). *Internet Usage Among College Students and its Impact
    on Depression, Social Anxiety, and Social Engagement*: A dissertation.
    (Doctoral dissertation). Indiana University of Pennsylvania, Indiana, PA.

Di Falco, J. (2000). *Symbols of Catholicism* (pp. 1–94). Barnes & Noble.
    New York, NY.

Divided: Survey finds split commitments. (1995, April 23). Fort Wayne (IN)
    Journal Gazette. Retrieved from www.rawstory.com/rs/.../poll-70-
    percent-religion-losing-influence

George, D., Mallery, P.& Pearson, B. (2005). *SPSS for Windows step by step: A
    simple guide and reference 12.0 update* (pp. 1–340). (5th ed.). New York,
    NY: Pearson Education, Inc.

Georgii, C. (2008, March 8).*Why some people don't vote: Reasons Some People
    Don't Vote.* Retrieved from http://www.helium.com/items/902505-why-
    some-people-don't-vote

GotQuestions.org. (n.d.). *The Bible has the answers, we'll find them for
    you!* Retrieved from www.gotquestions.org/astrology-Bible.html

Grandstaff, M. (2001, November 15). The impact of videogames on college
    students. *The Michigan Daily News.* Retrieved from www.michigandaily.com

Green, S. (2008, Oct 7). Opinion: The Effects of Negative Campaigning.
    Digital Journal. Retrieved from http://www.digital journal.com/
    article/260839

GunFreeKids.org. (2007). Campaign to keep guns off campus. Retrieved from
    www.GunFreeKids.org.

Haviland, W. A. (1996). *Cultural anthropology* (8th ed.). Fort Worth, TX: Harcourt Brace College.

Howlett, D. (1980). *The critical way in religion.* Buffalo, NY: Prometheus Books.

Hudson, W. S, & Corrigan J. (1992). *Religion in America: An historical account of the development of American religious life* (5th ed.). New York, NY: Macmillan Publishing Company.

Hughes, R. (1997, Spring). *American Visions: What America's greatest art reveals about our national character* (Special Issue). Time Special Issue.

Jenkins, O. B. (2004). *Cognitive and social culture.* Retrieved from http://orville jenkins.com/whatisculture/cogandsocialcul.html

Kacmar, K. M. & Carlson, D. S. (1997). Further validation of the perceptions of politics scale (POPS): A multiple sample investigation. *Journal of Management, (23)*(5), pp. 627–658. doi: 10.1177/014920639702300502.

Kaufmann, W. (1990). *Critique of religion and philosophy.* Princeton, NJ: Princeton University Press,

Kirszner, L. G., & Mandell, S. R. (1986). *Patterns for College Writing: A Rhetorical Reader and Guide* (3rd ed.). New York, NY: St. Martin's Press.

Krejcir, R. J., & Schaeffer, F. A. (2009). *Institute of Church Leadership Development.* Retrieved from http://www.churchleadership.org/apps/ articles/default.asp? articleid=55991&columnid=4545

Kumar, V., Aaker, D. A., & Day, G. S. (2002). *Essentials of marketing research* (pp. 1– 508). (2nd ed.). San Francisco, CA : John Wiley & Sons, Inc.

Kunkle, L. (2009). Ethics & pro-social values in Judaism, Christianity and Islam. Retrieved from http://abrahamicfamilyreunion.org/ethics-pro-social-values-in-judaism-christianity-and-islam

Lake P. F. (2002). The emerging crisis of college student suicide: Law and policy responses to serious forms of self-inflicted injury. Stetson Law Review (32)(1), Stetson University College of Law. Tampa Bay, FL.

Larimer, M. E., & Neighbors, C. (2003). Normative misperception and the impact of descriptive and injunctive norms on college student gambling.

Psychology of addictive behaviors by the Educational Publishing *Foundation* 2003, (17)(3), 235–243, doi: 10.1037/0893-164X.17.3.235.

LaRosa, J. (2006). Self-improvement market in U.S. worth $9.6 billion. *PRWeb—online visibility from vocus.* Retrieved from http://www.prweb.com/releases/ 2006/9/prweb440011.htm

Larose, D. T. (2005). Discovering knowledge in data, an introduction to data mining. (pp. 1–239). New York: NY: John Wiley and Sons, Inc.

Larose, D. T. (2006). *Data Mining Methods and Models* (pp. 1–344). San Francisco, CA: John Wiley and Sons, Inc.

Lindbeck G. A. (1984). The nature of doctrine: Religion and theology in a postliberal age (pp. 1–142). Philadelphia, PA: The Westminster Press.

Lippman, L., Michelsen, E., & Roehlekepartain, E. C. (2005). Indicators of child, family, and community connections: The measurement of family religiosity and spirituality. Search Institute. *Office of the Assistant Secretary for Planning and Evaluation, HHS.* Retrieved from http://aspe.hhs.gov/hsp/connections-papers04/ paper1.htm

Madrid, P., & Rahlwes, M., (2006). California Arkansas Graduate Survey of religion and marketing (CAGS). California State University, Long Beach, and the University of Arkansas, Fayetteville.

Markovsky, B., & Thye, S. R. (2001, Spring). Social influence on paranormal beliefs. *Sociological Perspectives.* (*44*)(1), 21–44, doi: 0.1525/sop.2001.44.4.2.

Maslow, A. H. (1970) *Religious, Values, and Peak-Experiences.* New York, NY: Penguin Group.

Merriam-Webster's Encyclopedia of World Religions. (1999). *Philippines*, New York, NY: Merriam-Webster, Inc.

Morgan, D. & Promey S. M. (Eds.) (2001). *The visual culture of American religions.* (pp. i–xi). Berkeley, CA: University of California Press, Ltd.

Mormon Church. (n.d.). *How do Mormons view gambling?* Retrieved from http://www. mormonchurch.com/69/how-do-mormons-view-gambling

New York College of Health Professions (n.d.). *Science of self-improvement and wellness.* Retrieved from http://www.nycollege.edu/academics/self_ improvement_wellness.php

Office of National Drug Control Policy. (n.d.). *Drugs & sports: Combating doping in sports.* Retrieved from http://www.whitehousedrugpolicy .gov/prevent/sports/

Ohlendorf, J., & Fehring R. (2007). *The influence of religiosity on contraceptive use among Roman Catholic women in the United States.* Marquette University College of Nursing. Retrieved from http://www.lifeissues .net/writers/feh/feh _28religion_contraception.html.

Parsons, M. J. (1987). How we understand art: A cognitive developmental account of aesthetic experience. (pp. ii–xi) Cambridge, UK: Cambridge University Press.

Patterson, F., Lerman, C., Kaufmann, V. G., Neuner, G. A. & Audrain-McGovern, J. (2004). Cigarette smoking practices among American college students: review and future directions. *Journal of American College Health.* Department of Psychiatry, University of Pennsylvania, Philadelphia.

Perreault Jr., W. D., & McCarthy, E. J. (2006). *Essentials of marketing, A global-managerial approach.* (pp. 1–622). (8th ed.). New York, NY: McGraw-Hill Higher Education.

Pew Research Center. (2008, August 21). Public support falls for religion's role in politics: Some social conservative disillusionment. *National survey by the Pew Research Center.* Retrieved from http://pewresearch.org/pubs /930/religion-politics

Pickford, R. W., (1972). *Psychology and visual aesthetics.* London, UK: Hutchinson Educational Ltd.

Pouliot, K. (2007, December 12). *Shopping addiction: When casual shopping becomes a compulsion.* Retrieved from http://www.foxnews.com/ story/0,2933,316610,00 .html

Psychology Glossary (2010). *Prosocial behavior defined.* Retrieved from http://www.alleydog.com/glossary/definition.php?term=Prosocial%20Beh avior#ixzz13c GWDAgZ

Putnam, R. D., Campbell, D. E. (2010). Losing faith: Religion politics—Young people are rejecting organized religion they see as too politically conservative. *Los Angeles Times*. Retrieved from ww.nd.edu/~dcampbe4/cv.pdf

Ramsden, E., (2009). Sensorlytics. *Affinity analysis: Identifying exploitable product synergies in sales data. In marketing, communication & analytic services for the sensors industry.* (pp. 1–10). Retrieved from http://www.sensorlytics.com /docs/affinity_ analysis-d09005a.pdf

Reed, M. P., & Dalmas, H. N. (2004, November 10). *Business executives view the politician: Negative feelings block cooperative efforts.* The Ohio State University. Retrieved from http://www.sciencedirect .com/science?_ob= ArticleURL&_udi=B6W45-4DS3K35-V&_user =10&_coverDate=10%2F31 %2F1968 &_rdoc=1&_fmt=high& _orig=search&_origin=search&_sort=d&_docanchor=&view=c&_search StrId=1505557780&_rerunOrigin=google&_acct=C000050221&_version =1&_urlVersion=0&_userid=10&md5=fbf71e3582640ba1940c37ae13a16 4f1&searchtype=a-bfn2#bfn2

Religion: Christian Dancing (1959, January 26). *Time Magazine*. Retrieved from http://www.time.com /time/magazine/article/0,9171,892104,00.html

ReligionFacts (n.d.). *Baptist lifestyle*. Retrieved from http://www.religionfacts.com/christianity/denominations/baptists.htm

ReligionFacts (n.d.). *Ethics & values of Jehovah's Witnesses*. Retrieved from http:// www.religionfacts.com//jehovahs_witnesses/ethics.htm

ReligionFacts (n.d.). *History of Presbyterianism and gambling*. Retrieved from http://www.religionfacts.com/christianity/denominations/presbyterian/ history.htm

SaeNgian, K. (2008, June 13). Researcher cites negative influences of hip-hop. Pittsburgh, PA: *Pittsburgh Post-Gazette*.

Schafer, L. (1997). *In search of divine reality: Science as a source of inspiration.* Fayetteville, AR: The University of Arkansas Press.

Schmidt, R. (1980). *Exploring religion*. Belmont, CA: Wadsworth Publishing Company.

Schmidt, R. (1988). *Exploring religion* (pp. 1–240). (2nd.). Belmont, CA: Wadsworth Publishing Company.

Shariff, A. F., & Norenzayan, A. (2009). *God is watching you: Priming god concepts increases prosocial behavior in an anonymous economic game.* Psychological Science: Department of Psychology, University of British Columbia, Canada. Retrieved from www.psychologytoday.com/.../when-god-is-watching-people-are-more-generous

Spohn, W. C. (2007). *Go and do likewise: Jesus and ethics.* (pp. 1–240). New York, NY: The Continuum International Publishing Group Inc.

Sports1234.com. (2009). *Hunting a Sign of Dangerous Behavior to come?* Retrieved from http://www.sports1234.com/outdoor-recreation/ 1571-6-outdoor-recreation.html

The Holy Bible King James Version (1998). Cedar Rapids, IA: Parson Technology Inc.

The Lutheran Church, (n.d.). *What is the LCMS view of gambling?* Retrieved from http://www.lcms.org/pages/ internal.asp?NavID=2130

The Methodist Church, (n.d.). *What is the history of Methodist concerns about gambling?* Retrieved from http://www.methodist.org.uk/index.cfm? fuseaction=opentogod.Content &cmid=1558

The Real Clear Politics Blog (2009). Retrieved from http://realclearpolitics.blogs. time.com/2009/04/09/the-fall-of-mass-attendance-but-not-us-religiosity/

The Treaty of Tripoli (1797). Approved by the Senate of the United States and President Washington

U.S. News & World Report (2001). Mysteries of Faith: Exploring the Bible With New Insights and Discoveries. (Special Collector's Edition). *U.S. News & World Report Inc.* Washington, D.C.

University of Wollongong (UOW). (n.d.). Conducted at the meeting of the School of Management and Marketing. Wollongong, Australia. Seminar Notice. Retrieved from http://www.uow.edu.au/content/groups/public/ @web/@commerce/@smm/ documents/web/uow041024.pdf

Way to Religion.com. (n.d.). *Comparison of Christian denominations' Ethical views.* Retrieved from http://www. waytoreligion.com/en/index.php? option=com_ content&view=article&id= 67&Itemid=109&lang=en

Wilkes, R. E., Burnett, J. J., & Howell, R. D. (1986). On the meaning and measurement of religiosity in consumer research. *Journal of the Academy of Marketing Science* (*14*)(1), 47–56, doi: 0.1177/009207038601400107. Texas Tech University.

Wulff, D. M. (1997). Psychology of religion classic & contemporary (pp. 1–288). (2nd Ed.). New York, NY: John Wiley & Sons, Inc.

Other Books by Same Author By
Royal Premier Publishing
Grandville, MI

1. College Students and Religion: How Todays College Youth View Religion.

2. What Today's College Students Think of Religion

3. Basic Marketing in the 21st Century

4. Marketing, Selling and Commercialization of Religion: How Religion in the 21st Century Has Taken Us to Greed and Ego

5. The Basics and True Meaning of Crucifix's and Crosses

6. The Humble Beginning of Christianity's Symbols.

7. Basic Step by Step Marketing Surveying

8. Basic Statistical Analysis of Survey Data

9. How Red and Blue States Differ

10. Smoking Drinking and Nightclubbing in College

11. Just the Basics: An Introduction to Feng Shui and it's Symbolism

12. The Basic Story Behind Your Families Family Coat Of Arms; A Step By Step Look At It's Symbolism and Meaning.

13. Ground Breaking Research on the Religious Meaning and Marketing of Iconography.

14. Just the Basics: Setting up your tablet to do what you what

15. Just the Basics: Increasing your Luck, The history of Lucky Gemstones

16. Just the Basics: Angels their place, and their historical beginnings.

17. Just the Basics: Selling on Craigslist the easy way

18. Just the Basics: Your Family Tree and How DNA Can Help

19. Just the Basics: How do you get a self-published book a Library of Congress Number.